The truest act of courage,
The strongest act of manliness
Is to sacrifice ourselves
In a totally nonviolent struggle
For Justice.
To be a man is to suffer
For others.
God help us be men.

CESAR CHAVEZ

March 1968

Photo by Ronald B. Taylor

CHAVEZ

and
the Farm Workers
Ronald B. Taylor

BEACON PRESS

BOSTON

Beacon Press books are published under the auspices
of the Unitarian Universalist Association
Simultaneous publication in Canada by Saunders of Toronto, Ltd.

9 8 7 6 5 4 3 2 1

Library of Congress Cataloging in Publication Data

Taylor, Ronald B
   Chavez and the farm workers.
   Bibliography: p. 333.
   Includes index.
   1. Trade-unions—Agricultural laborers—California.
2. Chavez, Cesar Estrada.   I. Title.
HD6515.A292C38   331.88′13′0924 [B]   74–16671
ISBN 0–8070–0498–7

This book
is dedicated to the farm workers,
may their collective strength
prevail.

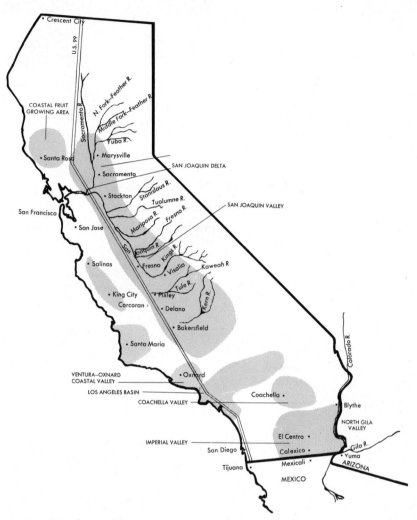

Map drawn by Fern Ross

CONTENTS

ACKNOWLEDGMENTS

This book includes the work of many people. To list them all would be impossible, but there are a special few whom I feel most indebted to. The first of these is my wife, Dorothy, who read and read again and argued and discussed the work and, in the end, took time to type the manuscript. This was a family effort; my three kids copy read and sorted pages and answered phones and contributed far more than they will ever know.

Obviously this book could not have been written without the cooperation of Cesar Chavez, the membership and staff of the United Farm Workers of America. They took time out from their important work to talk about *La Causa* and to show me the workings of the movement. Although getting appointments with Chavez was often a frustrating experience, once the interview started he was warm, candid, and helpful.

I would also like to acknowledge the farmers who agreed to interviews even though they were angered by my newspaper reporting and suspicious of my sympathies. While they cussed and fumed at me, in the end they explained their positions and I hope I accurately reflect their views.

One of my primary sources was the record laid down by the various newspapers reporting the farm labor struggles in California, Arizona, and Florida. Without the tiny Pixley *Enterprise* my knowledge of the 1933 cotton strikes would be incomplete; without the big Los Angeles *Times* many puzzling pieces of the conflict would have gone unnoticed;

without the efforts of the reporters working in the various farming areas, this work would not be complete. My special thanks to my own employers, the Fresno *Bee*, for giving me the time to work on this project and for making available the most complete library file on United Farm Worker history anywhere.

There is one special newspaper friend whom I want to credit—Harry Bernstein, the Los Angeles *Times* labor writer. Harry spent hours with me discussing, arguing, commenting on the rough drafts of my work. His knowledge of the labor movement gave me an extra dimension to work with in the writing of this book.

And finally I want to acknowledge the craftsmanship of Ray Bentley, the Beacon Press editor who made this work possible and put it into its completed form.

CHAPTER ONE : THE FARM WORKERS

On Tuesday, January 15, 1974, Pablo Navarro Arellanos got up sometime after midnight, as was his custom, and drove the old school bus through the dark streets into downtown Calexico. Even at 2:30 A.M. the streets were peopled with the hurrying shadows of farm workers crossing the U.S.–Mexican border from the sprawling, dusty, metropolitan Mexicali into this small California town. They walked quickly, in twos and threes, each carrying a lunch, a soda, and a water bottle in a plastic shopping bag; hundreds of men, women, and children headed for a dozen or more informal labor shapeups that transpire daily in the pre-dawn.

Pablo Arellanos, no longer a young man, considered himself lucky. Instead of having to hustle into the shapeup and then bend his back all day in the hot fields of the Imperial Valley, he worked as a bus driver and crew pusher for labor contractor Jesús Ayala. Although the bus wasn't in the best shape — the wiring was bad, the motor smells came up through the holes in the floor by his feet, and the emergency brake didn't work well — it was a good job. He worked long hours driving and working the crew, driving home, and then, cleaning and servicing the bus after the day was over; but the job paid more than field labor. It was a job that could lead to better opportunities. But Pablo Arellanos had no future; by dawn he would be dead.

Arellanos turned the bus north at the corner of Second and Imperial, drove a half block on Imperial, and pulled into the red zone, next to Hotel El Rey. Already a few people were waiting on the corner as Arellanos and the other drivers lined the old buses up and began recruiting their loads of workers for the day. The Ayala crews were working in the lettuce, near Blythe, a hundred miles north and east of Calexico, in the fields near the Colorado River. The work was thinning and weeding the crop with the short-handled hoes that kept the crews bent double all day.

That same morning in one of Mexicali's poorer *colonias* Lucia and Maria Mendoza had been awakened at 2 A.M. by the clatter of their alarm clock. They dressed quickly in the dark, putting on the loose-fitting work pants and long-sleeved shirts that protected them from the sun and dirt. They were teenagers, 18 and 17, and each hoped to earn $16 today, the same as their father, Manuel, and brother, Javier, who was 16. The girls stepped into the kitchen lean-to in the back of the small adobe house and began putting together the day's lunch of tacos, a thermos of hot soup, and bottles of soda pop. On this morning there would be only four bottles of soda in the big plastic shopping bag; Manuel, Jr., 20, could not go to work because he had gotten a traffic ticket and had to go to court in Calexico later in the day. The ticket would save his life.

At 2:45 the girls woke Javier and their father. The men dressed quickly, and, by 3 A.M., they were in their newly purchased secondhand station wagon, driving the mile and a half to the border. The car was their pride; they hoped later in the year to travel north in it, following the crops. They bumped through the rutted back streets, turned onto the paved boulevard through downtown Mexicali, and pulled into one of the lines of old cars and camper-pickups moving slowly through the massive, dull yellow building that straddles the border; they drove slowly in under the building, showed their green identity cards to U.S. border guards, and were waved on through the long S curve that brought them onto Imperial Avenue. They began searching for a place to park near the Ayala buses.

Though the Mendozas drove, most of the farm workers walked through the border each morning, crossed the block and a half to Second Street, then turned east, down across the tracks into *"El Hoyo"* — the hole — where the state department of employment operates a shapeup for 15 to 18 labor contractors. Each morning during the season as many as 100 farm labor buses and trucks leave from *El Hoyo* or the Calexico street corner shapeups with 3,500 to 4,000 workers; they haul them from 15 to 115 miles out into the fields. This same Mexicali-Calexico scene is repeated daily — in season — in a dozen different locations like Ciudad Juarez–El Paso or Reynosa–McAllen.

Manuel Mendoza and his family were trying for the best of two worlds, the cheaper living costs of Mexico and the higher wages of the United States. Like tens of thousands of others, the Mendozas moved to Mexicali from the interior of Mexico because they were desperately poor. Because Señora Mendoza was born in Texas, while her Mexican parents were working there illegally, she was a U.S. citizen. Using her status, Manuel Mendoza secured his immigration documents. One by one, the Mendozas obtained resident alien visas and I-151 "green cards" for Manuel, Jr., then Javier and the two girls. By 1974 Señora Mendoza was staying home in Mexicali to care for the five younger children, but for years she had worked beside her husband, leaving the children with her father as she and Manuel followed the crops clear to Salinas and Stockton.

On the morning of January 15th Manuel Mendoza parked just off Imperial Avenue. He and his children walked to the Ayala buses and boarded the one driven by Arellanos. They chose seats up front, on the left side, behind the driver. By 3:30 A.M. the bus was loaded. Arellanos leaned over, pulled the door lever closed, carefully edged the crowded bus out into traffic, and headed north, toward the lettuce fields near Blythe. Some of the 46 passengers settled down to sleep, others talked quietly, or stared out the window at flat, black emptiness dotted by occasional lights on barns or farm houses.

As the bus rumbled along, Luis Ramierez, 53, dozed in his second-row seat. Sometime just before dawn the bus lurched off the road, then back again. Ramierez was jolted awake. "It frightened me. I was wide awake after that. The driver seemed to be going too fast."

Most of the workers slept on. In the dark before dawn Arellanos was speeding north on Rannells Boulevard. He either did not know, or did not see, that this county road dead ends in a sweeping right curve onto 20th Avenue. Just beyond the curve is a drainage canal. The bus failed to make the curve, went up the canal embankment, and hurtled 56 feet through the air, smashing into the opposite canal bank. The impact tore all the bus seats loose, hurling workers forward in a tangle of arms, legs, seat cushions, and twisted metal that crushed Arellanos. After the impact the bus toppled over on its left side into the water.

One survivor said, "We began to hear the sound of water [rushing in through the broken windows] and everyone began to scream, for it was the sound of death itself."

Another passenger said the total darkness added to the horror: "At first I couldn't find my way out because there were so many people piled on top of me. And the seats were piled around us, like a prison. I couldn't free my hands from below the seats."

Nineteen of the workers — including Manuel Mendoza and his children — were trapped in the bottom of the tangle. Twenty-eight passengers managed to smash windows and wiggle free of the wreck; pulling and tugging, they helped each other. Most had serious injuries. It was 15 minutes before anyone could go for help. By then it was too late for the 19 who were still trapped inside. They drowned — in 28 inches of water.

The death of these workers — of Manuel Mendoza and his three teenage children — is not an isolated case. The transportation of farm workers, both on and off the farm, has been a national disgrace for decades. Each year too many men, women, and children die, or are injured, as they are hauled like animals to and from farm jobs.

The Blythe accident that killed 19 workers brought reactions of rage and indignation from Cesar Chavez and the

United Farm Workers of America. Many of the 46 Mexicans riding in the Ayala bus, including Manuel Mendoza, were members of the UFWA. Chavez, in Atlanta at the time of the accident, immediately flew back to Los Angeles, and drove to Calexico to personally direct the union's assistance to the families. The UFWA sent staff members to the hospitals to help the families of the dead and injured.

Señora Mendoza said UFWA representatives came to her home the day after the accident, bringing food and the offer of help. Within the next two weeks the union had loaned her $200 to support the family, and she said they had helped her make the funeral arrangements. The union also put her in touch with a sympathetic attorney who helped her file for workmen's compensation — the claims total $120,000 — and fend off the ambulance chasers working for shyster attorneys operating out of Los Angeles.

The aftermath of the bus accident was complicated by the struggle between the UFWA and the International Brotherhood of Teamsters. As the three-year-old UFWA contracts in the Coachella Valley began to expire, in the spring of 1973, the Teamsters started jurisdictional raids in the vineyards. The growers eagerly signed contracts with the Teamsters, contending the workers preferred the switch. Chavez called these grower-Teamster agreements "sweetheart contracts" and said this was another agribusiness move to get rid of the eight-year-old UFWA.

Technically, the 46 workers on the bus driven by Arellanos were Ayala employees, but they were going to work on a farm covered by Teamster contract. The Teamsters claimed 6 of the dead — including Manuel Mendoza — had been paying Teamster dues and therefore their families were eligible for a $2,000 death benefit each.

Señora Mendoza knew nothing of this death benefit. Manuel, Jr., said they had received some kind of postcard from the Teamsters, but it had said nothing of death benefits, only that they should call the El Centro office. They threw the card away. The family knew nothing about the Teamster contract at High and Mighty Farms. They were paid each day, in cash, and no mention of Teamster dues or payroll deductions was made.

Señora Mendoza and her son acknowledged that Manuel, Sr., had been a member of both the Teamsters and the UFWA, but they said he favored the UFWA cause. Señora Mendoza said her husband "was an aggressive man, who liked to talk about the union, liked to promote its cause."

Immediately after the Blythe accident the UFWA sent its own investigators to the scene and began to pressure the California Highway Patrol, demanding that criminal charges be filed against the labor contractor. The union asked for a federal investigation, and the National Transportation Safety Board sent investigators to examine the bus. They reported the bus seats were secured to the thin metal flooring only by sheet-metal screws, and because the screw holes were not reinforced the seats were held in place by only a single thread of each screw. On impact all of the screws tore loose. The seats became missiles of death.

The CHP agreed with federal investigators that, had the seats been more securely fastened, the death toll and the number of injured would have been reduced substantially. But the patrol considered this a coincidental fact. The cause of the accident according to investigators was excessive speed. Since the driver was dead, no criminal charges would be filed.

The UFWA helped plan a memorial mass and cortege for the dead that started in Calexico and worked its way back to Mexico, with farm workers carrying the caskets on their shoulders. Nearly 2,000 farm workers gathered at the Calexico National Guard Armory for the funeral Mass on Saturday, January 19. During the Mass Cesar Chavez delivered a eulogy, a stinging indictment of the agribusiness system itself:

> There have been too many accidents in the fields, on trucks, under machines, in buses; so many accidents involving farm workers. People ask if they are deliberate. They are deliberate in the sense that they are the direct result of a farm labor system that treats workers like agricultural implements and

6

not human beings. These accidents happen because employers and labor contractors treat us as if we were not important human beings. . . . The workers learned long ago that growers and labor contractors have too little regard for the value of any individual worker's life. The trucks and buses are old, and unsafe. The fields are sprayed with poisons. The laws that do exist are not enforced. How long will it be before we take serious the importance of the workers who harvest the food we eat?

Speaking in Spanish, his voice revealed the emotion he felt when he said, "We are united in our sorrow, but also in our anger. This tragedy happened because of the greed of the big growers who do not care about the safety of the workers and who expose them to grave dangers when they transport them in wheeled coffins to the field . . . brothers and sisters, the men and women we honor today are important human beings, because they are from us. They are important because of the love they gave to their husbands, their children, their wives, their parents — all of those who were close to them and needed them. . . . They were important because of the work they do . . . these terrible accidents must be stopped. . . ."

A few days later the Chavez eulogy, with some additional comments and observations, appeared under his by-line, in the Los Angeles *Times*. Agribusiness was outraged. Don Curlee, then executive assistant to the Council of California Growers, wrote a letter to the *Times* that said, in part:

This [Chavez's writing] is inflammatory, irresponsible, and unnecessarily harsh rhetoric that has no basis in fact . . . the bus was not owned, maintained, or operated by a grower, big or small. Only the shallowest, most reactionary thinking can associate this accident with greediness on the part of anybody.

Sympathy certainly is extended to the families of the victims, especially since they have been exploited in the publicity-seeking stunts of Chavez consoling them publicly.

7

The greater tragedy here is an intellectual and moral one, in which the demagog Chavez capitalizes on the deaths of people he purports to represent and seeks to use the occasion as a platform from which to spew his unfounded vilification of growers.

Growers have labored under this unrestrained and scurrilous type of attack for 10 years, a decade which saw the forced and coerced followers of Chavez membership in the UFWA reach a maximum of perhaps 60,000 and then rapidly wilt and fade to about 6,000 when the workers could choose an alternative union. . . .

The emotionally immature, undisciplined, and unreasonable approach of the UFWA has run its foul course, and its rhetorical chickens have come home to roost. The entire movement was created out of whole cloth, and beyond creating substantial wealth which can be tapped easily by Chavez and his cohorts, has accomplished practically nothing but a harvest of bitterness, distrust, and misunderstanding . . .

Curlee ended the council's position paper by briefly attacking the *Times* for using the "editorial tirade attributed to Chavez." Curlee's writing nicely sidestepped the fact that the agriculture industry has the third worst occupational safety record in the nation; only in the mines and construction trades are the accident rates higher. What farm work safety laws *are* passed are not enforced because the bureaus that police the farms are grossly understaffed and frequently directed by men sympathetic to agribusiness, not labor.

The entire exchange — Chavez's opinions and Curlee's responses — accurately reflects not only the relative positions, but also the mood of the struggle that has been going on since 1965, when Chavez and AFL-CIO organizer Larry Itliong led Mexican and Filipino grape workers in a strike against Delano grape growers. And certainly Curlee, by hiding the Teamsters behind the words "alternative union," put the jurisdictional struggle in perspective. The Teamsters were and still are the growers' alternative to Chavez.

The fact that both unions lay claim to the same workers is in no way inconsistent with the realities of farm labor. Many men like Manuel Mendoza joined both UFWA and Teamsters because they needed work. If they can find work in Mexicali the pay is about $2 a day; in the United States a man or woman can make that much in an hour or two. Sometimes workers must kick back some of their pay to the labor contractors to ensure a seat on the bus each morning. When the winter and spring work is over in the Imperial Valley the workers migrate north, up into the heart of California, and return in the fall. Sometimes the men travel alone or in crews; sometimes they move in family units.

Multiply Manuel Mendoza's family by 50,000, by 500,000, or by one million; spread them out from Brownsville, Texas, to San Diego, California; let them work and earn enough money to buy a tiny house in a Rio Grande Valley *colonia* or a California *barrio*, and start to put down roots, and then, in a year or two, take their money away capriciously, arbitrarily, and push them out on the road again, let them drift with the crops; land them in Oregon's Willamette Valley where the strawberries and the bush berries and the pole beans provide long months of work; bring in the machine harvesters and gangs of schoolchildren from Portland, keep the pay low, and put too many workers in each field, and slowly drive the migrant family out, on the road again. Do all of this over and over again, and you begin to get the sense of farm labor, the sense of desperation and futility, the feeling of powerlessness.

It is dangerous to make generalizations about farm workers because they come in all shapes, sizes, and ethnic backgrounds; each worker, each family is unique. Nothing is consistent about farm labor except its inconsistencies and the poverty and powerlessness of the workers. Annually the U.S. Department of Agriculture attempts to build a set of statistics to describe the farm labor force. Crop by crop, area by area, USDA statisticians construct elaborate sets of numbers and publish them. In the early 1970s there were nearly 3 million hired farm workers reported by the USDA; the total included housewives, schoolchildren, and college students earning

9

spending money, as well as professional farm workers. But within the total were 367,000 year-round workers who averaged 306 days of farm wage work and earned $4,358. That figures out to be just over $14 a day, and they get no vacations, holidays, or medical insurance. The USDA reported there were 187,000 migrant seasonal farm workers, and their average pay was $10 a day for men, $9 for women. The migrant family, counting the wages of the man, wife, and children, averages $3,350 a year. If these figures are meaningful, they indicate that the 554,000 men and women who depend upon farm labor for their living are competing with more than two million casual workers — the students, housewives, pensioners, and winos who come into farm work at the flush of the harvest season, when the most money is to be made.

But there are factors that the USDA does not report, factors that depress the wage structure and make farm labor even more chaotic. There are the illegal aliens, for instance, that are flooding north across the U.S.–Mexican border to work on the farms. The U.S. Immigration Service estimated 800,000 illegal aliens would be captured during the 1973–74 fiscal year. During the early 1970s this figure was increased 20 to 30 percent a year, and at least 60 percent of these illegal aliens work on farms.

A farm wife told me: "We couldn't get along without them."

A rural judge said: "The farmers in this area couldn't finish the crop harvests without them."

I asked one California fruit farmer how many illegals he had working on his farm, and I think his answer fairly represents the agribusiness scene in the San Joaquin Valley. He said: "How many? Oh, I don't know, 'cause I don't screen 'em, but I'd guess maybe 30 percent. Hell, they're here today and gone tomorrow, you never hold them long, they are scared they are going to get picked up. They have picked up some on my place, hell, I ain't scared of that. The only thing is, I don't like it when they [the Border Patrol] come into my place and run into my fields like cops and robbers, like somebody committed a crime. Hell, that's no good. . . . All I ask is that the border patrol keep their ass out of my field while we are working . . . they can come in at lunch, or before or after work . . . I couldn't care less."

Such attitudes are ingrained in the agribusiness system; the use of illegal aliens, the exploitation of child labor — a U.S. Senate committee estimates 800,000 children under 16 work on American farms — and the importation of foreign workers are essential if farmers are to continue to keep wages down. Elaborate myths are constructed to justify the resulting socioeconomic deprivation among the farm worker force. Whenever legislative proposals are advanced to help raise farm workers out of poverty, agribusiness is quick to appear in opposition, using the mythology of the family farm to cover its callous approach to labor relations.

Nowhere was this attitude more clearly expressed than in the 1965 hearings before the U.S. Senate Subcommittee on Migratory Labor when American Farm Bureau Federation senior lobbyist Matt Triggs appeared in opposition to bills that would bring farm labor under the National Labor Relations Act, tighten up child labor laws, and extend minimum wage coverage to farm labor. Senator Robert F. Kennedy, shocked by what he was hearing, interrupted: "You [the Farm Bureau] are opposed to virtually all of this legislation?"

Triggs: That is correct.

Kennedy: Do you feel there is a problem?

Triggs: Certainly there is a problem . . . it is a social problem. It was created in part by the seasonal and short-run characteristic of agriculture employment which we regret, but which we don't know what we can do about.

Kennedy tried repeatedly to get Triggs to define the problem and to come up with some recommendations for the subcommittee. Triggs finally responded, "I suggested education of individuals."

Senator Harrison Williams asked Triggs if the Farm Bureau supported any of the education bills that had come before the full committee on education and welfare.

11

Triggs: We have not favored extended programs of federal aid to education.

Kennedy, hardly believing his ears: Did you support President Johnson's federal aid to education bill?

Triggs: No. We did not.

Kennedy: Did you oppose it?

Triggs: We appeared in opposition to it.

Kennedy: Then we were wrong on that too. What do you suggest we do? What is your program to deal with this problem?

Triggs: We do not have any program to deal with the problem of migrancy. It is a difficult problem. We thought that the program of employing Mexican [national contract] workers in the United States . . . was a reasonably good approach.

Kennedy finally told Triggs: . . . this is the first time I have heard you, so perhaps this comes as more of a shock to me; to be opposed to a minimum wage, to be opposed to legislation which would limit the use of children between the ages of 10 and 13 for working, to be opposed to collective bargaining completely . . . to oppose all that without some alternative makes the rest of the arguments you have senseless.

In March of 1966 Harrison Williams brought the farm worker hearings into California, and it was here Kennedy got his first real look at Chavez and the farm workers. Chavez opened his testimony by pointing out, "Hearings similar to these have been called for decades, and unfortunately things have not changed very much in spite of them. The same labor camps which were used 30 years ago at the time of the La Follette committee hearings are still housing our workers. The same exploitation of child labor, the same idea that farm workers are a different breed of people — humble, happy, built close to the ground — prevails."

In a prophetic analogy, Chavez told the senators, "The Negro problem was the same way. People talked about it, people studied it for many years. I am sure that some very sincere people really worried about it. But nobody in the state capitals or in our nation's capital did anything about it

12

until one woman, Rosa Parks, walked to the front of the bus and touched off a revolution. Then men and women began freedom rides, and thousands of students came to help, and many people were needlessly maimed and slaughtered."

Under the leadership of Cesar Chavez, the California grape pickers had stood up and started moving toward the front of agriculture's economic bus in September of 1965.

CHAPTER TWO : THE UNION

In the spring of 1972 the United Farm Workers of America was at the crest of its power. Its president, Cesar Chavez, was a nationally recognized labor leader and the most prominent ethnic radical in the United States. What had been a ragtag coalition of Mexican and Filipino farm workers in 1965 was now a bona fide union within the AFL-CIO.

The UFWA had 147 contracts covering 50,000 to 60,000 jobs on farms in California, Arizona, and Florida, contracts with farms that ranged in size from 50-acre family operations to 50,000- and 100,000-acre corporate ventures by such conglomerates as Coca-Cola, Purex, Tenneco, United Fruit, and Hueblein. The union had a stable membership of 30,000 farm workers, and this number increased each spring as migrants from Texas and Mexico moved into the fruit and vegetable harvests covered by the UFWA contracts.

Chavez located the union's national headquarters in an old, abandoned tuberculosis sanitarium thirty miles east of Bakersfield in the Tehachapi Mountains. The rambling administrative buildings, hospital wings, and cottages house the 130 people who live in this place Chavez calls La Paz. In addition to the headquarters complex in the mountains, the UFWA had 26 field offices operating both hiring halls and farm worker service centers in the farming areas of three states; there were 33 boycott houses scattered across the United States; the UFWA had 600 volunteers, each getting $5 a week and expenses, working either on the staff or in the boycott. The average volunteer family needed $300 a month to survive, the single volunteers $50 a month. President Cesar Chavez and the UFWA executive board were also paid $5 a week. Chavez's expenses for 1972 totaled $5,144, an average of $426 a month for him, his wife, and three of his eight children who were still living at home.

Farm worker wages had been almost doubled by the union, and for the first time the workers were covered by a health and welfare medical plan that provided such benefits as $300 for childbirth and up to $400 for surgery. The union was establishing medical clinics and a prepaid health care plan. By the end of 1972 the Robert F. Kennedy Health and Welfare Plan — financed by 10-cents-an-hour employer contributions — had a $4.4 million reserve and was paying out $1.4 million a year in medical benefits. The plan — and the newly developing clinics and prepaid health care — were designed to meet the highly seasonal income patterns of the farm workers.

The union's administrative costs were running $175,000 a month. Income from the $3.50-a-month dues provided about $110,000 a month, on the average, and the rest came from regular contributions and sporadic fund-raising efforts. Each of the boycott cities was supposed to raise its own budgets, plus something extra for the general fund; but most of the boycott organizations were hard put to break even. Unions like the electrical workers, the rubber workers, and the county and municipal workers contributed on a regular basis; the United Auto Workers upped its contribution to $10,000 a week. Churches, synagogues, liberal groups, and individuals made contributions; and a considerable amount of Chavez's time was being spent traveling to generate this kind of support.

On the surface, the UFWA appeared quite strong, a young,

vigorous union that had somehow managed to wrest control of the work force away from more and more fruit and vegetable growers.

But Chavez warned, "We are not a union yet."

He was right. The UFWA had only captured control of a tiny portion of the total farm labor force, and that control was, at best, tenuous. The agribusiness employers in California, Florida, and Arizona were not accepting the inevitability of a Chavez-led labor organization's coming into their fields; if anything, the Chavez-led efforts from 1970 through 1973 had solidified the farmers' resolve to fight off the menace of organized farm labor. Most of California's lettuce growers had jumped into bed with the Teamsters when the grape growers signed UFWA contracts in 1970. By 1973 the UFWA grape contracts were expiring. Instead of renegotiating with the UFWA, the grape growers signed with the Teamsters and the fight was on.

The UFWA, financed by $1 million of its own money and $1.6 million donated by the AFL-CIO, struck the Coachella grape vineyards and a furious battle ensued. When the dust cleared, two UFWA members were dead, dozens were injured, 3,500 had been jailed, and the union had lost 133 of its 147 contracts. Some had simply expired and not been renegotiated, but most growers had switched to the Teamsters. The losses were staggering. The UFWA now controlled only 10,000 to 12,000 jobs in a scattered disarray of crops, and these 14 contracts were — from a reorganizing point of view — a liability to the boycott staff who would have to attack one brand of grapes while promoting another brand. It would all be very confusing to the consumer.

The loss of the contracts angered and disappointed AFL-CIO President George Meany; he had raised the $1.6 million for Chavez in the belief it would once and for all drive the Teamsters out of the fields and firmly establish the UFWA. The loss of the contracts convinced him that Chavez did not have the loyalty of the workers. In forming this judgment, Meany was trying to relate his Irish-Catholic, urban trade unionism to the problems of the United Farm Workers. But the problems of urban workers, with a century of trade union battles behind them, do not relate to the problems of the farm workers. The instability of agricultural labor — often one employer will have a 400 or 500 percent turnover in his work force in a single year — and the employer's absolute control over his workers has institutionalized a sense of chaos and futility within the workers. They expect the worst and adapt.

And then there is the problem of strikebreakers. Any labor leader, faced with the uninterrupted flow of legal and illegal aliens coming through the U.S.–Mexican border, would have had trouble sealing off the growers from the work force. But it wasn't the strike that Meany misread so much as it was Chavez's commitment to building a union that can take the absolute power away from the growers and place it in the hands of the workers. Where urban labor leaders like Meany deal in the art of compromise, meeting management on an equal footing to negotiate a wage increase or a week more of vacation, Chavez deals in guerrilla warfare. He is a revolutionary leader who decided he would not compromise those union structures the UFWA had created to seize control from the employer.

The structures were the hiring hall and the seniority system used to dispatch workers. Chavez admits he might have headed off the loss of the contracts — and the resulting strikes — if he and the rest of the UFWA leaders had been willing to compromise. But he said, "We had a choice and that choice was a weak, meaningless union or a fight for a strong union, with the possibility that we would lose it all. We gambled, and we lost all that we had gained in the 1970 contracts. But whatever we lost, we gained something too, because now the grape workers are really solid with us . . ."

He explained that many of the grape workers had been brought into the union through the 1970 contracts, and they had "never been really close to the union, not like the lettuce workers . . . then there was the Coachella fight and it really tempered them. Some of them went to jail, some were beaten, some were killed. We have a union now, which we never had before, a real aggressive group of grape workers . . . we won that, and that is quite a bit. We took a chance, and now we have a clear-cut decision: We know who is with us."

To some this may sound like Chavez was whistling in the dark. I don't think so; the fact that 3,500 farm workers were willing to go to jail for *La Causa* is a measure of strength. Chavez explained to me, "You don't know how far we've brought them. In 1962 the people were even afraid to look up when I came into the fields and began talking about a union; then, after we started organizing, they were afraid of the picket lines and the flag. (The union's flag is a black eagle on a red field.) This country has done a good job of making people afraid of strikes and anything red. Strikes are connected with disloyalty; red is associated with communism.

"Now they are not afraid of the flag; they accept the strike as an important part of their lives. Now when the courts bring those damn injunctions against us to cripple our picket lines they are willing to go to jail, they are not afraid of jail. When all of those men and their families were jailed — even the mothers and grandmothers went — we built a perpetual strike. They'll never be afraid again. Never. That's why when people ask if I am discouraged, I say: 'How can I be discouraged?' That kind of commitment you cannot destroy."

As he talked, Chavez got up out of the rocking chair behind his small black desk and started pacing slowly about the room, stretching against the ache of his back muscles. The office, in one corner of the big, rambling old administration building, is large, but sparsely furnished. Windows on two sides give a good view of *La Paz* and the mountains; the two interior walls are covered by homemade wall-to-ceiling bookshelves — painted red — that house an extensive library. The office floors are bare, paint-speckled hardwood, the furniture is secondhand — old kitchen and schoolroom castoffs. The chairs are for sitting, not relaxing.

Chavez is a deceptively small, soft-spoken man with tiny hands. At 46 his thick, straight black hair is touched here and there with lines of gray. His face is fuller now, the wrinkles at the corners of his brown eyes are deeper, the boyish look that once prompted him to grow a mustache — so he would look older to the people he was organizing — is gone. The pain of fasting and the fatigue of long days and impossible travel schedules have matured his appearance. He dresses simply, in soft, open-collared shirts, dark work pants, and scruffy shoes; for public appearances he will put on a white Mexican shirt with a Mandarin collar and bone twist buttons.

When he travels he is constantly flanked by two security guards and — unless the trip is by air — two big German shepherds. Chavez moves quietly in public, smiling, "how are you?" and shaking hands, pausing to listen to a question and give an answer. Because he is well known, his presence in a crowd causes a stir; yet he is almost unobtrusive. If he is with farm workers he is seldom up front; instead he will blend in with the crowd. In a line of march he will be somewhere well back of the leaders, walking with the people, listening to them, sensing their mood.

Chavez is not a great public speaker. He is a teacher, a visionary who is at his best in the give-and-take of a meeting with farm workers. He is gentle, frequently humorous, always persistent, sometimes ruthlessly sharp, seemingly arbitrary. There is never any doubt that he is the leader; yet the people in the meeting somehow convey the sense that they granted him the position, they project an air of expectation, and they impose upon him because he is their leader. Chavez is a listener; he hears the farm workers not only in group meetings, but afterward, if any of them wish to speak to him privately, he is available; and it is from these contacts that the structures of the union have come. While Chavez learned the lessons of farm labor and migrancy as a child of migrants, he has tested his own feelings against the will of the farm workers in countless meetings in every farming area of California.

Out of this he distilled his concept of a union. The hiring hall is the tool by which the UFWA intends to wrest the power away from the growers. And from the very beginning Chavez has openly declared that this shift of power, if it is to be successful, must eliminate the labor contracting system that has been used to dominate and exploit farm wage earners since the growers first imported Chinese coolie labor in the 1870s. The labor contractor is a middle man, a broker of muscle and sweat. He supplies farmers with workers and workers with jobs; he collects the cost of the labor from the farmer, deducts his "fee," and pays off the crews. The potential for cheating and exploitation is almost limitless; because unscrupulous operators have gouged the workers, California passed a series of labor contractor licensing and regulatory laws. But the legislature and former Governor Ronald Reagan have so shorted the labor-law enforcement staff, avaricious operators have little to worry about. Contractors not only charge for finding work, they house and feed and transport workers — all for profit. The contractor labor camps from New Jersey to Washington State are notoriously bad; the transportation frequently is unsafe.

Farm workers want to be rid of the contractor system. On the East Coast, in Texas, up through the Midwest, and in California, farm workers have told me one of their big goals is to purchase a car sound enough to travel independently, to be free of the contractor system that exploits them. The elimination of the labor contractor has been one of Chavez's goals from the beginning. During a 1966 rally he told workers: "We will not work under any labor contractor. The labor contractor is out. We will have a union hiring hall on a legal basis that will send men to jobs and those who live here the year round will have those jobs because they belong to us."

As the UFWA won its first contracts, it began putting together the hiring-hall system. The farmers under contract were required to give a general two-week notice to the hiring hall, indicating how many workers would be needed. The hiring hall would begin notifying workers that the jobs were opening up. Forty-eight hours before he needed the crew, the grower was to give the hiring hall a specific crew order, in writing. The dispatcher in turn notified workers — using a seniority list — and the jobs were held open for them for 48 hours. If some of these workers did not show up, then the dispatcher worked his way down the list.

Chavez likes to talk about the union, to discuss the concepts of union democracy. The hiring hall, the seniority system — with all its problems — and the grievance procedures all depend upon the union's basic building block, the *ranch committee*. The workers on each ranch covered by contract elect five workers from within their ranks to represent them in their dealings with both the employer and the union staff. On the giant conglomerate operations more than one ranch committee is needed to represent the workers adequately.

In Chavez's mind, the ranch committees — and the great mass of workers they represent — are a separate structure within the UFWA, and they must remain separate from the administrative staff if the union is to survive. It is the ranch committee that sets and administers the policy on each ranch; all of the ranch committees, meeting together in convention, create the broader union policies; and during the conventions — held every second year — they elect the union officers and the board of directors. Chavez, with the consent of the directors, hires the staff and establishes the administrative machinery.

He said, "We have to preserve the ranch committee. They must have direct representation at the convention. They not only have the right, but the responsibility, to deal with their own internal problems. They deal with the membership directly. They are *involved* at all levels of grievances, but they must be *responsible* for the first and second steps of the grievance procedures."

Chavez stopped pacing the floor, turned purposefully back to his desk, sat down and reached for a pen, took out a yellow scratch pad, and made a quick line across it: "See, we've had to fight these companies to make them talk to the ranch committees." He made two lines, as if underscoring his spoken words to add emphasis. "The companies wanted to come direct to *La Paz* and have us straighten out the problems, but we can't do that."

He made another line with his pen: "Because we are dealing with people most of whom have never been to a meeting before, we had to start from scratch. We didn't have rules for the ranch committees. They made them up as they went along . . ."

This frequently created unbearable strain between management and labor. Farmers, accustomed to dealing with absolute authority, now had to meet with a committee of workers if there was any question about an order or a contract clause. When problems arose between the committee and the farmer, the farmer would reach for the phone and put in a call to La Paz. Although Chavez has this deep-seated belief that each ranch committee must be the one to handle the problems on its own ranch, he frequently had to step in to keep things from blowing up. He had to quell wildcat strikes and bring the committee into the grievance procedures spelled out in their contract.

But his problems weren't just with labor and management relations; there was internal conflict also. Chavez said, "There was a big drive on to get rid of one of our guys in the Poplar hiring hall. I sent Richard [Chavez's brother] out there to see what was happening. On first examination, Richard said he did not feel that Al [the hiring-hall supervisor] had done anything wrong, that he was just enforcing some rules over there."

The hiring hall had been forcing migrant workers returning from Mexico to pay the $3.50-a-month back dues before they could be dispatched. Union regulations required all members to keep dues current; they were paid in quarterly installments, and a small stamp was affixed to the back of the union membership card to note the paid-dues status of each worker. But Richard Chavez also discovered that a ranch committee — over the Poplar staff's protests — had been skirting the seniority system to help get cousins, aunts, and uncles on the payroll. Before the union signed its contracts, such nepotism was an established part of the farm labor scene. Any worker

21

who could supply 10 or 15 reliable workers on demand had a good chance of becoming a crew boss or foreman. He not only helped relatives and friends — frequently bringing them up from Mexico or Texas — but he could also advance his own position. The most ambitious men sometimes built up two or three crews and then moved into labor contracting. Such a system was built on paternalism that was frequently despotic, avaricious, and exploitative.

Chavez backed up his Poplar hiring-hall staff, calling the ranch committee to task. "We told them the rules were theirs; they had made the seniority system, and we were there to follow it."

In another area, a ranch committee had been using a nearby unorganized farm as a place of extra work for union members. When the unorganized farm signed with the UFWA these "extra jobs" were technically no longer available to outsiders. The newly organized ranch had its own ranch committee and job structure, but the bigger, older committee tried a raid on the jobs. Chavez heard about it and ordered the offenders to report to La Paz. "I told them one more time and I would strip them of their authority. I am very tough when it comes to protecting individual rights."

Once he starts explaining the ranch committee structure, it is hard to get Cesar away from the subject. He would answer other questions, talk of other things, then in midsentence say, "There's one more thing I want to tell you . . ." and we would be back on the subject again. For instance, in Delano, where there were 30 ranches under contract, there were 150 ranch committeemen setting policy for the Delano hiring hall's service area.

Chavez explained that it would be more efficient to have a 15-man representative board, "but if we do that the big ranches will elect the guys and the little ranches will not be represented. Then say if ranch 28 down the list in size has a problem but has only 60 people involved, the more pressing problem on ranch three or five, with 1,000 workers, will get the service.

"What we are doing is taking each factory, no matter how

big or small, and giving them their own executive board. We can't do that unless we computerize the administration and have a large central staff. But we are starting something that I think is very dear. We are giving these guys on the small ranches a voice."

A knock at the office door interrupted him. An aide opened the door halfway, looked in, then came on in carrying what at first glance appeared to be a carafe of thick orange juice and a single glass. Chavez thanked the aide and, pouring a glass, asked, "You know what this is? . . . carrot juice."

"Is it good?"

"Oh, tremendous." He handed the full glass toward me, "Try it, I'll drink out of the jar."

As we took a carrot juice break Chavez started explaining another of his passions, a vegetarian diet. "I don't drink water, you know? I haven't had a glass of water in two weeks; the only water to touch my mouth is when I brush my teeth. This [holding up the jar of carrot juice] is the best water you can get. Let the plants take it up, takes all the impurities out."

The only processed foods Chavez eats are cottage cheese and bread; he eats a lot of greens, watercress, avocados, hot potato soup when the weather is cold. Although he gets up before dawn and starts work, his first food intake is at mid-morning: "I take yeast, two heaping teaspoons of yeast, with lemon and hot water and honey, so that when I go for lunch I am ready to start digesting, the moment I start eating. I eat fruit first and I eat food second, the fruit goes underneath and gets your digestive things going."

Once, following a 25-day fast, Chavez suffered horribly from a disabling back problem that lasted for a year; despite the best efforts of several doctors, the twisting pain continued sporadically, he said, until he started his vegetarian diet: "I claim my diet had a lot to do with my good health; that is how I got rid of my back problems. Oh, the doctors helped, I know . . ." He let the words trail off as his thoughts shifted slightly, "If I am nervous or irritated, I take carrot juice or celery juice and it's better than a tranquilizer."

When Chavez is traveling, Richard Ybarra, the young chief of security, takes along a supply of fruit and vegetables and a blender. Ybarra is Chavez's son-in-law and constant companion; on the road he doubles as a travel secretary and boss of the young Chicanos who guard Chavez and handle the logistical chores. When they are driving, they take the two guard dogs, Boycott and Huelga. They always take two cars, and sometimes three; Cesar and Richard Ybarra — and the two dogs — ride in the station wagon and Cesar works. Frequently he will ask an aide or an associate to ride with him so they can discuss a project or a problem. When they are flying, Ybarra handles all the logistical chores by himself; he sometimes brings an assistant to help set up security and to drive the cars they rent or borrow on a whirlwind tour of Ohio or New Jersey or Texas.

Chavez is never left alone, even when he is home, at La Paz. The concern for Cesar's safety began increasing after Martin Luther King and then Robert F. Kennedy were assassinated by gunmen. Kennedy was particularly close to Chavez and the farm workers, and his death left a deep impression on the UFWA staff. Then, in the summer of 1971, U.S. Treasury agents warned Chavez they had uncovered what could have been a plot to take his life. An informant had told the agents some unnamed Delano farmers had put up $25,000 to have the farm labor leader killed and some of his personal files burned. Nothing was proven and both the Treasury Department and Department of Justice dropped the case, turning what evidence they had over to local law enforcement agencies.

Not long afterward, a UFWA supporter gave Chavez the two German shepherd guard dogs, Boycott and Huelga. Roving security patrols were established around the union headquarters at La Paz, and a 24-hour security gate was posted at the front entrance. Chavez's small wood-frame house is surrounded by a high chain-link fence; inside the fence a third, more aggressive, guard dog — Red — is allowed to roam. Chavez has learned to accept all of this and has taken an active interest in the dogs. He has learned to train them himself, and he takes great delight in showing off their obedience skills.

Walking along a road shaded by oak trees, Chavez talked about the dogs, then pulled a small choke chain out of his pocket and shook it, gently. Boycott and Huelga, running off a way, stopped, perked up their ears, caught the sound of the chain, and returned to Chavez's side. By voice command he ordered them to heel, sit, stay, lie down. He was quiet with them, but insistent. Direct. The dogs showed no indecision or confusion; they obeyed quietly, instantly.

Pleased with their performance, he called them over and showed them a great deal of affection. He straightened up and said, "Come on, I'll show you the kennels."

Out behind the administrative complex, and off to one side, is the big kennel where he keeps a half dozen young German shepherds. "I train them myself, you know. It's very easy. It only takes 5 minutes a day with a dog, that's all. You start with 20- or 30-foot leash, try to get him to go for a temptation, like a cat or a squirrel, so he'll run. When they hit the end of the leash, they learn. You pull them in, give them a lot of praise, a lot of affection; and they get the idea that they must depend on you, not the leash."

Talking with staff people around Cesar you get the impression the dogs are for security. They do look menacing. But Cesar said the dogs had no security training; they are not guard dogs, but his companions. Red, by his own aggressive nature, is not trusted by anyone but Chavez and Ybarra — when I, without knowing this, climbed into a car with Red and just verbally pushed him over and sat down, Ybarra became visibly concerned for my safety. The dog apparently had grudgingly accepted me because of my lack of fear; I didn't repeat the mistake. Red normally bristles and barks when strangers approach the car he's riding in, or the house he's guarding. On the other hand, Boycott and Huelga are quiet. They are used to travel, and, whether at La Paz or a rally in some farming town, they lie on the floor, or move lazily around the room, ignoring the hands that reach out to pet them.

La Paz is an unlikely setting for a trade union headquarters. But it is a symbol of Chavez's unique concept; somehow he equates the movement he leads with some kind of agrarian social reform. As he walks through La Paz he makes it obvious he feels something for "the land." There are 300 acres here, rolling, grassy hills studded with big oaks. The place once belonged to Kern County, but advances in the treatment of tuberculosis made such isolated hospitals unnecessary. The big medical units, staff housing, central steam-boiler plant, and the administrative buildings fell into disrepair. The county put a $2 million price tag on the place, but no one wanted to buy. The price was lowered, then lowered again and again. Someone in the union heard a farmer was quietly buying the property from the county for $201,000. Cesar called a movie producer friend who had said he wanted to help the UFWA buy a farm someday; the producer agreed to put in a bid for $205,000, the farmer upped his bid, and the contest was on. The movie producer won at $232,000. The county officials had no idea the down payment was a gift to the union, and that the UFWA would work off the sale price on a lease-purchase agreement.

Cesar laughed, "When they found out a month later that a Hollywood Jew and a Delano Mexican had gotten together to beat them, they were mad as hell."

Chavez renamed the place La Paz — the peaceful place — and in 1971 pulled the central UFWA staff into the complex. This reduced the Delano "Forty Acres" administrative unit and hiring hall, the medical clinic, and cooperative gas station to a field-office status. Not everyone in the union hierarchy approved of the move, but Chavez's arguments prevailed. In addition to administrative space, he had been seeking some place to start a union training center, a place where farm workers could be trained to administer their own union. The big old buildings at La Paz would provide that space.

La Paz is staffed by the $5-a-week volunteers. They live in the old staff housing or in trailers purchased by the union. The former hospital unit has been converted to a transient hotel for the constant stream of people coming through La Paz: farm workers come here for training, Anglo volunteers pass through on the way to a boycott assignment or a staff job in a field office. The full-time La Paz population fluctuates between 100 and 150, as people come and go. Many are married and usually both parents work at staff jobs. There is a nursery school–day care center for the younger children, and the school-aged kids are bused into the small town of Tehachapi, 10 miles farther back in the mountains.

The ethnic mix at La Paz is Anglo-Chicano, with an occasional black or Puerto Rican. Although the names and numbers change rapidly, on one day in 1974 the list of residents at La Paz showed 76 Anglo and 30 Spanish surnames. Most of the Chicanos are farm workers who have come into the union full time; Anglo volunteers are a mix — some are young, long-haired New Left, others are middle-aged couples who have taken a month or a year and given themselves over to the cause; there are union carpenters and painters here for a week or a weekend; high school and college students come to offer their sweat on weekends and during school vacations; 25 law students came into the union's legal department for the summer of 1974.

La Paz is in many respects a commune and Chavez thinks in communal terms. He frequently speaks in the "we" context and envisions a self-sufficiency and sense of community that is disquieting to some of his followers. Privately there are those who argue that La Paz has removed the union leadership from the fields and farming towns where the farm workers live. Some feel the intense pressures of living in a tightly controlled isolated community are too great. Chavez, they say, has absolute control over not only their work, but even their private lives because of the pace and example he sets.

For Chavez, La Paz is a refuge, a home where he can escape the public, highly politicized aspects of his life and focus on workaday union problems. But La Paz is also a hobby, a distraction, a place where he can experiment with his instincts for agrarian reform. He has imported four hives of bees and located them on a knoll, away from the buildings. And he tends them personally.

Bees?

"Sure, for the honey. I eat honey like a bear. Honey is so expensive now . . . oh, it's expensive; $5 a quart. And I use a lot of it, every morning I have a pint or two of hot lemon juice with honey mixed in."

As Chavez talks about honey, and beekeeping, it is obvious he has studied the subject intensively, and I'm impressed, once again, with his ability to single-mindedly tackle one subject at a time, focusing his attention entirely on what is at hand. Walking the La Paz pathways, he stops and talks to a woman tending a flower bed and he is a gardener, talking to a gardener; out, traveling and making speeches and meeting with supporters and holding press conferences, he is a politician given over to the rush of 18-hour days, moving through a constantly changing set of places and people; in meeting with farm workers he is the gentle teacher, the interested listener who has the time and patience to cultivate the ideas of his fellow workers, developing them into usable policies; to the farmers, in negotiations, Chavez is mercurial — sometimes an angry, swearing man who will concede nothing, sometimes an amiable, reasonable person willing to reach agreement.

The farmers who have negotiated contracts with him say that at the bargaining table he frequently uses four-letter words, but interestingly the farmers don't repeat those words in direct quotes — although they, themselves use the same words as frequently. What they seem to try to imply is that Chavez is a man who has been proclaimed a saint when in fact he is not. The farmers don't like the hiring hall, or the seniority system or the ranch committee structure. One complained angrily, "They are so goddamn democratic they can't get a goddamn thing done."

Another grape grower, Steve Pavich, of Delano, said, "The union officials were just like mosquitoes behind a guy's ear. They bothered the shit out of you, but you had to put up with it . . . they fought you on seniority, on grievances, on the dispatch system. It got so when we got a grievance, we filed it in the wastebasket. If they felt strongly enough about it, we would hear from them again."

Pavich, 24, is taking over the 500-acre family vineyard from his father. He said, "I went to school with José (the supervisor of the Delano hiring hall). He was kind of a nice kid until he got involved in this union thing . . . people get in those union things and their egos get all involved . . . this power thing they got is really hell . . . goes to their heads.

"Where before they were nothing, you know? So now they are in the limelight. They got all this power. They just whip on you, they been whipping on me for three years," young Pavich complained in an angry voice. According to Pavich — and others like him — the hiring hall and seniority system created havoc with work patterns and traditional farming practices. It was for these reasons, they said, that as the UFWA contracts expired in 1973 the grape workers began switching to the Teamsters.

Pavich, like most farmers, is angry over the press coverage he feels has been pro-Chavez. After cussing me individually and the press in general for nearly 10 minutes, Pavich challenged me to go into the fields and talk to the workers during the 1973 harvest season. I accepted the challenge.

In the course of one morning I talked to 10 workers in five family groups. Almost without exception they said they preferred the Teamsters — if they had to have any union at all. These workers were migrants — from Michoacan, Mexico — who come up just for the grape harvest, staying on each ranch only as long as the best picking is available, then they move with the season.

One weathered old man, the father of eight children who were all at work in the vines, summed it up: "Chavez has been a good leader for the workers, but the people working under him have not been so good for the workers."

Why?

The problem was with the dispatch and seniority systems, he said. These migrants travel in family groups. Everyone, including the younger children, work, and, over the years,

29

they have developed employer contacts and working patterns. The UFWA, when it won the grape contracts in 1970, covered this work force. To work they had to pay $3.50-a-month dues — including those months spent back in Mexico each winter — and be dispatched through the hiring hall.

The old man sighed. With the UFWA he had received some medical benefits — though he felt the $300 allowed for childbirth should have been higher because his wife had to have a Caesarean section. He acknowledged that without the Chavez-led union, wages and working conditions would not have improved as they have. But the hiring hall would not dispatch the family right away, they had to wait, then sometimes they would break up the family, making them take jobs on different ranches rather than allowing them to work as a group. He concluded, "With the Teamsters is like no union at all. With the Teamsters you are free. If you do not make it at one place, you can go someplace else. There is no problem with the back dues, the *patron* [farmer or labor contractor] takes it out of your wages."

The Teamster contracts set wages at rates comparable to the patterns established by the UFWA, but they allow both the farmer and the farm worker to return to the pre-UFWA labor relations power structure. The growers can, under Teamster contract, use farm labor contractors, they can work families — including children — and illegal aliens without interference from the union. The hiring hall is abolished and with it any meaningful seniority system for seasonal workers. As the growers switched to the Teamsters, the number of illegal aliens employed on California farms increased at a startling rate.

One illegal alien, working on a Delano grape ranch, gave the UFWA a sworn statement that said in part: "Each month eight dollars are deducted from my check. I am told this money goes for dues to the Teamsters union. I signed a card for the Teamsters when I was told by the company that I will be fired if I do not sign. The only thing I know about the arrangement is that they take the eight dollars from me every month and when I die thay will send death benefits to my wife and kids in Michoacan, Mexico."

Historically the influx of migrants into any crop was encouraged by the growers because it kept the wage structure depressed; local workers could not organize and demand higher pay if the growers had ample supplies of workers who — because of poverty in Mexico — would work for low wages in farming areas of the United States. The impact of large numbers of migrants — whether legally or illegally in this country — was like that of a stone dropped in a still pool, the economic ripples spread, reaching the farthest corners of the pond. Chavez felt the key to reversing this economically depressing effect was to guarantee the jobs for local workers.

Chavez said, "The big fight we have — and we didn't solve it the first time around — is that the local people . . ." His voice trailed off, then he picked up the idea from another angle. "See, it is not the dispatch card or the dues so much; it is that we don't send the migrant worker out if he doesn't have seniority. That's where the problem is at; though they don't say it, they blame the dispatch system and the hiring hall, but they don't talk about the real issue, seniority."

Chavez admitted there were problems in individual hiring halls and that the payment of back dues did create problems, but he pointed out these things were being worked out, the dues structure was totally revamped by the ranch committees meeting in convention in the fall of 1973. Chavez said, "The big fight is still the seniority system, we computerized the lists of people. The grower had nowhere to go with excuses because we had him right on his own records. We fought like hell to get these local guys hired first.

"What has been done is the families come, the migrants, and they come for the picking only, they bring a cousin or a brother and his family. So they have their own work force and they will come for the picking, where the best money is, and they will take off after the best is over . . . so what these guys from Michoacan are talking about when they say the dispatch or the hiring hall is the seniority system, we won't

31

let them work until our guys with seniority have the jobs. We feel if we don't have that, we don't have a union."

The problems of the migrants in competition with the local workers is most critical in places like the Delano-Earlimart area, where large numbers of former migrants have settled and become a permanent part of the work force. These men and women work thinning and pruning and tying the vines during the cold of winter; these are the relatively low-paying jobs, compared to the harvest pay scales. At harvest such workers make the bulk of their income; their wives and children can work in the harvests, supplementing this income. Once the UFWA contracts had been signed, the strongest of these workers became members of ranch committees. Sylvestre Galvan was one of these. Galvan was a former migrant, a member of an extended family group that once traveled as a crew sufficient unto itself. The family settled in Wasco, and Galvan became a tractor driver on one corporate farm. His wife and relatives worked seasonally on the same farm. From 1970 to 1973 Galvan was a member of the ranch committee and was in the thick of the struggle to strengthen the workers' position with their employer.

One of the first major confrontations between the ranch committee and the farm management came during the harvest of the highly perishable plum crop. Ranch supervisors insisted on hiring migrants — they wanted a quick surplus of workers to get the crop off in a hurry — rather than waiting for the dispatch of local workers. The union had a "48-hour rule" that gave the workers with seniority a two-day chance to claim their jobs. The delay was intolerable to the supervisors; in addition to getting the work force over a two-day period, the ranch also had to take the older, slower workers. The foreman wanted the chance to select only the fastest workers and to push them with speed-up tactics outlawed by the union. The ranch committee would not tolerate such tactics.

When the seniority system prevailed, despite the hassling, the ranch management lowered the piece rate, contending the slower workers were not worth more. The rate was so low

the slowest workers were not making the guaranteed mini-
mums, and the ranch committee once again stood up to
management. In the midst of the hassling the ranch supervisors discharged 28 workers, including Galvan. Five hundred
workers walked off in protest. The 28 were rehired and the
piece rate boosted.

How did Galvan feel about the hiring hall?

He said, "The ranch committee worked with the Delano
hiring hall staff and the seniority dispatch came first. The
migrants from Mexico and Texas didn't like it when they
couldn't go right into the fields. Before the contract they used
to come right on in, brown nose the boss, and get on, but now
the seniority protects those of us who stay the year round and
work the cold weather jobs too . . ."

I have watched the ranch committees work, sat through
some of their grievance procedures where field workers on
the committees confront management on an equal footing.
Sometimes such confrontations were stalemated; neither side
could give enough to reach settlement, and the issues were
taken to arbitration. Sometimes the workers used wildcat
strike tactics and had to be ordered back to work by Chavez
so that the grievance procedures could work. But frequently
the issues were resolved, and, for the first time, workers had a
real voice in their working conditions.

Nowhere was this more obvious than among the black
citrus workers in the Florida orange and lemon groves owned
by Coca-Cola's subsidiaries, Minute Maid and Hi-C, now
under contract to the UFWA. Throughout Florida, farm
workers are little better than rented slaves; historically they
have lived in unbelievable poverty and have been powerless
to do anything about these conditions.

A 1970 NBC-TV documentary, "Migrant," focused on the
problems of the citrus workers, including those employed by
Coca-Cola. Coke President J. Paul Austin, in a surprisingly
frank response, testified before a U.S. Senate subcommittee
that the migrant workers did suffer malnutrition, physical
privation, and a "profound sense of futility." Austin said he
discovered the facts of migrant life in the Coke groves in

1968, after "I began reading more and more about the crusade of Cesar Chavez in California."

Austin ordered Coke's farm labor practices improved. At about the same time Chavez ordered his cousin Manuel Chavez to go to Florida and begin organizing the citrus workers. Manuel Chavez concentrated on the 25,000 acres in the Minute Maid and Hi-C groves near Avon Park and Indiantown in southcentral Florida. Most of the workers were black, and at first they were suspicious of the square-set, tough-talking Chicano. But he is persuasive, and persistent, and workers began signing cards. By the spring of 1972 Manuel Chavez could prove to Coke management that the UFWA represented the majority of the 1,200 workers. Coke signed a contract, guaranteeing the workers $61.50 a week, work or not; the workers were given such fringe benefits as paid vacations and medical benefits. The union established a hiring hall and service center.

The workers and the company management negotiated a piece-rate adjustment system that daily allows the workers a voice in establishing the rate of payment for harvesting the fruit. Mack Lyons, UFWA Florida supervisor and a former DiGiorgio farm worker from California, said the Florida citrus workers under contract are now averaging $5,000 a year, double what they used to earn. In addition, the contract seniority system provides year-round work for most of the crews. These former migrants — they traveled north each summer "on the season" — now spend the year moving from one grove to another on Coke property. Company-provided transportation — big, clean buses equipped with toilets and drinking water — allow the workers to return home each night. During the lemon season the workers travel two hours each way, but prefer this to living in labor camps.

One lemon picker, asked how the union had affected his life, replied: "It means a whole lot. I feel damn good about it. Lots of protections I never had before. Since I been here I just feel free on my job. I wake up in the morning and I know where I am going. I don't have to meet the boss with my head down no more."

Another lemon picker talked as he worked, pulling the fruit from the thorny trees, dropping it into the big picking bag strapped to his upper body. "It used to be the bull [foreman] jump you. All that bullshit. They try to pull you [keep wages low] and tell you if you don't want to pick, get the hell out. Now they can't do that."

From Florida to California the workers complained about the speed-up systems formerly used, and those who support the UFWA agree with the Chavez concepts of seniority and a hiring hall system. Those workers who have been in the struggle to organize a union, and who have worked under contract, have a growing awareness of their collective power. Ernesto Loredo, a former migrant from the Rio Grande Valley of Texas, is a strong union member; a picket captain during the time of strikes, he has led 285 men and women in acts of civil disobedience that ended in their mass arrest and jailing.

Loredo, his wife, and children once traveled in a family group that numbered 18, moving through Midwest harvests, traveling seasonally into Arizona and, at the end of the cotton season, back into Texas. In the early 1960s they started migrating into the California fruit harvests, spending their winters in Woodville in a Tulare County Housing Authority labor camp. The camp was a half-hour drive from Delano, where Chavez was living as he started organizing the National Farm Workers Association in 1962.

Loredo recalled, "Cesar came to the camp, but he did not try to convince us we ought to join. He just tried to show us we had a problem . . ."

It was difficult for me to understand his point. It seemed obvious to me that farm workers had all kinds of economic and social problems and that they certainly should be the first to know about them. Loredo tried to explain that being poor was a way of life and that the working poor were convinced the problems they faced were foreordained by a social system they could not control or even influence.

"We thought that always you had to suffer and be hungry. That was our life."

I asked, "You mean you had to be convinced this was a problem?"

"Yeah. Yeah. I think that is why Chavez is so great. He doesn't bullshit you. He just say, 'Look, you know, people call you a son-of-a-bitch in front of your wives, your mothers, and they don't have the right to do that.'

"I had accepted that as a way of life. So what was new? So then he convinced us something has to be done, that we do not have to take that. He tells us we can do something about that, and then he turns and goes away, just saying 'I'll see you, huh?' He doesn't tell us to join him, or nothing, so naturally we had to go to Delano and hear more." He grinned.

Then Loredo's deep brown face took on a serious, yet peaceful, expression, "He started shaping my life. I changed. I completely changed. I am a different man now."

And it is true. Ernesto Loredo is a different man. He is a leader himself, a quietly determined man who says, "In the United Farm Workers we see the solution to our problems . . . before it was really something else, you know? And so we are willing to do anything we can. Some of us put our jobs on the line, whatever it takes. Some of us put our lives on the line to see that we have a union . . . there is no other way."

CHAPTER THREE : A BLOODY PAST

The history of farm labor is redundant. Masses of impoverished people have been imported into the work force and exploited. Low pay and intolerable working conditions, hunger and privation, are the rule for those who must work for wages on the farm. Periodically these powerless workers become restive. The farmers tolerate some unrest, but when the workers show signs of open rebellion, the agribusiness labor system begins to purge and recycle itself.

First, the farmers psych themselves up for the traumatic confrontations; the current work force is discredited and given a pejorative label; the once efficient Chinese coolies become quarrelsome Chinks, the "industrious" Japanese become sneaky Japs, and the "perfect workers" — the Mexicans — become dirty, lazy Spics. When the most aggressive workers walk out on strikes, the farmers cry out against the "outsiders," "agitators," and "Communists" who are leading the workers astray, and the war is on. Judges outlaw strike activities and mass meetings and local law enforcement moves in; too often, wherever workers gather mob violence erupts. Guns fire. Clubs split heads. Blood. Mass arrests. Terror. Violence. The strikes are broken, the leaders jailed or run out of the county. A labor shortage is declared, and recruiters seek out a new powerless minority.

When the 1965 table-grape harvests started in California's Coachella Valley, 100 miles north of the Mexican border, the Filipino farm workers, who had been migrating with the crop for 30 years, found their wages were lower than those of the Mexican nationals being imported under federally supervised programs. The Filipinos struck, and their wages were increased. But when the harvest moved north into the San Joaquin Valley the farmers there were paying the lower wages. The Filipinos went out on strike again and the farmers began to react; it seemed the historic patterns would once more be repeated. But they were not repeated. The grape strikes did not go according to history. From the very beginning this labor unrest began to take on new form and shape; the new element was a permanency, a structural form that would endure beyond the immediate walkout on one farm or set of farms.

Although it was the Filipinos who started the strikes, it was Cesar Chavez and his newly emerging National Farm Workers Association that established the concept of a permanent, social service–oriented farm workers union. The strike was not of Chavez's choosing, but time and circumstance forced the NFWA to join with the striking Filipinos. The fact that all of this happened in California is not accidental or coincidental; the right man — Chavez — was in the right place — Delano, California — at the right time.

California — specifically the 200-mile long, 60-mile wide San Joaquin Valley, located in the heart of the state — is one of the few places in the nation where such a struggle could take root in 1965 and grow. It is here, in the flat, fertile lands that were once an inland sea — an extension of San Francisco Bay — that the future of agriculture has always been written. Here, in the nation's richest farming counties, the myth of the family farm takes on its industrialized, agribusiness proportions.

California farms produce $8 billion in food and fiber; the state supplies a quarter of the fruit and vegetables for the nation's market baskets. The average California farm is an irrigated, specialized operation covering nearly 600 acres. But the average is small potatoes when compared with the large operations within the southern half of the San Joaquin Valley, the primary territory of the Chavez-led farm workers' union.

For example, the Giumarra family corporations operate 11,000 acres in a checkerboard of ownerships and leases that sprawls across Tulare and Kern counties. The family farms 6,000 acres of vineyards and 5,000 acres of orchards and row crops; there are packinghouses, cold-storage plants, and a winery within the family corporations to process and market the farm output. According to John Giumarra, Jr., the family lawyer and spokesman, the Giumarras employ 200 farm workers the year round, and seasonally this figure will reach 2,000 during the peak of harvest.

The Giumarra payroll records reflect the transient, unstable nature of the agribusiness labor force; the company will hire 8,000 farm workers in a year just to maintain the needed supply of labor. Some will work a day, some a week or a month; some will be fired, most will be laid off after a specific job has been completed. Prior to the advent of the United

38

Farm Workers there had been no union job protection, no call-back procedures, no seniority systems to stabilize the work force. A 400 percent labor turnover in farming was not uncommon.

The Giumarras represent *successful* family farming. But they are not typical of large-scale, industrialized farming operations like Anderson Clayton Company (50,000 acres) and J. G. Boswell Company (110,000 acres). The Tejon Ranch sold 2,225 of its 290,000 irrigated acres for $518,000. The biggest "farm" in California is the old Kern County Land Company, now a part of the Tenneco conglomerate. Tenneco farms 128,000 irrigated acres in the valley as part of a 1.4-million-acre agribusiness operation in California and Arizona.

These are the "Factories in the Fields" that Carey McWilliams wrote about in the late 1930s. This is industrialized farming, where each acre is mechanically and chemically pushed to yields that stagger the imagination.

To push these yields so high farmers invest great sums of money for irrigation water, seed, fertilizers, pest-control chemicals, chemical growth stimulators, and chemicals to improve the cosmetic appeal of the fruit or vegetables. But the most costly input is labor. These factories — whether 200 acres or 20,000 acres — require large crews of workers for relatively short seasons. Mechanization cut labor costs and made the individual farm worker more productive — one worker in 1950 produced food for himself and 15 others; by 1967 the figure was for himself and 41 others and still climbing. Machines push workers out of jobs — the cotton-picking machine, alone, eliminated more than 1 million hand-labor jobs in the 1950s. But, in California — and particularly in the San Joaquin Valley — the number of farm jobs is increasing because the number of acres of irrigated farming is increasing dramatically. In 1939, California had 4 million acres of irrigated land. With the construction of the state and federally financed California Aqueduct and the Central Valleys Project canals this figure has doubled; there

39

were 8 million acres of irrigated land in California by 1972, and the figure should reach 10 million by 1986.

The net result is an increase in jobs. The U.S. Department of Agriculture reported 190,000 hired farm workers in California in 1968; by 1973 that number had increased to 213,000. (The same trend is beginning to show in the national farm labor statistics). Whether they are called seasonal workers, permanent workers, or migrant workers, these are the "hired hands." Only a small percentage of this force is used on traditional "family farms." Most are employed in the "Factories in the Fields."

McWilliams wrote:

> What has long been termed "the farm labor problem" in California may be said to date from the introduction of intensive farming with the attendant requirements for an abundance of cheap, skilled, mobile and temporary labor. The rudiments of the problem, as it exists today [1939], existed in 1886. From 1886 to the present time the problem, in so far as the growers were concerned, has simply been to recruit and maintain this supply of labor . . .

Nearly four decades later these words are still true. It is frustrating to look back 35 years to McWilliams's work and realize *he* was looking back and reporting the "worker's plight is nearly as wretched today as it was 30 years ago." Trying to explain California's violent farm labor history, McWilliams wrote,

> . . . to realize what is back of the terror and violence which breaks out periodically in the farm valleys, it is necessary to know something of the social history of California . . . [It] is in many respects a melodramatic history, a story of theft, violence and exploitation. It completely belies the sense of peace and lassitude that seems to hover over rural California.

He referred to the land baronies created out of questionable Mexican land grants or carved out of United States land laws between the 1840s and 1880s. The land swindles, the schemes of private empire that were worked in the western United States became legends, and created a prototype for using and misusing governmental largess. But the story of California's land schemes is another subject, for another time.

The point to be made here is that most farm jobs are found on industrial or corporate farms and the number of these farms — hence the number of jobs — is growing. Historically these jobs have been so poorly paid that the workers have been kept in economic servitude. The awful conditions shown in Edward R. Murrow's TV documentary *Harvest of Shame* are hard to differentiate from the conditions in John Steinbeck's *Grapes of Wrath*; yet two decades and 3,000 miles separate these journalistic efforts. (The documentary was filmed in 1960 among black East Coast migrants, the book written about Dust Bowl "Okies" flocking into the California harvests in the mid-1930s). These same deplorable conditions caused Japanese fruit pickers to walk out of California orchards in 1902; black sugar-cane cutters rebelled against intolerable wage and working conditions in Louisiana plantations in 1896, and one of the first farm labor strikes ever reported occurred when Chinese workers refused to harvest the Kern County hop crop in 1885.

The Chinese hop pickers were members of a tong — an association of an extended family group from a specific province of China. In California the tongs — controlled by wealthy Chinese merchants — acted as the workers' agents and as a labor contractor for employers, profiting from both.

With the completion of the transcontinental railroad, the dry land grain farms in California gave way to the more profitable fruit and vegetable crops that could be marketed in the East. Fruit farming required gangs of laborers for the brief harvest seasons, and the Chinese contracting system was refined and expanded. Mexican and Indian workers were brought into the crops and more Chinese were imported. Late in the 1800s a series of labor disputes, then an economic depression, triggered anti-Chinese rioting, and the coolies were driven from the fields. They were replaced by young

41

Japanese men, who were declared better suited for the work.

In the Midwest an army of grain harvesters worked their way north each summer up through the Great Plains, creating legends of the "bindle-stiffs" and the hired harvest hands. These were the unskilled European immigrants who worked sporadically on industrial assemblylines, or in lumbering and mining or on railroad maintenance gangs. Because they had no marketable skills or trades, organized labor unions had little interest in these men. But the Socialists were concerned. They created the International Workers of the World, one of the earliest unions to attempt to organize the proletariat.

The "Wobblies" organized from the top of soapboxes on downtown street corners, near the factory gates, out in the fields — wherever they could find exploited workers. Labor historian Philip Taft wrote, "The ability of the iww leaders to mobilize large, unskilled masses to display their poverty and suffering was of a high order, but they failed in the elementary ability needed to build a permanent organization . . ."

The iww set the pattern for a half century of farm labor organizing efforts. And Taft's critical observation remained true. None of the farm labor union efforts left anything behind except the memory of violent confrontation. The iww organizers moved with the workers, in the textile mills, in the lumber mills, in the fields, taking advantage of existing strikes, exerting leadership wherever they found the proletariat in rebellion. In 1912 they were in Lawrence, Massachusetts, mill strikes and in 1913 they were in the New Jersey silk workers' strikes. In the summer of 1913 Wobbly organizers Blackie Ford and Herman Suhr were with destitute farm workers' families in California. That summer there were 10 unemployed men for every job, people were hungry and desperate, entire families groveled for work, accepting any wage.

When the Durst Brothers advertised they needed 2,700 workers to pick their hops, near Wheatland, thousands of people responded. Within days 3,800 men, women, and children showed up at the Durst farm. E. B. Durst allowed the workers to camp on a low, unshaded hill; he supplied tents, at 75 cents a week. There were only 9 outdoor toilets, the water wells were inadequate, and soon went dry. A relative of Durst's sold lemonade at 5 cents a glass. Durst established a company store to sell groceries at inflated prices.

There was no garbage disposal, no sanitary system established. Soon the camp was filthy. Disease spread. Although he had advertised for 2,700 workers Durst really needed only 1,500. There wasn't enough work to go around; the picking rates were dropped from $1 a hundred to 90 cents. Over half the workers were destitute and were living from day to day, cashing in their daily pay tickets at the company store. The workers — from a half dozen different ethnic backgrounds, speaking seven different languages — were earning $1 a day, or less.

Ford and the other IWW organizers in the camp began to call meetings. Committees were formed and workers drew up a list of demands protesting the living conditions, the overcrowding, lack of water and sanitation. The final protest was over low wages.

Durst rejected the demands and called the law. Armed deputies, accompanied by the district attorney (who was also Durst's private attorney), confronted the workers during a mass meeting. They were there to arrest Ford and the other IWW leaders. The workers' mood was sullen, angry. A deputy sheriff fired a pistol in the air intending to "sober" the people, to cow them into submission. The shot had the opposite effect. The mob went wild; more shots were fired. The posse fled in terror. When it was over, the district attorney, one sheriff's deputy, and two workers were dead. No accurate count of the number of wounded and injured was ever reported. That afternoon and evening hundreds of workers and their families packed up their camps and scattered. Anyone who had fallen in with the IWW now was a fugitive.

Months after the riots, Herman Suhr, Blackie Ford, and two workers were put on trial for murder. The two workers were acquitted, but Suhr and Ford were sentenced to life in prison. Carey McWilliams wrote:

> Wheatland was not a strike, but a spontaneous revolt. It stands out as one of the significant episodes in the long and turgid history of migratory labor in California. For the first time the people of California were made to realize, even if vaguely, the plight of its thousands of migratory workers.

In 1914 and 1915 the iww turned away from California and focused its efforts on the Midwestern grain belt's "bonanza farms" — the large enterprises owned by outside investors. As the grain ripened in the southern plains an estimated 250,000 itinerant workers began following the harvest season from south to north.

For decades the wheat harvesters had protested the low pay and miserable conditions. They conducted sporadic strikes — small, unorganized, unsuccessful efforts. Prior to the 1914 season, the iww established locals in the small towns that flanked the wheatbelt, and, as the harvest advanced up through the plains, the organizers were ready. The iww's strategy was to work farm by farm, area by area, demanding $3.50 a day, striking where necessary.

The tactics worked. In 1915 a wage of $3 to $3.50 a day prevailed and membership in the union expanded. Members' dues put $14,000 in the war chest, and the 1916 harvest was even better for the workers. The nine locals had, in conference, created the Agriculture Workers Organization 400, and by 1917 it was boasting a membership of 70,000.

The Midwestern farmers responded: iww organizers were beaten and run out of town. Newspapers editorialized for vigilante committees and a supply of "reliable firearms." In farm communities, iww offices were raided and destroyed. In 1917 agents of the federal government raided the iww central headquarters in Chicago and arrested scores of people on charges of violating the Federal Espionage Act. A federal judge handed out sentences ranging up to 20 years, and fined the iww $2.3 million. The iww was beaten.

After World War I California farmers found Japanese workers were no longer uniquely suited for laboring in the fruit orchards and vines; they had become restive, "sneaky," and "overly ambitious" to own their own farms and compete. The Japanese — like the Chinese before them — were aliens and therefore could be outlawed by a sympathetic Congress. The Alien Exclusion Laws were duly amended and the farmers turned their attention to the docile, low-bending Mexicans who were proclaimed uniquely suited for "stoop labor" in the fields.

In the late 1920s, the *Pacific Rural Press* reported an average of 58,000 Mexicans were brought in yearly to work the crops; by 1930 state population figures revealed 250,000 Mexicans living in California. The same kind of importation was going on all along the border, in Arizona, New Mexico, and Texas. McWilliams wrote:

> . . . the large farms used Mexican labor as their main source of cheap, easily exploitable farm labor, beating down wage rates and forcing cities to assume the burden of supporting the Mexicans during the period of "hibernation" [those months when there was no work]. . . . In 1928 the Mexican labor was earning 35 cents an hour, but with the depression this sank to 15 cents an hour . . . these rates [do not] adequately reflect the miserable conditions of the Mexican labor . . ."

The Mexican workers in the Southwest were treated like the Negroes in the South; the prejudices were summed up by a Texas farmer this way: "God created the Negro race to labor and marked them so you'd know them. If he hadn't intended it, he'd have made them white, and the Mexicans, too . . ."

An executive of the California Fruit Exchange, commenting on Mexican labor during the same period, was just a bit more sophisticated when he summed up the same feeling:

> Mexican casual labor fills the requirements of the California farm as no other labor has done in the past. The Mexican

withstands the high temperatures of the Imperial and San Joaquin Valleys. He is adapted to the field conditions. . . . [He] does heavy field work, particularly in the stoop crops of vegetables and cantaloupes which white labor refused to do and is constitutionally unsuited to perform . . .

When the seasonal harvests ended, the poorly paid workers had to fend for themselves. They headed into the cities, or nearby farm towns; frequently they were destitute and had to seek welfare assistance. The farmers were dumping their workers into the cities in the off season, using the state and county welfare systems as their unique form of unemployment insurance. But the cities and counties rebelled; they did not want the unemployed Mexicans. Life became hell for these workers. Pushed and shoved, deprived of the last shreds of human dignity, they rebelled, just as the Chinese and Japanese had rebelled. Early in 1928 the cantaloupe workers in the Imperial Valley formed *La Union de Trabajadores del Valle Imperial*. They sent letters to the growers, and to the Chambers of Commerce in Brawley and El Centro, asking for a cent-and-a-half increase in the piece rate or a flat pay rate of 75 cents an hour.

A state labor investigator reported: "The difficulties which the Mexican laborers have been experiencing with the labor contractors are undoubtedly responsible for the organization of the union . . ."

The growers refused to talk with the workers. A strike followed. Sheriff's deputies moved in, arresting strike leaders, shutting the union offices, and outlawing further strike activity. The strike was crushed, but not the spirit of rebellion.

In 1929, the Depression pushed large numbers of unemployed urban workers into the farm labor market. With the growing availability of "white" workers, the growers began to pressure the Mexicans to leave the country. Welfare departments began to purge their rolls of aliens. Working with city and county governments — and supported by agribusiness politicians — the federal government began a mass deportation of Mexican aliens.

From 300,000 to 400,000 Mexicans and Mexican Americans were herded south, across the border. Those Mexicans who escaped the dragnet, those U.S. citizens of Mexican descent who remained in farm work, were intimidated, and once more docile. But the farmer was no longer worried about Mexicans; he now had a bountiful supply of poor white workers. The urban unemployed came out of the Eastern cities into the Cape Cod cranberry bogs, breaking the strike of the black workers who were attempting to build a union. In Idaho the state and federal government helped the pea farmers break a strike by turning out all of the able-bodied men and women on relief, creating a surplus of hungry, destitute people who would work for just enough to buy a meal for their children. The use of welfare recipients as strikebreakers became a common tactic throughout the West.

The Great Depression and the years of drought and dust storms in Oklahoma, Arkansas, and Texas drove thousands of yeoman farmers off the land. Broke, hungry, and poor, these white families loaded their old cars and trucks and headed west, on Route 66; they became the Dust Bowl Okies, and tens of thousands of them flooded into the California farming valleys, further depressing the wage rates and overtaxing the parsimonious welfare systems. The Okies, Filipinos — who had been imported during the late 1920s — and the Mexicans had to compete for the low-paying jobs.

A special U.S. Commission studying agricultural unrest in the Imperial Valley reported:

> Living and sanitary conditions are a serious and irritating factor. . . . [We] found filth, squalor, and an entire absence of sanitation, and a crowding of human beings into tents or crude structures built of boards, weeds, and anything that was found at hand. . . . [In] this environment there is bred a social sullenness that is to be deplored but which can be understood . . .

47

The plight of the Okie, Filipino, and Mexican workers in the Imperial Valley attracted the Communists; the Los Angeles chapter of the Trade Union Unity League sent organizers into the valley. The TUUL had been formed by the Communists as a national organization to assist in the development of individual unions; eventually the TUUL was to become a federation of these unions, a red AFL-CIO. But from the North Carolina textile mills to the Imperial Valley farms, TUUL organizers were tagged by undercover operatives and arrested by police before their movements could take hold. In the Imperial Valley, in 1930, the TUUL formed the Agriculture Workers Industrial League, established its headquarters in Brawley, and sent out a call for workers to come to a farm worker conference on April 20. On April 14, law enforcement officers, backed by farmers, raided the AWIL and rounded up 100 of its leaders and suspected followers. Seven of those arrested were convicted of Criminal Syndicalism, and sentenced to San Quentin state prison. Criminal Syndicalism made it a crime to advocate or conspire to take over government *or industry* by violent action.

Pat Chambers, one of the TUUL organizers sent into the Imperial Valley, recalled: "There was some leakage [informers] inside our Los Angeles operation, so when the organizers showed up in the Imperial they were arrested. I found out later I was working with the guy [informer], not knowing he was on the Police Red Squad."

Chambers, now 73, describes himself still as "an old-school radical, like the old-time Socialists who relied on human beings, on developing self-concept." Chambers spoke fluent Spanish, as the result of working on construction jobs in Mexico, and he felt at ease among the field workers. His abilities in organizing workers made him a special target for the red hunters. Chambers explained the AWIL was just an exploratory attempt to organize field labor, and out of it came the Cannery and Agriculture Workers Industrial Union, which would attempt to organize both field labor and workers in the sheds and canneries.

The CAWIU organizers began following the farm work force

in 1931; using the IWW tactics, they moved in on spontaneous strikes, giving leadership and seeking out sympathetic townspeople to supply workers with food and shelter. The first major CAWIU-led strike took place in the fall of 1932, in the fruit harvests near Vacaville. The strike leaders were jailed. Masked vigilantes broke six of the strike leaders out of jail, took them out into the countryside, flogged them, shaved their heads, and poured red enamel paint over them.

The following spring 3,000 pea pickers went out on strike in the DeCoto–Hayward area, and CAWIU organizers, including Chambers, helped establish a strike camp. The strikers lived in old cars, tents, or out in the open. A communal kitchen cooked whatever organizers could beg from the liberals in nearby communities like San Jose. Armed deputies patrolled the road to keep strike agitators from talking to strikebreaking workers in the fields. Chambers said he worked primarily at night, contacting workers in their camps, holding clandestine meetings in woodsheds and garages.

The DeCoto pea-picker strike was finally settled, with some gains for the workers, and this success prompted strikes in the cherries near Mountain View and Sunnyvale, and in the apricots and peaches in Merced, Sacramento, and Gridley. The strikes forced wages higher, but CAWIU was not recognized as a union, and men like Chambers left no permanent organization behind them.

By August, Pat Chambers had drifted with the fruitpickers into the Tulare County peach harvest, and there he led the Tagus Ranch workers in a successful strike. Tagus had been paying $1 for a 10-hour day, but with the fruit ripe on the trees, the farm management quickly agreed to pay 25 cents an hour, for an 8-hour day. Word of this doubling of the wages spread up and down the San Joaquin Valley, triggering more strikes. Other growers were furious.

The mood within the agribusiness communities in Tulare County and the valley was ugly; the Depression had struck hard at commerce, businesses were closing, the farms that had heavy debt loading were going bankrupt, taxes were delinquent, and county governments were hard pressed to meet their own expenses.

The labor problems agitated by CAWIU dominated the street-corner talk in small farming towns like Pixley, but strikes weren't the only topic of interest. The June 30, 1933, issue of the Pixley *Enterprise* reported farmers in the area were forming an organization to apply for federal crop "set-aside" payments; the U.S. Department of Agriculture was paying from $6 to $12 an acre to retire land in an attempt to cut production and stimulate prices.

The same issue of the *Enterprise* reported the Tulare County Board of Supervisors, sitting in the courthouse in nearby Visalia, had voted to trim $40,000 from the welfare budgets because tax delinquencies had cut county income. Board Chairman Alfred Elliott — a spokesman for agribusiness whose political ambitions would soon carry him to Congress — ordered the county welfare director to require all welfare recipients to purchase fresh fruit and vegetables and can or preserve them for winter consumption as a condition for staying on relief.

Chairman Elliott's concern about the high cost of welfare knew little bounds; he suggested welfare mothers should be sterilized, and in a speech he explained, "The transient Mexican families are a large source of the problem. While this form of labor may be cheaper, it is poor economy to import workers from the south [Mexico] and then have to take care of them all winter . . . at taxpayers' expense."

Pixley was in the heart of a large cotton-growing area; for miles in any direction great fields of green cotton plants stretched to the horizon. Each fall 15,000 to 20,000 men, women, and children migrated into cotton harvests, living in the rickety cabins in cotton camps furnished by farmers, or on ditch banks in tents. They swarmed like locusts over the stalks, trying to earn enough to survive the coming winter.

In 1933 the San Joaquin Valley Agricultural Labor Bureau — made up of representatives from all six valley counties — set the picking rate at 60 cents a hundredweight, which was 20 cents higher than the previous year but 40 cents below the demands of the Cannery and Agriculture Workers Industrial Union.

When the farmers refused to set the rate at $1 per 100 pounds, CAWIU organizers quietly rented a 40-acre farm near Corcoran, 30 miles west of Pixley, and laid out a strike camp. Streets were marked off, adequate toilet facilities were dug, a water supply was established, and a sanitation supervision system planned. Meetings were held among the workers, and committees were formed to coordinate the strike activity in each of the six counties. A date was picked, October 4. As the strikers were evicted from their camps, or driven off the ditch banks by lawmen and vigilantes, they were to come to the strike camp, where food and shelter would be available.

On Wednesday, October 4, a one-column headline on the front page of the Visalia *Times Delta* read: "Cotton Picker's Strike Started Today in Tulare County Fields." The story reported that 14,000 pickers had left their jobs and that three CAWIU organizers, two of them Mexican, one Anglo, had been arrested near Earlimart by Pixley Justice Court Constable Delos Howard. Pat Chambers and the other organizers formed workers into car caravans early each morning and set out through the back roads seeking crews at work. When a working crew was spotted, the caravan stopped, a picket line was set up along the road, and the pickets tried to talk — or yell — the strikebreakers out of the field. Frequently frustrated by the distance, strikers would rush onto a ranch, only to be confronted by armed farmers, sheriff's deputies, and Constable Howard.

The CAWIU efforts were successful; the cotton strikes spread through the entire valley, strike camps were set up near Wasco and Arvin, and the newspapers reported 18,000 pickers had walked out of the fields. The entire harvest was brought to a standstill.

The mood of the entire valley was reflected by the Fresno *Bee* on October 6. The *Bee*'s editorial writer agreed workers should get:

a fair day's pay for a fair day's work, [but he noted] our people are getting exceedingly weary of the activities of professional Communist leaders, mostly from New York, who are motivated by no honest desire to improve working conditions, but rather propose to feather their own nests while promoting the cause of social anarchy and red revolution. . . . They loaf between working seasons and then descend upon the scene like vultures who have smelled carrion from afar. Why should they have such wide tolerance?

The tolerance didn't last long. The next day's Fresno *Bee* story was headlined: "Ranchers Arm as Precaution; Strike Trouble Spreading." Four agitators were arrested in Madera, Kern County farmers were driving cotton strikers out of the camps, and, on October 9, growers from Kern, Tulare, and Kings counties met in Corcoran to work out strategy. The growers refused an offer by a state deputy labor commissioner to mediate the dispute; they refused to meet with the union negotiators. A mob of 70 farmers tried to break up a workers meeting in Woodville, and, in the melee that followed, the outnumbered farmers were badly beaten and had to flee for their lives. Farmers who traded in the city of Tulare declared it to be a "hotbed of Communists." Chambers had his office in Tulare and he had considerable support from liberal townspeople. The "Farmers Protective Association" took out ads in local newspapers, contending the city police force was allowing 6 to 8 known Communist agitators to hold meetings in the city. The ad warned:

We the farmers of your community whom you depend upon for support feel that you have nursed too long the viper that is at our door. These Communist agitators must be driven from town by you and your harboring them further will prove to us your non cooperation, and will make it necessary for us to give our support and trade to another town that will support and cooperate with us.

The date was October 10, 1933. By late afternoon the main street of Pixley, 17 miles to the south, would run with blood. A light rain had fallen the day before, the first to cool the air and end the long, hot summer. By dawn on the 10th the CAWIU striker car caravans were out, running the back roads, seeking out any strikebreakers.

One of the caravans found a group of Mexican workers picking the cotton near Pixley. The strikers stopped and set up a picket line. The farmer later testified in court that there were about 200 strikers, and that a delegation of 30 came onto his property to talk to him. They did not know that Constable Delos Howard had a posse of armed, deputized farmers waiting, at the ready. The farmer ordered the strikers off the farm, and, according to testimony given later, the strikers started to leave. Constable Howard came up and suggested the farmer sign trespass complaints and have the entire group arrested; the strike leader turned and protested Howard's suggestion. A fight started and the pickets rushed in to help, but they were met by the posse of armed farmers; they turned and fled. Seventeen strikers were arrested and transported to the Pixley Justice Court.

The Pixley Justice Court was not far from the CAWIU meeting hall. Both buildings faced onto Highway 99, the town's main street. The court was housed in an old cafe; the union meeting hall was an old two-story brick structure that had a storefront downstairs and an abandoned hotel upstairs. Across Highway 99 was a large open lot that served as a rallying point for the union. Just beyond this vacant lot was the Southern Pacific Railroad freight and passenger station.

Years later, Delos Howard walked me through the scene, explaining that nearly 1,000 CAWIU strikers were mobbed up on the big lot in front of the railroad station. Howard and a deputy sheriff had barricaded themselves inside the justice court to keep the mob from rescuing the 17 arrested strikers. Howard said a worker delegation had come to the justice court door and demanded the prisoners be released. Howard telephoned both the Tulare County Sheriff's Office in Visalia and the California Highway Patrol, asking for help. The requests were turned down because the police agencies were tied up with strike activities elsewhere.

The posse that had helped bring the 17 strikers into the

justice court had driven back out into the fields before the CAWIU organizers and the workers heard about the arrests and started gathering in protest. Pat Chambers, working in his Tulare office, received a phone call warning him that the situation in Pixley was about to blow up. He said years later, "I knew then that the use of violence was inevitable, that it had to be expected, and you could not let the threat of violence slow you down."

Chambers, accompanied by a San Francisco news photographer, drove to Pixley. He estimated there were 400 or 500 workers milling about the big lot in front of the train station. Like the IWW organizers he admired, Chambers climbed up on a box and started talking; pulling the workers around him, he launched into a verbal attack on the system, trying to divert their attention from the prisoners in the justice court. His goal was to distract their anger, to pull them away from mob action into some kind of planned demonstration. But it was not to be. The farmer posse had returned to Pixley. Parking their cars on the edge of the lot, they listened to the harangue.

Chambers said that when he saw the farmers drive up, he started moving the crowd, telling them to cross the highway and enter the CAWIU hall, where they would begin to make some plans. Chambers recalled, "The minute I said 'let's go into the hall,' the meeting broke up and we started across the highway. It was then that the farmers opened fire."

W. D. Hemmett, one of the strike leaders, testified later that the armed group of farmers advanced toward the union hiring hall. Just as the first man of the advancing farmer group reached the edge of the highway, opposite the union hall, Hemmett said, "I told him not to shoot into the hall, into the women and children in there. He shoved the rifle toward me and I grabbed it by the barrel and shoved it toward the ground.

"Just then a Mexican fella grabbed the rifle, and I grabbed the pistol that the next farmer had, we started scuffling and wrestling around while I tried to get the gun. . . . [While] we were scuffling I heard a shot and I heard Delfino Davila

54

shout: 'Bill, run, they've got me.' I look around in time to see him fall. I let go and run into the building."

Gunfire crashed and exploded, blotting out the screams and shouts as workers scrambled into the building. Hemmett and others ran through, and on out the back. The farmers killed Davila and another man, Delores Hernandez; they wounded eight others, including Mrs. Isabella Ward, 47, of Pixley.

On October 11 the strikers called a rally in Visalia, on the steps of the courthouse, to demand murder charges be filed against the growers. About 300 showed up to listen to Chambers list the dead and wounded and harangue the agribusiness establishment. At that time five ranchers had been disarmed and arrested. The 17 workers who had triggered the episode in Pixley had been moved to the Visalia jail. Eight farmers eventually stood trial and were acquitted. Their defense lawyer, in his opening argument, set the tone: "The strikers had sent out a call to assemble in Pixley to take matters in their own hands. They formed a veritable army and marched on the justice court and defied the majesty and sovereignty of the state of California by serving upon it insolent demands which the state could not have granted without surrendering to the mob . . ."

The farmers testified it was someone within the strikers' headquarters building who fired the first shot, that the farmers were, in fact still the "posse" legally formed by the deputy sheriff, and they only returned the fire once the opening shot had been fired.

The district attorney, in his closing arguments, tried to impress upon the jury that it was the strikers who took all the casualties, "We must remember two men were killed and at least eight persons were injured . . . and in spite of reports of shots from the strike headquarters how very little damage was done to the farmers on the west side of the high-way . . ." But the jury of agribusiness peers voted for acquittal.

Chambers, when I asked him about the farmers' contention that the strikers had guns, said: "They didn't have a single gun. Look, I'll be the first one to condemn any individual who in any way tries to use violence on the part of strikers . . . any bastard who even takes a step in that direction I would consider an *agent provocateur*. He would be leading a bunch of working people to slaughter. The only way to defeat violence is for workers to stand still, no matter what happens."

The cotton strikes continued until late October. The shock of the Pixley killings drew national attention to the strikes. State and federal officials tried to get both sides to sit down and talk, but the farmers resisted. Their position was expressed by the secretary of the Agricultural Council of California:

A campaign of intimidation, finally culminating in bloodshed and rioting, has paralyzed California agriculture at the height of the harvest season. For weeks past, due to the activities of radicals and agitators in inciting farm laborers . . . [heavy] damage has already resulted and millions of dollars in crop losses are inevitable if this condition is permitted to continue. . . . [The farmers] have the right to expect that the law abiding element of labor will purge labor's house of communists who have brought discredit upon them by this reign of terror . . . [That] the farmers in some sections have struck back is not a reflection on the farmers so much as a reflection on labor leaders and public officials whose inability or unwillingness to cope with the situation made it necessary for the farmer to protect himself and his property . . . [With] the cotton harvest getting underway . . . with 196,000 bales on the stalk it is essential officials deal firmly and promptly with the strike condition . . .

Chambers issued a statement:

The fight of the starving cotton pickers is a fight against starvation wages and a recognition of their union. The workers will not be misled by charges of communism. . . .

[In] every strike the charge of agitator is made by those serving the interest of the bosses in order to continue exploitation of workers . . .

Despite the rhetoric and anger, the efforts of state and federal mediators began to have an effect. A fact-finding commission suggested a 75-cent-per-100-pound compromise, and the San Joaquin Valley Agriculture Labor Bureau accepted the offer. In a last-ditch effort to establish union recognition, CAWIU leaders attempted to drag their feet, but the battered, starving farm workers in the Corcoran camp would tolerate no more action. CAWIU accepted the 75-cent offer and a hand-scrawled sign was nailed to the Corcoran strike camp gate: "THE STRIKE IS OVER."

CHAPTER FOUR : CHAVEZ: THE BEGINNING

The cotton strikes of 1933 were a qualified success. A ragtag army of 18,000 workers — many of them Mexican immigrants recruited into California agriculture — had stood up to the combined efforts of the San Joaquin Valley agribusiness establishment and won a 15-cent-per-100-pound increase in pay. To the average picker the sum itself was insignificant — it meant 30 to 45 cents more a day — but the victory was important. Workers had proven they could stand fast against vigilante terror tactics. Reacting to this limited success, the California Farm Bureau and the state Chamber of Commerce formed a three-man committee to investigate the "labor trouble" and make recommendations. Their report: Ninety percent of the strikes and labor disturbances that had taken place in 1933 had been caused and financed directly by Moscow for the sole purpose of sabotaging American production. The committee recommended formation of a new statewide farm organization to fight the red menace. The first chapter of the Associated Farmers was formed in the Imperial Valley, prior to the 1934 vegetable harvest season. The association signed a mutual-aid pact with local law enforcement agencies and placed association members on call to assist lawmen in suppressing any labor strife. The CAWIU organizers moved into the Imperial Valley as the workers began harvesting the vegetables. A strike was called. The Associated Farmers' reaction was swift: Posses dispersed crowds of workers with tear-gas bombs, 87 "agitators" were arrested, and vigilante groups flushed 2,000 men, women, and children out of the strike camp and burned it to the ground. In July of 1934 a big posse raided the Sacramento Workers Center, operated by CAWIU. The raid netted 18 "agitators," including Pat Chambers. They were all charged with criminal syndicalism; eight eventually stood trial, were convicted and sentenced to state prison. Chambers, and the others, served two years before an appeals court overturned their convictions and ordered them set free. But CAWIU was finished. The vigilante tactics had succeeded; the Communist Party ordered its unions disbanded and directed its organizers to go underground.

The strikes did not stop. Nor did the fascism. Carey McWilliams wrote:

The wave of violence launched by the Associated Farmers in 1934 swept on into 1935 and 1936 with organized vigilante groups crushing one strike after another. . . . [No] one who has visited a rural county in California under these circumstances will deny the reality of the terror that exists. It is no exaggeration to describe this state of affairs as fascism in practice. Judges blandly deny constitutional rights to defendants and hand out vagrancy sentences which approximate the period of the harvest season. It is useless to appeal, for by the time the appeal is heard the crop will be harvested. The

58

workers are trapped, beaten, terrorized yet they manage to
hold out . . .

Towns like Salinas and Stockton and Madera were mobi-
lized on a warlike basis; the Associated Farmers were the
militia, the California Highway Patrol — mounted on white
motorcycles — the cavalry, the sheriff's deputies the shock
troops. There is a strong temptation to detail more of the
strikes, but there is danger in dwelling on the violence; it
tends to distort the total agricultural scene. The strikes were
the highly visible exceptions, not the rule. Most of the
workers were too poor, too hungry, too intimidated, to stand
up. The work force was, by this time, a tattered blend of
black, white, and brown families. They moved here, drifted
there, camping out under the bridges, agreeing to work for
the hated labor contractors just because housing went with
the job.

This was the California of Librado and Juana Chavez.
They had been small landowners in Arizona's north Gila
River Valley, north and east of Yuma. Half of their quarter
section (160 acres) was farm land, and they had grown
vegetables, corn, milo, and alfalfa and kept a few cows to
milk and horses to pull the plow. But the land did little more
than feed them. There were debts and back taxes. As the
Depression deepened, their financial problems grew worse.

The second of Librado and Juana Chavez's children was
Cesar Estrada Chavez, born March 31, 1927. He was 10 or 11
when the deputy sheriff came to the old, rambling adobe
farmhouse. Cesar Chavez recalls, "He had the papers that
told us we had to leave, or go to jail. My mother came out of
the house crying, we children knew there was trouble, but we
were confused, worried. For two or three days the deputy
came back, every day . . . and we had to leave."

They loaded the family car, taking what they could,
leaving behind most of what the family had acquired. "We
had these corrals, they were made of rails and those rails
were our swings, that was where we would play, after we had
watered the horses and cows. We kids did that, that was our

job, to water and feed the stock. Before we left, the big tractor came and started knocking down these corrals. That crushed me. I didn't really know what was happening . . ."

From Yuma, the family crossed the Colorado River, driving north and west seeking work. They were penniless migrants now, a part of the "Grapes of Wrath." The only work they knew was on the farms. They stopped in Brawley, in the Imperial Valley, to "tie carrots." The carrots are harvested by a machine that turns up the earth, exposing the root. Workers, using raffia twine, tie up the carrots in bunches and put them in containers to be hauled out of the field. Families were paid according to the number of bunches they tied each day.

Families working in the carrots furnish their own raffia. Chavez said, "We used to have to buy the raffia on the job, take it home, and soak it overnight, so the next morning we could split it three ways. That way it would go further and we wouldn't have to buy so much . . . you know what the whole family could make in a day? A dollar, maybe $2 if things went right. Ooh. It was bad. I don't know what kept those workers from revolting . . ."

From the carrot fields near Brawley the family migrated north and west, toward the Pacific Ocean. They harvested vegetables in Oxnard and moved north and east, up into the San Joaquin Valley, driving 200 miles to reach the grape harvests near Fresno. There, they went to work for a labor contractor who housed them in an old camp and, week by week, stalled them when they asked for their pay. The contractor told the Chavez family he would pay them when the farmer paid him, but, one morning, near the end of the season, the contractor simply disappeared. The family was left destitute.

In the late fall, cotton was the only crop left that could provide any work at all, and then it would be meager. Cotton was the San Joaquin Valley's major crop, and, from fall through winter, 15,000 to 20,000 migrants could keep alive in this harvest. The first picking provided "good money," if the workers could pull 300 to 400 pounds a day; by late October the families were in the second picking, and by November, when the Chavez family had scraped up enough gas money to drive into Mendota, there was little left but cleaning up the cotton remaining on the stalks and on the ground. A family, working hard, could make just enough to get through the winter.

It was in the cotton camp, near Mendota, that the migrant life began to take hold of the Chavez family. Cesar Chavez recalled, "We couldn't play in these camps like we did on the ranch. We had been poor then, but we had a big adobe ranch house, with lots and lots of space. We [his brother Richard, his cousin Manuel, and Cesar] had a special place we would play, by this tree that was our own. And when we built things — playhouses, bridges, barns — we could come back the next day and they would be there . . ."

"Home" in a migrant cotton camp was a 15-by-15 tarpaper-and-wood cabin set flat on the ground; row upon row of these cabins formed camp "streets." The cabins were furnished with a single electrical outlet, dropped from the bare ridgepole. Life in these camps was miserable, especially in the dead of winter, when there wasn't enough food, when the camp streets were rutted quagmires; when the rainwater formed great shallow ponds around the communal water faucets and outhouses. In many of these camps there was a "company store" run by either the labor contractor or the farm owners. The workers lived on credit, and worked when they could.

It wasn't just the physical setting, or the skimpy life so much as that life had no consistency, no permanent features, no continuity. The Chavez family lived here for a while, there for a while, establishing a base in Brawley, another in San Jose, and another, finally, in Delano, but always moving on.

Chavez recalls: "I bitterly missed the ranch. Maybe that is when the rebellion started. Some had been born into the migrant stream. But we had been on the land, and I knew a different way of life. We were poor, but we had liberty. The migrant is poor, and he has no freedom."

With the migrancy came the feelings of economic and ethnic prejudice. Chavez said, "I still feel the prejudice; whenever I go through a door, I expect to be rejected, even when I know there is no prejudice in there . . ."

When the family was living on the farm they were sheltered from this sort of thing. Chavez recalls the second year the family was on the road, they were in Brawley. He was 11 or 12 (exact dates and places fade into the larger patterns of migrancy) and shining shoes for extra money. The police would not let the Mexican shoeshine boys into the "white side of town."

"I was shining shoes and selling papers. On Sunday we would go to Mass early so we could get on the street and shine shoes. When we finished, we would give our shoeshine kits to the Chinese man who owned a store. He'd keep the boxes for us when we went over into the Anglo side of town.

"We went this one time to a diner, it had a sign on the door 'White Trade Only' but we went in anyway. We had heard they had these big hamburgers, and we wanted one. There was a blonde, blue-eyed girl behind the counter, a beauty.

"She asked what we wanted — real tough you know? — and when we ordered a hamburger, she said, 'We don't sell to Mexicans,' and she laughed when she said it. She enjoyed doing that, laughing at us. We went out, but I was really mad, enraged. It had to do with my manhood."

Relating the incident triggered other memories. Once the family had been driving through a remote corner of the San Joaquin Valley's west side. For miles on end there was nothing but brown hills and flat, dry desert. When they came to Devil's Den, a crossroads intersection, with a service station and a cafe, they stopped for gasoline and Librado went into the cafe to refill a thermos of coffee, ignoring the "White Trade Only" sign. When the counter girl ordered him out, he tried to explain all he wanted was to refill his thermos, but she yelled, "Get Out."

Cesar said, "It happened again, in Bakersfield, about the

same way. And what really hurts most of all is to see someone you love rejected like that."

As the Chavez family moved through the harvests, ranging as far north as the Sacramento Valley and as far south as the Imperial Valley, they learned their only weapon was their ability to quit, to withhold their labor. Like most migrants, they participated in scores of small strikes. The workers — either as individual families or as an entire crew — would ask for higher wages. If they were rejected they would quit in anger, stalking off the job.

Chavez said of his father, "He would walk off whenever he heard the word *huelga* [strike]. He was strong on the idea of unions, even though he didn't know what a union was."

Cesar recalled, "We were in Sacramento once, in the tomatoes. It was one of the best seasons we had ever had, but the foreman gave this young guy hell for complaining about a mix-up in the box count. They had not given him credit for picking as many boxes as he thought he had, so he quit. Walked out. And we walked out with him.

"We felt good. Lose a day's pay, or two, but we felt we had kept something that belonged to us . . . our dignity. After we had learned the tricks we would not stand for any shit from anyone. We tried a lot of jobs. The worst crop was the olives; the olives are so small you can never fill the bucket.

"The worst crop for pressure, for selective picking, is the table grape. Unless you have a lot of skill, you feel the pressure. Picking apricots can be the same thing."

Cesar stopped talking for a second. Characteristically he speaks in phrases and thought patterns frequently interrupted by a new train of thought. His mind seems to be working both out in front of what he is saying and behind, checking, weighing what he has said.

"Oooh. No. The worst crop is not olives; the worst is the work of the short-handled hoe." In 1942 the family was working with these short-handled hoes, bent double, thinning cantaloupe. The children were paid 8 cents an hour, the parents 12 cents. Construction workers at the time were making three or four times that wage. There were five workers in the Chavez family — the parents, Rita, 17, Cesar, 15, and Richard, 14. The two younger children, Vicki, 8, and Lennie, 6, stayed in the car. Just thinking about the back-breaking indignity of the hoe with the 18-inch handle makes Chavez fume: "When I see crews bent double, working those goddamn hoes . . . I get mad. There is no need for such cruelty. I never want to see that again, not until I can do something about it."

As the Chavez family traveled, Mrs. Chavez tried to keep her children in school as much as possible. By the time Chavez had dropped out in the 8th grade he had attended so many schools he can never give an accurate count. Sometimes he recalls 30, sometimes 40; the number varies with the telling as Chavez relates his educational background. The classrooms looked the same; the teachers seldom took notice of the migrant children passing through.

Chavez said, "I think that was the worst, not being noticed. The schools treated you like you didn't exist. Their indifference was incredible. When you went into school for the first time the principal and a teacher would discuss where they should put you, right in front of you. It made you feel like you weren't important.

"Then they wouldn't let you talk Spanish. In P.E. they would make you run laps around the track if they caught you speaking Spanish or a teacher in a classroom would make you write 'I won't speak Spanish' on the board 300 times, or I remember once a teacher hung a sign on you that said 'I am a clown, I speak Spanish.' "

In the fall of 1943 the Chavez family moved into the Fresno County raisin harvest, near Biola. The pay was a nickel a tray for cutting and spreading the grapes on paper trays to dry in the 100-degree September sun. Richard and Cesar, working as a team, would start in the vines at dawn. They would work at top speed until 8:30 A.M., when they would stop for a little breakfast, then back again, working as hard as they could until early afternoon, when the heat became so fierce the thick, loose earth burned their feet. By early afternoon they could make 200 to 250 trays each, and they were proud of the $20 to $25 a day they contributed to the family income.

The Chavez family returned to Delano that winter, and established a home there. He said, "We had a house on Ellington and 8th Street. There was no development there then, to speak of, and the town itself had maybe 2,500 people. It was a wide-open town with a red-light district with maybe 20 houses . . ."

He said the whorehouses attracted the servicemen and truck drivers off Highway 99. The truckers used to park their big rigs in front of the Chavez's driveway while they went across the street to get a quick bounce in a squeaky bed. When the truckers ignored the family protests, Cesar went to the Mexican Society — a group of older men who had been in the Mexican revolution — and asked them to do something.

The old revolutionaries told Cesar to go home, that he was too young to do anything, and besides, the whorehouses were legal, they were a part of the government in Delano. Young Chavez didn't like the answer, but he could think of nothing else to do. A few nights later he went to the movies in a downtown theater. The audience was segregated. The Anglos sat on one side of the main aisle, the Mexicans on the other.

"I really hadn't thought much about what I was going to do but I had to do something. We were supposed to sit on the south side. I moved over to the north side, but this usherette wouldn't let me sit down.

"I told her, 'Don't touch me, I got a ticket,' and I sat down. She called the assistant manager and he came down. He was hostile and he told to get up, or he would break my arms. When I didn't move he called the manager and he raised hell. It was dark inside and all these people were turning around, looking to see what was happening."

Finally the police were called. They came in, and when Chavez refused to move, they pried his hands loose from the armrests and dragged him out. They took him to the police station. Cesar's friends in the theater called his father. The police kept young Chavez for about an hour, then warned him not to cause any more trouble and turned him back over to his father. Angered and frightened by the confrontation, he wanted to take some kind of legal action, but he did not know how. He knew no lawyers. The incident was put aside, but not forgotten.

The humiliation, anger, and frustration of being powerless made deep impressions on Chavez. He was and still is *Mexican* in the California-migrant–farm worker sense of the word; this Mexican-ness was the only thing he knew from the time the family was displaced from their Arizona farm until he joined the Navy, in 1944. When Cesar reported for basic training in San Diego he had just turned 17, and had never been away from his family; for him the prejudices were clear cut, brown vs. white, but in boot camp in San Diego, he discovered prejudices had other dimensions.

"I saw this white kid fighting, because someone had called him Pollock and I found out he was Polish and he hated that word Pollock. He fought every time he heard it. I began to learn something, that others suffered, too," Chavez said.

Chavez served in the South Pacific, at the tag end of World War II. As a coxswain's apprentice he worked on the small boats, ferrying ship's pilots in and out of the harbor. He recalled, "Once or twice we picked up fliers who went down in the water." He was transferred to Guam, where he worked on the beach, in a paint shop; he was taking tests for a third-class painter's rating when he was discharged in 1946.

After his discharge he hitchhiked to Delano: "I tried a job just as soon as I got back. I went out to the Good Morning Ranch . . . it was a big vegetable farm, I went to cut celery . . . ooh my God, it was awful. I left in two hours. I couldn't keep up with the crew . . . I was soft. I quit about 10:30 . . . it was animal like.

"I went home and I stayed. I remember we were getting those 52-20s. [Discharged servicemen got $20 a week for 52 weeks, unemployment insurance.] And I just took in the scene, and rested. But finally I got worried because everybody else in the house was working. So I went back to work

. . . I think it was in the cotton . . . cold . . . oooh it was cold."

By his own admission Chavez was never more than an average cotton picker (he could pull 300 to 350 pounds a day, counting a few clods and gourds thrown in for extra weight), but cotton provided the family with winter work. During the late 1940s they needed every cent they could scrape together because the work patterns in the San Joaquin Valley were changing drastically. Each spring and summer there were more and more workers in the orchards, vineyards, and fields; where 10 families could work all day finishing out a block of peaches, there would be 20 to 30 families and the work would be completed by noon. Sometimes, when they pulled up to a farm, they were told there was no work at all, but out in the field they would see large crews of single men — *Braceros*.

The *Braceros* — the word means "arm" or strong arm — were Mexican-national contract workers, imported under special treaty with Mexico, to work for specific periods in specific "labor-short" crops. The *Braceros*, first used during the World War II labor-short years, were becoming the "ideal" farm labor force; they replaced the troublesome "Okies" who were off in the defense plants building bombers or tanks. These rural Mexican men, coming from the poorest of circumstances, living in farmer-operated camps, dependent upon farmers for food and transportation, were totally subservient. They could not rebel, and when the work was over they were shipped back to Mexico. Any *Bracero* who protested working or living conditions had his contract terminated and he was swiftly repatriated.

The farmers in Texas and California liked the *Bracero* program so much that by 1945 they were ordering 50,000 contract workers. Ten years later the number had reached 300,000 *Braceros* a year, and this number did not include the *illegal* aliens who were flooding into the farm labor market. As the farmers recruited the *Braceros*, they also attracted tens of thousands of impoverished Mexicans from the villages all over rural Mexico. Those who could not get on the *Bracero* lists paid smugglers to help them slip through the border. In 1945 the U.S. Border Patrol captured 69,000 illegal aliens in the United States; as the demand for *Braceros* rose, the numbers of illegal aliens also rose; by 1953 the farmers were importing 200,000 *Braceros* into the farming states, and the Border Patrol was capturing 800,000 illegal aliens, most of them farm workers.

Numerically the *Braceros* were never more than a minority of the total work force; in California and Texas at the peak of the harvest season, one worker in three was a contract Mexican national, but this statistic did not measure the impact the program had on farm labor. *Braceros* dominated some crops, like tomatoes. The local tomato pickers then had to seek work in other crops, like grapes, where there were already enough workers. With more than enough workers the grape farmer had no reason to increase his pay scale. The key to the vicious cycle lay in the farmers' ability to set "prevailing wages" so low local workers would not work the crop; this produced the "labor shortage" needed to certify the crop for *Braceros*, and it produced a surplus of workers in other crops that had a chilling effect on the total farm wage structure.

The effect of this could plainly be seen in the San Joaquin Valley. Along the west side of the valley and down into Kern County the large row-crop farms used most of the Mexican aliens, and during the late 1940s the prevailing wage on the west side was 80 to 85 cents an hour. The state average at the time was a dollar, and many of the small family farms along the east side of the valley were offering "a dollar and a dime" to attract workers away from the corporate farms. As the cost of living went up and farm wages remained the same, or sagged, the local workers became angry and rebellious.

In the fall of 1947 — as the Chavez family moved into the Delano grape harvest — the DiGiorgio Fruit Corporation workers near Arvin went out on strike. The news spread quickly: 1,100 workers on this big ranch had asked for a 10-cents-an-hour pay hike, for grievance procedures, for a seniority system, and for recognition of their union, the

National Farm Labor Union. The NFLU was an affiliate of the American Federation of Labor, and from the outset other members of the federation began to support the farm workers' strike with money, clothing, and food. Urban churchmen and liberals took up the workers' cause, volunteering time, money, and supplies.

The muscle and guns of the Kern County Sheriff's Office moved onto the DiGiorgio property to protect agribusiness from the rabble, but there was relatively little violence. DiGiorgio was working 130 *Braceros,* and when they walked out with the strikers, sheriff's deputies and federal officials talked them into going back to work — a violation of the U.S.–Mexico treaty agreement. *Braceros* could not be used to break strikes. The union protested the *Braceros* were working illegally and they were finally removed, but not until DiGiorgio had successfully recruited other strikebreakers from as far away as Texas. The farm was also using illegal aliens. Goaded by NFLU reports, the U.S. Immigration Service raided the DiGiorgio properties 19 times in 1948 and 1949, netting 315 illegal aliens at work.

While most of NFLU's attention was focused on DiGiorgio, the union's chief officers, Hank Hasiwar and Ernesto Galarza, put organizers in other crops in other areas; and Galarza began his personal crusade against the *Bracero* program.

In the fall of 1949 the San Joaquin Valley Agriculture Labor Bureau set the cotton-picking rate at $2.50 a hundred, down 50 cents from the previous season. The NFLU capitalized on the anger this move generated among the cotton pickers, calling a general cotton strike throughout the San Joaquin Valley. The workers — many of them veterans of 1933 — responded, and strike camps were set up throughout the valley. It was in this strike that Cesar Chavez got his first taste of a major farm labor strike.

Chavez's role in the last major San Joaquin Valley cotton strike was small, and, characteristically, while he recalls the events, he does not remember the date. "My participation was very nil, you know. I think it [the strike] was in 1946 or 1947. . . . The strikes were in the cotton in Kern, Tulare,

69

Kings, and I think in Fresno too . . . a little bit of Madera too, maybe. We were picking cotton in Kern County, just by Highway 43, you know? Where a . . . a little place outside Delano on the way to Wasco . . . just across the Santa Fe tracks . . ."

Cesar was describing the place as each detail popped into his mind, but he could not recall the name of the place, and, while I know the valley well, I couldn't place it either. He went on, ". . . ah, there's a little school there . . . ah . . . Pond. That's it, Pond. Just across the track, you know where the Pond store is . . . okay. We saw this huge caravan [strikers cars] . . . I thought the whole world was there . . . must have been probably a couple hundred cars, you know? And they had, well, the strike was on and they had loudspeakers . . . and we joined immediately, most of the people joined the strike. We caravaned with them, and we wound up in Corcoran, about four in the afternoon.

"There was a rally, in a big, open field. We felt pretty good. The strike went on. We caravaned about six or seven days, maybe, more or less. The whole family. Finally — there were no strike benefits or anything, we were not asking for any — but after a few days we made an agreement: My dad, my mother, and the rest of the family would go into the grapes, and I would stay with the strike . . .

"We had an old Model A Ford and they took that to work. They gave me the better car and I went for another week or two. A lot of people were there in the beginning, but they began to leave. But I stayed there, and I wanted to do something, but no one told me what to do, you know . . . there was no . . ." His voice trailed off.

Several times Cesar started to say there was no leadership in the strike, but he could not bring himself to criticize. He described the car caravaning — a tactic left over from the 1930s — and the afternoon rallies. "There was a meeting every day, just a meeting, you know. Some very good stuff was developed at these meetings, but I wanted to do more than just be there. I wanted to help. I didn't know anything about unions." He voluntarily worked in the strike camp, watering dusty streets, sweeping out the headquarters. He recalled, "In those days I was pretty quiet and reserved, so I wasn't noticed."

The strike lasted a little more than two weeks. Then, with the help of the state mediation service, the NFLU succeeded in getting the Agriculture Labor Bureau to reverse its decision. The picking rate was set back at $3 a hundred pounds. The cotton pickers went back to work. Chavez drove back to Delano, to join his family in the grape harvest. But the whole experience had been unsatisfactory, unsettling. The strikes, the picket lines and caravans, the meetings in the afternoons, all had whetted his appetite, but it had been so disorganized. He wanted to learn how to avoid the mistakes he felt the NFLU had made, but there was no one to help him.

Two months later, when a special subcommittee of the House of Representatives' Education and Labor Committee announced it would hold hearings to investigate the DiGiorgio strike, Chavez was again pulled away from work by the desire to learn. The hearings, held in the posh Bakersfield Inn, 30 miles south of Delano, on November 12th and 13th, had been arranged by Kern County's Congressman, Thomas H. Werdel, at the behest of the agribusiness community.

The special investigating subcommittee was chaired by Congressman Cleveland Bailey, of West Virginia; the other members were Congressmen Leonard Irving of Missouri, Tom Steed of Oklahoma, Thruston Ballard Morton of Kentucky, and Richard Milhouse Nixon of California. Nixon, a freshman legislator, carried the ball for the DiGiorgio interests; the game plan was simple — put the union on trial.

The leadoff witness was H. L. Mitchell, the controversial president of the NFLU. The National Farm Labor Union was an outgrowth of the Southern Tenant Farmers Union, organized by Mitchell and other old-time socialists in the middle 1930s, in the Mississippi River Delta.

World War II pushed the STFU into the background, but after the war Mitchell began rebuilding the union in the South. He flirted briefly with the CIO, then turned to William Green, president of the AFL, for support. Green was attracted to the farm workers cause, and in 1945 he prevailed upon the AFL executive council to issue a charter to Mitchell's union. It was renamed the National Farm Labor Union. It experienced some success in the next two years in the South and then decided to spread out of the South into a national effort. California, specifically the San Joaquin Valley — and more specifically the DiGiorgio Fruit Corporation — was singled out because it was representative of corporate agribusiness.

At the time the DiGiorgio company farmed 11,000 acres of vines and orchards in the Arvin-Lamont area of Kern County; there were another 4,400 acres of vines 30 miles to the north, near Delano, and two large fruit orchards 300 miles further north, in the Sacramento Valley. The corporation assets were listed at $19 million and its gross revenues at $18 million. Mitchell testified the company shipped 10 million boxes of fruit, and 500,000 cartons of vegetables a year.

As Mitchell completed his testimony, Nixon began his chores:

> In your statement, you spoke of cases of malnutrition and starvation, will you please tell the committee what specific cases on DiGiorgio ranch you would like to put in the record at this point . . . are there many on DiGiorgio?

Mitchell had no specific cases on DiGiorgio property. Nixon — as if impressing a jury — repeated the question in slightly different form three more times to make it "perfectly clear" that Mitchell was not testifying these or other sins had been committed on DiGiorgio's sacred ground. As other union witnesses were called to testify, Nixon zeroed in on their allegations of poor housing, poor working conditions, poor wages, establishing that DiGiorgio was indeed no worse than any other corporate employer.

During the hearing Associated Farmers past president R. F. Schmeiser testified:

> Regardless of the affiliation of the NFLU with the AFL, the farmers are naturally suspicious of the intention of a union

headed by H. L. Mitchell . . . formerly a member of the executive committee of the Southern Tenant Farmers Union, of the CIO and according to pages 679 to 682 of the 1938 report of the House Un-American Activities Committee, an associate in that work with Donald Henderson who is reported as a known communist, and former professor of economics at Columbia University . . .

. . . and when Hank Hasiwar [NFLU's western director] is known to have studied economics at Columbia University while Henderson was teaching there. . . .

The NFLU had been cleared both by an investigator from the House Un-American Activities Committee — a committee that Nixon was then serving on — and by a state joint fact-finding committee. Earlier in the hearings this fact was pointed out, and even Nixon — the man who was making his reputation rooting out the evils of communism — was aware "there was no finding of Communist control involved in this particular strike."

While Nixon failed to point this fact out to Schmeiser, he did make good use of the friendly farmer witness to establish the evils of the historic farm labor organizing efforts.

Nixon: I understand the reason for forming [Associated Farmers] in the beginning [1933] was violence. Was there any violence?

Schmeiser: There was some violence, prior to the time we organized, yes. There were several individuals killed.

Nixon: There were?

Schmeiser: Yes.

Nixon: I understand there was destruction of farm property?

Schmeiser: Yes.

Nixon: Hay stacks were burned and things of that sort? Is that correct?

Schmeiser: That is true.

Nixon: And these incidents led up to the organization of your organization?

Schmeiser: I have quite a few pictures taken by myself and others showing the destruction by fire . . .

Nixon never asked who had been killed; he was not eager to establish for the record that it had been farmers who had shot down farm workers in Pixley. What was important was to make it clear that there had been destruction of property and to leave the implication that such actions were part of labor's plans. From that point the justification of the Associated Farmers would naturally flow as a defense against red-tainted aggression.

Throughout the hearings Nixon worked hard with the agribusiness witnesses to establish the impression that the DiGiorgio workers did not in fact want to strike, that outside agitators had stirred up trouble and led outside forces in picket-line and boycott activity, generally disrupting the tranquility of the peaceful valley. Robert DiGiorgio summed it up when he stated flatly the company knew its workers well and, as a result of constant communication with them, knew they did not want a union.

To counter such allegations, the NFLU put James Price on the stand. Price, wounded during the strike, testified he personally had worked for DiGiorgio for ten years, that the nine members of the NFLU Local 218 board of directors had a total of 75 years of labor invested in DiGiorgio. He and other workers detailed shoddy housing, poor sanitation, and low wages as their reasons for striking. But the committee was not listening. It was not here for workers, but to justify agribusiness.

It was during these hearings that the Nixon Doctrine of Agribusiness began to evolve. It is here that he began the foundation for his anti–farm labor biases, with such statements as:

In agriculture where we will have, say, one crop a year, the union going out on strike when that crop has to be harvested would not only be in a position to hold a gun to the farmer's head but also be in a position to destroy the entire crop . . .
. . . Agriculture labor has been exempted from all labor

relations [laws] ever written. The evidence before the sub-committee shows that it would be harmful to the public interest and to all responsible labor unions to legislate otherwise. The evidence shows that a strike of any serious proportions in agriculture would choke off interstate commerce in necessary foodstuffs, would cause incalculable harm to the public, and would antagonize public opinion to the cause of trade unionism . . . the subcommittee finds that the exemption of agriculture labor from the labor management relations act is sound . . .

CHAPTER FIVE : EARLY ORGANIZING

To a young farm worker like Cesar Chavez the power of the growers appeared awesome. They could summon congress-men to do their bidding, their politicians passed laws favoring agribusiness and blocked legislation that could benefit farm workers, farmers routinely called on the courts and law enforcement agencies to protect their interests. When farmers needed a supply of water — to supplement the deep wells that were sucking the underground dry — they asked for and received *billions* of federal and state dollars for dams and canals to import water from great distances.

Subsidized irrigation systems, subsidized transportation networks, subsidized research and development of crops and machines, and subsidized marketing all contributed to the "progress" of the San Joaquin Valley. Valley farming communities grew into prosperous agribusiness cities, and the farmers turned some of their capital to banking and other business and some of their time to politics. Agribusiness control was absolute.

The farm workers and their families never shared in this progress; they were never a part of the farming community.

They lived on the fringes of the cities in rural slums, or far out on the flat landscape, in labor camps. Some families purchased cheap alkali land and put up some kind of home in one of the dozens of isolated farm worker shantytowns that dot the landscape but never appear on maps. Almost all of the farm labor housing was substandard; most did not have indoor plumbing. A few of the shantytowns had no water supply at all, and the residents hauled their water miles in old five-gallon milk cans and stored it in the kitchen, or on the back porch.

A few workers broke out of the farm employment patterns. They became postmen or janitors in the *barrio* or ghetto schools, or maybe they saved enough to set up a one-chair barbershop or open a tiny store inside the *barrio*. The barber, the janitor, the postman, and storekeeper became symbols of upward mobility; they were singled out by the agribusiness establishment as the *spokesmen* for the poor; occasionally such men were invited to join the Lions Club, and maybe — after many years of testing — they could be trusted to sit on the school board.

By the time the DiGiorgio strike was called in 1947 Cesar Chavez was 20 years old. Although he had had some contact with Anglos while he was in the Navy, he had slipped back into the *barrio* culture, back into the economic ebb and flow of Mexican farm workers' life. Hard physical labor was a thing of pride. Men were tough. They not only endured, they *appeared* to thrive on hardship. The families were close knit, and competitive. Sons in their late teens and early 20s tried hard to outwork their fathers. The fastest picker in the field was *someone*. If a crew had a picker who made 800 pounds of cotton a day, and a nearby crew had someone who could do 900 pounds, a rivalry would develop.

The exploitation the Chavez family suffered at the hands of labor contractors made Cesar rebellious. There was nothing he could do but bury his frustrations in work. He was powerless against his employer, but he could take pride in the business of helping the family survive. Both he and Richard were seriously courting two Delano girls. Cesar's love was

Helen Fabela, and, on October 22, 1948, they were married. Helen and Cesar stayed with the Chavez family, moving and working, and moving again. Fernando, their first son, was born in San Jose. The work patterns and places blurred with the moving. By late fall of 1949 they were in the San Joaquin Valley cotton, and Helen watched her husband throw himself into the NFLU cotton strikes, then come away frustrated.

By spring of 1950 they were back in San Jose, in the *barrio* called *Sal Si Puedes* — "get out if you can." It was a rough neighborhood, full of hunger and rundown houses and frustration and unemployment. For Cesar and Helen, it was not an easy time; work was almost impossible to find, yet they had to have money to meet the expenses of a growing family. Their oldest daughter, Sylvia, was born that year.

Sal Si Puedes spawned several *pachuco* gangs, street gangs of young *barrio* toughs who preyed on each other and the *gabachos* who came into the *barrio*. Some writers have implied Chavez had become a *pachuco*, but that seems unlikely. A *pachuco* was usually a street-wise urban kid who had to *at least* act violent to survive the gang culture. Chavez was rural and small — five feet six inches — and slightly built. He looked very young and he wore no self-inflicted gangland tattoos on his hands and arms. Although he was rebellious, he was also shy, soft spoken, and there was none of the braggadocio so characteristic of the *pachuco*.

He recalls: "I didn't get in any fights. There were a lot of fights, and I was around. You know? I was never with any one gang . . . I just didn't get in any fights . . . I *was* beaten up a couple of times.

"I don't know if I didn't fight because I couldn't, or what." Cesar was characteristically thinking in phrases, sorting through his thoughts, narrowing the focus down to one incident that would serve as an example. He had been seated at a dance when the assailant struck. "The guy almost knocked me out. I don't know. My reaction was to cover my face, then I began to feel the kicks . . ."

Why had the guy hit and kicked him?

"Oh. Well. You know. Just to get it on. We knew who the

guy was; by that time my friends were taking care of him. Beat him up, too. The police came and wanted to take me to jail. I told them I didn't do anything. I had to talk my way out of that."

Certainly nonviolence was not a philosophical or moral belief with him yet. But Chavez was already beginning to exercise a kind of leadership that began to attract the attention of others. And it was during these years — the late 1940s and early 1950s — that a series of loosely connected events began to take place, bringing Chavez in contact with a half dozen people who would become vitally important to "La Causa" . . . the cause of the farm workers, 15 to 20 years later. In retrospect, these events have a special significance to both the farmer and the farm workers; they are the beginnings of the Cesar Chavez mystique and the roots from which the power of the United Farm Workers has grown.

One man served as a catalytic agent in this sequence of events, Fred Ross. He was a tall, thin, community organizer who had been in California since the Great Depression, helping the poor, the dispossessed, the ethnic minorities fight prejudice and poverty. Like most people attracted to such work, he lived a hand-to-mouth existence, shifting from one job to another, as funding ran out or projects changed or were disbanded. In 1946 his job with the American Council on Race Relations evaporated due to lack of financing.

Coincidentally two men playing pinochle in a Chicago suburb were discussing community organizers. Saul Alinsky explained he was looking for a good man to help the miners fight the copper combines in Montana. His pinochle partner, a University of Chicago professor who was a member of the American Council on Race Relations board of directors, said a man named Fred Ross was out of work. Alinsky asked a few questions, liked what he heard, and wrote Ross, offering him a job with the Industrial Areas Foundation.

The IAF, founded by Alinsky with funds donated by liberal industrialists like Marshall Field, already had an impressive — if radical — record for helping the poor organize into power blocs. Alinsky believed the only way the poor were going to get what they needed was through strong, militant organizations of their own. Alinsky wrote:

> This kind of organization can be built only if people are working together for real, attainable objectives . . . [You] can't go outside of people's actual experience . . . you must approach them on the basis of their own self interest. We say "Look, you don't have to take this; there is something you can do about it . . . but you have to have power to do it. And you'll only get power through organization. Because power just goes to two poles — to those who've got money, and those who've got people. You haven't got money, so your own fellowmen are your source of strength."

Alinsky repeatedly warned his organizers that the groups they worked with had to have many issues going at one time. The organization that had but one issue soon ran out of ways to confront that issue. The Alinsky techniques were radical; they met the power sources head on, manipulated them, outflanked them, created issues that were diversions. At the same time he emphasized the need to avoid complexities and confusion.

To emphasize the point he once said: "Do you know what being poor means? It's not very complicated. It means not having any money."

Ross liked the Alinsky style, but he did not want to go to Montana copper mines. He had another, more important, project in mind. The Mexican American *barrios* in East Los Angeles were seething. For 30 years, tens of thousands of Mexicans coming in to work on farms and the low-paying city jobs had ended up in "East L.A." the Spanish-speaking population in Los Angeles outnumbered those of most of the major cities in Mexico. In the *barrios* there was almost open warfare between the *pachuco* gangs and the city police, siding with soldiers and sailors stationed in nearby camps. Gangs of pachucos and servicemen fought wherever they met. The situation climaxed when sailors and police swept through the *barrios,* beating anyone who looked or acted as if he might belong to a *pachuco* gang.

Ross convinced Alinsky that the Mexican aliens and Mexican American citizens suffered the rankest kind of discrimination, that police brutality was a fact of life in the barrios, and that the people wanted to do something about it. Alinsky agreed, and Ross moved into East Los Angeles. Patiently, he began walking the neighborhoods, talking, listening, identifying what the people felt they needed. He was handicapped by his inability to speak Spanish, but sometimes he could use this to his advantage, getting a young, aggressive *pachuco* to go along to interpret.

Ross said, "The people of East L.A. had no power. They had no vote. Too many were not citizens, and the citizens were not registered to vote. But the big fights then were with the housing authority, to eliminate segregation, against the police, to eliminate brutality. We were instrumental in bringing the grand jury investigation of the police department."

As Ross identified men and women who had leadership ability, he began to use a new organizing tool, the "house meeting." It was something he developed, almost by instinct. When he found people who were already trying to take action, he would meet with them, suggest they bring in a few friends to their home to talk over the problems. The talk would develop a course of action; others were urged to call meetings. As the numbers increased, Ross would suggest they organize into a larger group, made up of the people from a dozen or more house-meeting groups. The larger organization was called the Community Services Organization. By 1951 there were three cso chapters in Los Angeles.

During that first year the IAF ran out of funds. Ross turned away from Los Angeles, casting about for another job. The American Friends Service Committee needed a fund raiser for its California Federation for Civic Unity, in the San Francisco Bay Area. Ross took the job, on the condition that he be allowed to spend a good part of his time organizing a cso chapter in the *barrios* of nearby San Jose. The AFSC

80

agreed, triggering the first of a series of ecumenical coincidences that influenced the farm labor movement.

The other side of this coincidence began within the Catholic Church, where there was a developing concern over the exploitation of Mexican farm workers. In the middle 1940s Archbishop Lucey of San Antonio was arguing "a very general lack of labor organizations, the absence of good legislation and the greed of powerful employers have combined to create in Texas widespread misery . . ." In 1945 in Chicago the American Board of Catholic Missions underwrote the formation of a Bishops' Committee for the Spanish-Speaking, but it wasn't until 1949 that the Church became directly involved.

Two priests, Fathers Thomas McCullough and Donald McDonnell, argued successfully for the creation of a "mission band" within the San Francisco Archdiocese to work with the rural poor. Four priests were assigned as pastors to the seasonal farm workers; they carried portable altars, said the Mass in farm labor camps, took open-air confessions, trained catechists to instruct adults and children. Both Father McCullough and Father McDonnell ministered to the *Braceros* and began to see the need to teach the Catholic Church's social doctrines on labor. Father McCullough made his base in Stockton; Father McDonnell moved into San Jose and was working in the *barrio* called *Sal Si Puedes*.

Taking advantage of his clerical garb and calling, McDonnell moved through the *barrio*, knocking on doors, asking questions. He met Cesar Chavez this way; Chavez, who was eager to learn anything he could about labor organizing, sat up talking to the priest until past midnight. Chavez said, "He told me about social justice and the Church's stand on farm labor and reading from the encyclicals of Pope Leo XIII, in which he upheld labor unions. I would do anything to get the Father to tell me more about labor history. I began going to the *Bracero* camps with him to help with the Mass, to the city jail with him to talk to the prisoners, anything to be with him . . ."

The AFSC willingness to allow Ross to work in the *barrios*

brought him into contact with Father McDonnell. Ross recalled: "I didn't speak Spanish then, and I wanted to meet some of the working people, not the so-called leaders of the community. Father McDonnell took me around for a month, just meeting people and getting the feel of the community."

Cesar was not in the *barrio* at the time. He, Richard, their sister Rita, and their families had gone north "to work in the woods" near Crescent City. They had heard that wages in the timber industry were better, and, because Richard was quite good with wood tools, they decided to give it a try. Helen Chavez remembers this as one of the worst years of her life: "It rained all the time. The weather was always bad and the wind would blow, *hard.* I'd hang the wash out to dry and the wind would blow the clothesline down, and everything would get all muddy."

Fernando and Sylvia were still very small, and Helen was pregnant again. "We had this wood stove and you had to chop wood all the time, to cook, to keep warm, everything." Their third child, Linda, was born in Crescent City on January 21, 1951. Richard, Cesar, and Rita's husband Joe worked as lumber handlers, or at times they helped out in a cabinet shop, but they were not "making it" so they headed back south, into farm work again.

By 1952 the IAF once again picked up Fred Ross's salary and expenses, and he concentrated on building a strong CSO chapter in *Sal Si Puedes.* Through the contacts established with the help of Father McDonnell, Ross had 80 or 90 people holding house meetings and he was seeking more. A friendly public health nurse, who knew Helen Chavez through the well-baby clinics she ran, suggested Cesar and Helen might be interested. Fred knocked on their door several times, talked briefly to Helen, but couldn't make contact with Cesar.

Cesar wanted no part of the *gabacho* and would leave when he saw Ross approaching the house. Ross was persistent. Helen finally put her foot down: She would lie no more; if Cesar did not want to talk to the man, then at least tell him so.

In later years, as he repeated the story, Chavez would explain that social workers, students writing reports, reporters, and professional do-gooders frequently came into the *barrio* to peek and probe, to observe cultural patterns among the poor, to take notes and write papers about hunger or school dropouts or teenaged gangs.

Such intrusions were deeply resented by the people of *Sal Si Puedes,* no doubt. But that wasn't the only reason for ignoring Ross. Most *barrio* residents had a deep distrust of, if not genuine dislike for, Anglos. To a young man like Chavez the Anglos were *gringos* or *gabachos,* and not to be trusted. But Ross persisted and Chavez finally agreed to a house meeting. He wanted to teach this *gabacho* a lesson; Cesar invited some of the *barrio* toughs to come, to drink beer and raise hell with Ross.

But it didn't work out that way. Ross, who looks like a scholar, began to talk; he knew the problems of the *barrios* and the fields, and somewhere along the line Chavez began to listen. Cesar says now, "He knew the problems as well as we did. He talked about cso and then about Bloody Christmas, you know, when some drunken cops down in L.A. beat up some Mexican prisoners. I didn't know about cso but I knew about Bloody Christmas. Some cops actually had been sent to jail for brutality and it turned out this miracle was thanks to cso."

The *barrio* toughs still wanted to give Ross a bad time, but Chavez turned them off, told them to stay and listen, or leave. By the time the meeting ended at 9 P.M. Chavez wanted to help organize cso. Ross, obviously pleased, asked when Cesar wanted to start.

"Right now."

Ross took him to another meeting that night, and, sometime after midnight, after dropping Cesar off at his home, Fred Ross wrote in his journal: "6 P.M. to Alicias. To the home of Cesar Chavez: very responsive. Agreed to become a deputy registrar. Chavez has real push. Understanding. Loyalty and Enthusiasm. Grassroots leadership quality."

From that night on, Cesar Chavez was Fred Ross's shadow.

First he had to learn that power was not a mysterious force, that it developed naturally as large groups of people worked together. The job of the organizer was to get the people to come together, to cultivate leadership within the group, and then set that leadership free to exert its own influence. Such work took three and four meetings a night; hours were spent talking and listening, days were spent persistently working, planting the seed of an idea, and patiently cultivating it.

The cso was not a union — in the organized labor sense of the word — but to Ross "we did have a sense of union in that we were getting people together to exert civic pressures on public officials to get roads paved, stop signals installed, so kids wouldn't get killed. We organized a union to oppose police brutality, urban redevelopment, all of those things that were irritants, that were making life miserable for the people."

Chavez was a volunteer. He worked for wages by day and as a deputy registrar at night, going from house to house getting people to register to vote. But he also went to as many house meetings with Fred as possible. He said, "All the time I was observing the things Fred did, secretly, because I wanted to learn how to organize, to see how it was done. I was impressed with his patience, and understanding of people. I thought this was a tool, one of the greatest things he had."

Once volunteers like Chavez were working pretty well on their own, Ross would take off to another part of town, or another community. Chavez was alternately working as a lumber handler in nearby yards, picking fruit, receiving unemployment insurance, and spending most of his time and energies getting people registered to vote. Ross wrote Alinsky and asked for money to hire Chavez. Alinsky was reluctant because funds were short, but in the end agreed to pay $275 a month.

Chavez was never trained by Alinsky. He never attended any Alinsky school for radicals, as the John Birch Society and most agribusiness spokesmen would like to believe. Ross said, "The only kind of help or training Cesar got from Alinsky was the same kind of training I got from him. Every six months or so Saul would come out, either to raise money, or attend a conference. We would get together and talk. Being around Saul like that, we did learn some of his concepts, his tactics, the use of power and strategies in conflict organizing."

Cesar Chavez had found his life's work: conflict organizing. The intensity of his commitment was measured in a small incident that occurred on September 11, 1953. For several months Ross had been working in DeCoto, a small town near San Jose; but he had also been ranging through the farm labor communities to the south, in the Salinas Valley. On September 11 he received an urgent call from King City. The Mexican American youngsters in the high school had been having trouble with the Italian American farmer kids. A fight had resulted and one of the farmer's sons, a well-known high school football player, had been killed.

King City was about to come apart at the seams. Could Fred Ross come down? Bring some help? Fred picked Cesar up and they drove nearly 100 miles south, to the tiny farming town. They interviewed the young Chicano who had been arrested for the killing, did what they could to cool the tempers, got lawyers, organized the Mexican American community into a concerted effort to resolve the issues. After a long, hectic day and night, they were driving back to San Jose when Cesar suddenly sat bolt upright in the car.

He had forgotten Helen. She was pregnant, and, when her labor pains had started, he had taken her to the hospital in San Jose. Then, in the excitement of getting to King City, he had forgotten her. Helen recalled, "When he dropped me off at the hospital I asked him to get me a bottle of alcohol so I could have a back rub. That night the other women in the hospital got their backs rubbed, but I didn't." That night Anna, their fifth child, was born.

Chavez was out of the fields and moving away from farm labor; he was away from the family for extended periods; as Ross gave him assignments he submerged himself in them. He was in charge of organizing DeCoto, while Ross attended to the problems in King City; then he went into Oakland, and the urban jungles on the east side of San Francisco Bay unnerved him. The people were tougher, more suspicious, and it was difficult for them to accept this slight-built country boy as the organizer sent by cso to help them. Chavez grew a mustache to make himself look older, he wore suits and ties, but he never felt at ease as an urban organizer. From the San Francisco Bay Area he was sent into the San Joaquin Valley to organize the *barrios* tucked off in an isolated corner of each valley town. Cesar was back with the rural poor again, with the farm workers, conducting house meetings, studying, and evaluating his own techniques. He and Fred Ross were not together much anymore as each worked different areas of the state, establishing cso chapters in Madera, Visalia, Hanford, Salinas, Oxnard — the list was long. The organization grew and held conventions and established a statewide base of power. The cso registered a half million Mexican American voters, it guided 35,000 in citizenship classes and naturalization, but more important it provided the people with a sense of power. In places like Visalia, cso became "the voice" of the *barrio* and it exerted pressures on city hall, on the school board and county government.

In Stockton, Father McCullough had organized a group of Mexican American farm workers into the Agriculture Workers Association. The association had come out of the disappointment that followed the abortive tomato strikes in 1950. That year the National Farm Labor Union, guided by Hank Hasiwar and Ernesto Galarza, was concentrating on the *Braceros* in the tomato harvest; the NFLU called a strike both to protest the low wages and the use of *Braceros* to displace the local work force.

Father McCullough was acting as a *Bracero* pastor at the time, moving daily through the remote *Bracero* farm labor camps, offering the rites of the Church, and talking to the men about the NFLU strike.

McCullough explained, "The *Braceros* were deeply troubled, they had made great sacrifices to come to this country; I knew that. They had families back in Mexico, most of them.

So it wasn't an easy thing. They came to me and said, 'Padre, what should we do? This strike, is it good?' I just talked with them about their rights under the Natural Law to band together with other workers. The operator of the camp came around. He saw the men sitting there and he frowned, and he said — I remember his exact words — '*Al trabajo o a Mexico!* [To work, or to Mexico!]' The men looked at me, at him, and they said, '*A Mexico!*' And that was that. Back they went, making wry fun of themselves the way Mexicans do when they are unhappy."

The tomato strikes were no more successful than any other NFLU effort. When McCullough could not get organized labor to commit itself to a long-term fight, he began to form the Agriculture Workers Association — with the help of a young woman named Dolores Fernandez Huerta. McCullough worked out of St. Gertrude's Church, and Dolores Huerta worshiped there. She was a Stockton girl; her mother ran a hotel-boardinghouse in a low-income, farm worker neighborhood.

Fred Ross completed his work in King City and turned his attention to Stockton. Through Father McDonnell he was put in touch with Father McCullough and through the priest, he met Dolores Huerta. The AWA was sputtering along, with a few hundred members meeting and talking, and it could be a good starting place for CSO. Ross asked Dolores to help. She agreed.

Dolores Huerta is tough. Once she had made the commitment, the organization of farm workers became the focus of her life; next to Chavez she is the most controversial figure in the farm labor movement. She is the union's chief negotiator; she is constantly on the move, crisscrossing the nation, giving speeches, bolstering boycott efforts, confronting farmers and politicians. I caught up with her at the AFL-CIO convention in Miami Beach, at the Americana Hotel. As we talked, George Meany's voice rolled over the auditorium, calling the roll on a vote. Dolores, outfitted in a smart red dress trimmed in white, her long black hair streaked slightly with gray, was here both as a delegate and a lobbyist seeking support for the farm workers.

She recalled: "When Fred started organizing us in Stockton, Cesar was in DeCoto. I hadn't met him yet and Fred kept talking about Cesar this and Cesar that and what a great organizer Cesar Chavez was. Finally he took me up to DeCoto to see him, and you know afterward I couldn't even remember what he looked like. I was very unimpressed. Fred had talked so much about this great organizer, and I found Cesar was very shy. The first two or three years I knew him it was difficult to have a conversation with him. He didn't speak up at meetings. cso, the way it was structured, was very bad. All the officers were — well, wherever there was a chapter, the president was on the executive board.

"Cesar was a staff person. The only people who had any say-so were these presidents of these chapters, so Cesar never spoke or said much. It was strange. Everyone knew that wherever he was, things happened . . ." Dolores tried to give an example of what she was talking about. "cso got some money, so we were going to put Cesar to work [at that time he was still paid by Alinsky's IAF] . . . Gilbert Lopez insisted Cesar would have to give daily reports and Lopez put a lot of strings on him.

"Cesar never objected. He sat there and took all this stuff. The effect was that it made a lot of other people get up and defend what Cesar was doing . . . and it worked." The fact that Dolores remembered how Cesar finessed Gilbert Lopez after 20 years is also a comment on the man's impact on people. The tactic also demonstrates something of Chavez's approach to organizing — he is frequently obtuse.

Chavez's impact on Gilbert Padilla was totally different. Padilla, a thin, curly-headed man of 45, is a UFWA vice president. He was a migrant worker, the son of migrant workers. By the time he met Chavez he had already begun his own rebellion: "When I got out of the Army, I went back into the fields. I had left for the Army from the labor camp near Los Banos and I was getting 85 cents an hour then. When I got back, the wage was down to 75 cents an hour, but the *Braceros* were getting 90 cents. That's when I led my first strike [1947]. We didn't get very far."

Gil left the fields, tried the dry cleaning business with his brothers, then came back into the fields in 1955. He got a job as foreman, supervising crews, checking off the work, for a labor contractor. "The guy was supposed to be a friend of mine. We were drinking buddies when I was in the cleaning business. He had a lot of money. Well, when the first week was over, he gave me $48. So I said to him, 'Willy, how much you paying me?' He said, 'A dollar an hour.' I said, 'Yeah, but I'm on the street at 4:30 in the morning, picking people up!' He said that the pay didn't start until we got to the field. I told him he was taking Social Security from my check, but he had forgotten to take down my Social Security number. I was getting hot, man. He knew it. He pulled $20 out of his pocket and gave it to me, not as wages, but to keep quiet. That's the kind of mind labor contractors have. If he did that to me, think what he did to the others . . ."

Gil was still working in the fields, in Kings County, and living in Hanford in 1957. In the south end of this county are the great cotton and grain farms, the J. G. Boswell Company (100,000 acres), the Salyer Land Company (90,000 acres), Southlake Farms, Westlake Farms, and a dozen others. The cotton-picking machines were successfully replacing thousands of hand pickers. Without cotton to carry them through the winter, the migrant farm workers faced hunger and the humiliation of trying to get counties like Kings to provide some kind of welfare subsistence programs.

Gil said, "Cesar came around to talk. He came to the house with some guys and I asked what it was he wanted to do. He was talking about service center kinds of things, helping workers with insurance forms, Social Security or welfare problems, driver's licensing and citizenship classes, and I wasn't interested. But then he starts talking about labor contractors and minimum wages and unemployment insurance for farm workers and I got interested. Right then. I started with him then."

Gilbert Padilla joined CSO that night. "Cesar stayed around

for about a week, and I would hang around and see him operate. There was a new chapter of cso starting in Hanford and he wanted me to help. He went around, talking to people about the basic problems, the real problems of the community. He was talking about how some day the people should have some sort of representation in the political structure. And we were thinking that if we could get someone elected, then we could get some laws that would help farm workers."

From 1957 through 1961 Gilbert worked as a volunteer, conducting house meetings, organizing voter-registration efforts, helping people with problems. Chavez acted as an area coordinator for such work throughout the valley. In 1959 cso had enough in its budget to hire Dolores Huerta full time, and then in 1961 Gilbert became the third paid staff member. He was assigned to Stockton, Dolores was shifted to Los Angeles, and Cesar was made executive director not long afterward. Ross continued to function as an IAF organizer assigned to cso. At the time Dolores Huerta moved to Los Angeles she still did not know Chavez well.

She said, "cso had been given some money by the packinghouse workers, I think it was $20,000, to go into the Oxnard area and help the local workers get their jobs back from the *Braceros*. Cesar took the job, and I was curious to see what he had been able to do." She went to Oxnard and what she saw "really turned me on. I wanted to help him organize and I wanted him to tell me what he was doing, but he wouldn't because I guess he hadn't got to the point where he'd thought it through."

Like Cesar, Dolores is a student of organizational techniques. Once she made this comparison between Fred Ross and Cesar Chavez: "Fred is a dogmatic type of organizer. Things are structured. Cesar is more like a conductor of an orchestra: something is happening here, and something over there and something somewhere else, and he knows what the hell is going on all over. Cesar is a real strategist. Fred organizes through people. Cesar organizes through events. He is more like a pool player."

She pointed out that Fred has infinite patience and

Dolores Huerta speaks to night rally of farm workers.
Photo by George Ballis

Gil Padilla (with cigarette) conducts outdoor meeting
in Rio Grande Valley. *Photo by George Ballis*

Chavez and UFW attorney Jerry Cohen.
Photo by Ronald B. Taylor

persistence, that he built support for cso as he organized people. "We were getting a lot of donations, foundation money, and we had a lot of volunteers. This was mostly all Fred's work." He had gone to the rank-and-file in the labor union locals, to the congregation members in churches, and to the members of liberal organizations, patiently talking and explaining. These people were gently brought around to a supporting position *before* cso went to the union officials, the church pastor, or the organization president to seek support.

Fred explained, "That way, you have their own people, on the inside, working for your request."

I asked Cesar about the cso organizing effort in Oxnard.

"Oh. Yeah. That is a beautiful story. We could have had a union there. We *had* a union there. It was just a matter of moving in. cso was very close to the labor movement. They supported us and the cso board of directors was afraid to move into a labor thing because they were afraid the labor movement would ask why.

"I was working for the cso, and I didn't want to say they were wrong and that I was going to go ahead. I wouldn't do that, so we lost. For all practical purposes we had a union going, and we lost.

"You will recall I was sent there. We got some money from the packinghouse workers. They had a drive going to organize the packing sheds. They had elections, and they had won something like 20 sheds. The growers had started court maneuvers against them, to destroy the union. By the time we came there, in 1958, the packinghouse workers union was pretty weak among the people in the sheds.

"I was sent there to organize the field workers and the community. This was to be a help to the union. We were not going to organize the packinghouse workers, but once we were there and they joined cso . . . [he dropped whatever thought he had and switched the subject in midsentence] . . . when I arrived there, what I found out immediately was the people there had *tremendous* complaints against the *Braceros. That issue was just bubbling.* You know?"

At the time, there were 85,000 *Braceros* working in

California; although they made up only about 30 percent of the total seasonal work force, the *Braceros'* concentrations in specific crops depressed wages. In west Fresno County, local workers complained farmers were paying 25 cents a box to harvest the small pear tomatoes. At that piece rate the pickers couldn't earn the $1-an-hour minimum guaranteed by the *Bracero* contracts. Because of these contracts the growers were forced to add $15 to $18 a week to the *Braceros'* paychecks, but the local workers had no such guarantees and if they were not satisfied with 60 to 75 cents an hour they could make at the piece rate, they could look elsewhere for work.

A Stockton potato grower explaining the need for *Braceros* told a Los Angeles *Times* reporter, "It is the farmer who has the problem of finding workers available and willing to do farm work when he needs them at pay rates which are based on their productivity rather than either their needs or the number of hours they spend in the field." He argued farm profits depended upon a cheap supply of labor and *Braceros* offered that labor supply.

Chavez said, "In Oxnard, the *Braceros* had it all. Many of the local workers were out of jobs and those who were working were afraid. In order to work they had to go through a lot of bad discrimination. I would hold house meetings and I got a lot of talk about the *Bracero* problems. So I reported back to CSO headquarters, saying this was the big issue. Labor is the big issue. The wages are low, the working conditions terrible . . . 65 to 80 cents an hour in 1958. Oh. Miserable.

"After a month, every single time I went someplace, they would complain about the *Braceros* and I began to shift my emphasis and I began to deal with those *Bracero* problems. They had more *Braceros* in that area than they did anywhere else in the United States. They had a big camp, and they sent the *Braceros* to work at 5 A.M.

"The local workers in the *colonias* and *barrios* were really getting a bad time. They couldn't get jobs on local farms unless they had a dispatch slip from the state Farm Labor

Placement Service office in Ventura, but that office didn't open until 8 A.M. From Oxnard to Ventura is about 12 miles. By the time they got the papers filled out and got back to the field the *Braceros* were out there working. The jobs were filled."

Legally the *Braceros* could work only if there was a labor shortage in a specific crop or a specific area; the Oxnard farmers contended they were short of workers and the placement service certified this was true. The certification was required by the U.S. Department of Labor. The labor department also required both the placement service and the farmers to make sure the *Braceros* were not displacing local workers. By placing all their job orders through the FLPS, and by ordering crews to report at 5 A.M., the farmers were manipulating the local workers, making it next to impossible to get work.

Chavez explained, "A lot of times the people would go out to the fields at 5 A.M., show the referral slip they had gotten the day before, but the farmer — or the field boss — would say they were sorry, that dispatch slip had been dated for the day before, it was no good now . . . or if the guy did get a job with the *Braceros*, the crew boss told the *Braceros* to speed it up. They were all very young and they could speed it up and the guy would get fired because he couldn't keep up, or he'd quit.

"We had almost every farm worker family in that city tied up, tied into the CSO as members. We went into the fields where the *Braceros* were and held sit-ins. We used to sit in right in front of them. The police would come and take us to jail. After maybe four or five months of fighting, we were able to have the Farm Labor Placement Service move the office halfway between Oxnard and Ventura.

"Then we had a march from Oxnard to the Farm Labor office. We got dispatch cards almost all day, maybe 600 or 700 of them, and we burned them. Built a bonfire and burned them. That got a lot of publicity. The big thing we were fighting for was 'gate hiring.' The growers had this thing, they would not hire workers directly, they made them go through the association and the association referred them to the Farm Labor Placement Service. The law required that the farmers hire local workers first. We said that if the farmer was using *Braceros*, he should hire local workers at the gate to make the preferential hiring policy meaningful. And we forced the farmers into gate hiring.

"In the *barrio* we opened an office in a big storefront. And by the time we got through, we were forcing the farmers to come pick up their workers there, in front of the store. I was there 13 months, and oh, hell, I learned a lot, an awful lot, there. By the time I left we could have converted to a union. Any farm worker that wanted a job could get a job. Growers called our office, just like a hiring hall, and we would tell them if they wanted workers they would pay $1 an hour and they *would* pay $1."

The Chavez-led efforts had been so successful that the formation of a small union was easily within CSO's grasp. But the CSO board of directors would not allow Chavez to take the needed steps to convert the efforts into a permanent power structure. Instead, he was directed to turn the farm worker organization over to the local United Packinghouse Workers and return to Los Angeles to assume his new duties as CSO executive director. The Oxnard field worker organization disintegrated within a few weeks, and, from that time on, Chavez was no longer satisfied with his work in CSO.

Fred Ross explained, "When Cesar was working with CSO, he was working with hobbles on. He was subject to an executive board that did not understand what he was trying to do. He was working harder than he ever had in his life in Oxnard, just killing himself, but the CSO board didn't understand that. They weren't interested in agriculture. The board was made up of a couple of lawyers, a school administrator, urban guys like that. He would come in and make glowing reports about what was happening in Oxnard and they would ask him about a typewriter that had disappeared from his office, little crap like that."

As Chavez moved into his new CSO job, another force was trying to make itself felt in the farm labor scene; the AFL-CIO executive council decided to take a direct hand in the battle to organize farm workers. Rather than depend upon small, weak independent unions like Mitchell's NFLU, the AFL-CIO created the Agriculture Workers Organizing Committee. Jack Livingston, AFL-CIO director of organizing, and his assistant, Franz Daniel, came into California personally to supervise the establishment of the AWOC. Stockton was picked as the national headquarters; Norman Smith, a crusty old United Auto Worker who had helped organize the Ford Motor Company, was named AWOC executive director. A well-funded organizational structure was mapped out. Smith's first job was to establish and charter eight AWOC locals; each local was to have at least 200 members, and this membership had to come from the stable community served by the local. Daniel said that while migrants were not being excluded — they could join the local in their home town — the emphasis was on the stable work force.

These locals were to be created by the AWOC staff, from the top down, and the staff would direct the local operations until such time as the worker membership was firmly established and capable of governing itself. If not democratic, the plan at least sounded very efficient. The problem was that Livingston, Daniel, and Smith did not know anything about agribusiness or farm labor. Their ignorance made their efforts absurd. The first AWOC organizing efforts took place in the fall of 1959, and the very first problem was finding farm workers to organize. The farm labor force didn't flow in and out of factory gates, where Norman Smith's ample voice could reach them. In fact there was nothing in Smith's considerable experience in the industrial union movement to prepare him for his task.

The AWOC organizers, equipped with cars and gasoline credit cards, were sent out to find farm workers, and, when they returned empty-handed, they were sent out again into the flat, empty-looking countryside. They could find no place to focus their attention; when the farm workers were in the fields they were so far removed from the public roadways they could not be seen, and the organizers could not legally trespass to deliver their message of liberation. When the day was done the workers went off in a dozen directions; the ebb and flow of workers on any ranch was so diffuse, so chaotic, so unpredictable, the organizers couldn't get a toehold. They were not a part of the *barrios* or *colonias* and the few efforts they made at establishing worker contact there were rebuffed; the farm workers were suspicious of outsiders.

Smith started hanging out around the one place where part of the labor force was concentrated, the pre-dawn shapeup on Stockton's skid row. Each morning dozens of farm labor contractor buses would line up on the streets and hundreds of "day haul" workers would come to this spot seeking work. It was the same from Philadelphia to Belle Glade, Florida's, "loading ramp" to Stockton and south to Calexico's *"el hoyo"*; these farm labor shapeups offer work to anyone who can physically climb aboard the bus; many of the workers in the Stockton skid row shapeups were winos or single workers so down on their luck they had no other choices. This was where the AWOC began to focus its organizational efforts.

There is no question about Smith's good intentions; his problem was he just didn't know what to do with the farm workers. But the AWOC had a couple of things going for it; one was the Filipino men who had been imported in the late 1920s to work the vegetables and the table grapes; they were already "organized" into cohesive groups that had lived and worked together for nearly 30 years. They were single men who lived in camps and spoke so little English they depended upon their crew leaders to communicate with both employers and the outside world. Among this group of Filipinos were men like Larry Itliong and Andy Imutan who wanted to improve the workers' lot and who had learned the rudiments of labor organizing by putting worker protests together. The AWOC hired both men, and they built AWOC "locals" among the Filipino grape and vegetable workers.

There was a second cohesive group, the "cherry pickers." These were Midwestern and Southern Anglos who specialized in "ladder work" in the fruit harvests. They were the self-styled fruit tramps. They said they suffered "white line fever" because they could not tolerate immobility and had to follow the white line down the road. The cherry pickers heard about the AFL-CIO AWOC coming into the farm work force, and in 1959–60 they began to strike the cherries, the plums, the peaches, and the olives. After they walked out of an orchard they would call AWOC headquarters and ask for help. Their biggest strike occurred at the Podesta Farms near Stockton. The cherries were "dead ripe," but the farmer refused to give in and the workers would not pick the crop. Podesta lost a $100,000 crop and the strike triggered a rash of walkouts in other tree crops.

The AWOC goal that summer was $1.25 an hour. Organizers made little effort to gain union recognition, or to form the 8 locals that Daniel had talked about. The "fruit tramps" carried the ball, within the orchards, the Filipino AWOCs struck the vegetable crops. The farmers reacted haphazardly. The old members of the Associated Farmers had by this time turned their farms over to sons and were retired; but when the strike lines came out, these old warhorses reached for their pick handles and charged. However, times had changed, the sons retained control, calling meetings to form new alliances. The newly formed farmer associations hired professional managers and issued public statements. The associations set uniform farm wages and, when AWOC pickets appeared, dispatched strikebreaking crews. The farm labor forces controlled by growers became highly mobile. The strikes were weak, unplanned efforts. As the fall olive harvest was completed, in Tulare County, Smith turned the AWOC attention south, to the Imperial Valley winter lettuce crops.

On November 22, 1960, California Farm Bureau President Louis Rozzoni told a Fresno State College conference on industrial relations that "the growers are immovable. They will not be coerced into signing union contracts. Unionizing farm labor is simply not feasible. Agriculture is different from other industries. It cannot set its price at the consumer level."

Smith also spoke at the conference. He grandly predicted that as soon as the AWOC finished off California agribusiness, it would move into Texas "where farmers pay 50 cents an hour. Then we'll go into Louisiana and drive the Long family nuts. They are only paying 30 cents an hour down there . . ."

But first Smith had to show some success in California. With the help of the United Packinghouse Workers, the AWOC organizers moved into the Imperial Valley lettuce harvest. The AWOC-UPHW plan was based on the federal regulations that prohibited the use of *Braceros* on ranches under strike. The strikes were focused on the Bruce Church operation, and the U.S. Department of Labor ordered 565 *Braceros* off the farm. Farmers from central California made up a 40-car caravan of workers and drove into the Imperial Valley to help the growers. By February the U.S. Department of Labor had certified 17 different lettuce strikes, and 600 more *Braceros* were removed from these ranches.

While this was some measure of success, the strikes did little more than slow the harvest. The farmers suffered some losses, but not nearly enough to bring them to the bargaining table. As the harvest ended in the Imperial Valley and the crews moved north to Salinas, the strikers followed. The threat of the strike, plus internal financial problems, caused one big lettuce grower, Bud Antle, Inc., to make a surprise move: He signed a contract with the International Brotherhood of Teamsters covering his field labor operations. The Teamsters then loaned the company $1 million. The Salinas Growers-Shippers Association denounced the labor contract and kicked Antle out of the association. The other lettuce growers stood pat, and the AWOC-UPHW efforts sputtered and died.

The AFL-CIO executive council asked the AWOC for an accounting of its successes, as measured by dues-paying members and contracts with employers. When it saw the lack of results the executive council ordered AFL-CIO president George Meany to close down the AWOC operations. While Meany and the executive council may have considered the AWOC dead, the workers had other ideas. The "fruit tramps" would not let their union die. The Anglo and Mexican fruitpickers had been ignoring Smith and were really running things themselves, on a local basis. They and some of the AWOC central staff called a conference in the tiny village of Strathmore, in Tulare County, to see what could be done to save the union. The 200 workers who attended assessed themselves $2 each and they sent a delegation back to the AFL-CIO's midwinter convention in Miami Beach. One of the four delegates elected to go was Mrs. Maria Moreno, the mother of 12. In an impassioned speech before the full convention she told how her family had literally been starving, how her 19-year-old son had not eaten for days, so that his smaller brothers and sisters could share the potato peel soup or boiled greens. She was a citrus picker, from Tulare County; rains had idled the family, there was no work available, and the anger she felt for a society that would allow her children to starve made itself felt as she spoke to the nation's labor leaders.

On her return to California she proudly reported, "Mr. Meany told us if we keep going we will soon have our union built. He said there would be as much money as needed. He told us to tell the people back home he was going to back us all the way."

Meany ordered a tough, old, cigar-chewing organizer, Al Green, to replace Smith, who was retired. Ironically, in the shakeup that followed, Al Green kicked Mrs. Moreno out of the union because she had not been keeping adequate records as she organized new members and collected dues. Green had no more feel for farm workers than Smith had. He was a gruff trade unionist, used to the wheeling and dealing and compromising in the smoke-filled back rooms of the Stanislaus County labor movement. Like Smith, he found the shapeup on skid row the only visible target for his organizers; Green set out to organize the labor contractors, and he had them deducting AWOC dues from the workers as they climbed on the buses each morning. Green was no more successful at building a viable farm labor union than his predecessor had been. Through the efforts of organizers Larry Itliong, Ben Guines, and Andy Imutan, the Filipino vegetable and grape workers were a cohesive force, but they were a small minority. The fruit tramps became disillusioned and dropped out. To the great mass of the farm labor force the AWOCS were meaningless.

There were other forces trying to influence the lives of farm workers. The American Friends Service Committee in the mid-1950s wanted to start a farm worker community-development project somewhere in the nation to demonstrate that these low-income families could, with technical assistance, improve their living conditions. The San Joaquin Valley was selected, and a community organizer named Bard McAllister was hired. He moved into Tulare County, in 1956, and set about exploring the dozens of remote farm worker villages that flyspecked the landscape. There were villages of blacks, villages of whites, villages of Mexican Americans. Theirs was a do-it-yourself kind of poverty; they hammered and nailed shanties together, dug pit toilets, hauled water for miles both for domestic use and to irrigate the tiny garden patches. When they got some money saved they drilled shallow wells and added a room onto the shack. The communities were called Pumpkin Center, Teviston, Cotton Center, Three Rocks, Weed Patch, Linaire, Tonyville. Whether populated by blacks, Chicanos, or Anglos, they all looked the same; each had a store or two, usually attached to a service station, and the houses were laid out along rutted dirt streets. McAllister helped communities organize water districts, and he conceived a self-help housing program for farm workers.

The California Migrant Ministry — a cookies-and-milk extension of the Northern and Southern California Councils of Churches — had come into some money, and, in 1959, it was decided the migrant ministers should get into some community-development projects. Up to that time the CMM had "ministered" to the spiritual needs of the migrants, taking food and clothing and sermons into the farm labor camps; but the new migrant ministers wanted to begin attacking the social ills that kept migrants impoverished, malnourished, and unorganized.

Wayne C. Hartmire, a divinity student at Union Seminary in New York City, was being considered for the job of CMM executive director. During the summer of 1959 Hartmire came to California to learn community development from CSO. He was assigned to the Stockton area. Each of the new migrant ministers-to-be was given such an assignment; they would work with Cesar Chavez, or Fred Ross or Gilbert Padilla or Dolores Huerta. Hartmire spent as much time as he could with Ross and Chavez: "It was a mind-blowing experience. We'd work all day, go to meetings at night, and then afterwards, sit around and talk about what had happened."

Hartmire lived in the run-down hotel operated by Dolores's mother just off Stockton's skid row, but he traveled all over the state, attending CSO meetings. Because of Chavez's influence on the CSO, much of the emphasis was on farm labor. Hartmire, to learn more, began attending AWOC meetings. At the time Larry Itliong was organizing the asparagus workers. Hartmire recalled, "When Larry had a strike up in Salinas, I went up to try to find out what it was all about. All that was sort of an interesting thing that was going on in agriculture, but we gave no direct assistance to the strikes then. It wasn't as though we were involved. We had a much closer relationship with the Conference on People Who Follow the Crops."

This "conference" was a movable meeting, held once or twice a year, sponsored by the AFSC, the CMM, urban churches, liberal groups, and individuals who were "concerned." The conference brought both farmers and AWOC leaders together to argue; it invited state and local officials to present position papers and reports on the scandalous housing and living conditions. But essentially the "conference" was powerless, and as long as the voice of liberal conscience was weak it was tolerated by the larger agribusiness community.

In addition to the conference, the AFSC and the CMM, each summer, sponsored "work projects" for liberal high school and college students who wanted to donate their time and

103

sweat to a farm worker community project. These youngsters would live in a makeshift camp on the edge of a farm worker settlement, and they would hammer and nail on a community hall or set up summer recreation programs or day care centers for the children.

Hartmire remembers: "By the end of the summer these volunteers were so frustrated, they had seen so much real pain and misery and suffering and . . . they were just sick, seeing what was happening to people in the camps and they were bright and full of love and just knew what they were doing was not getting at the problem. . . . [They] used to push us, ask us what we were going to do about the problems they had seen.

"The most sensitive of these kids would point out nothing was going to change until the workers had a union. AWOC was not hacking it, and the kids wanted to know why the Migrant Ministry was not doing it. . . . My mind was just not ready for that. I had all kinds of theological reasons for not going that route. Labor organizing was someone else's job. These kids didn't know how relatively incompetent we were, how tough organizing would be . . . Cesar knew, but we didn't."

That comment, *"Cesar knew,* but we didn't," struck me. I asked why he felt Cesar Chavez could have known the problems that he was still five years from facing.

Hartmire paused, and thought. "Yeah. That's interesting. I don't know. Well, probably I am giving him too much foresight, credit. I have a tendency to do that. He usually operates by the seat of his pants and afterwards it seems like he was running on foresight."

As the migrant minister's role changed, as the CMM trained its new "worker-priests" and put them with the farm workers, Hartmire's perspective on the church role in labor organizing began to change. He took over the CMM executive director's job in 1961, and, as he hired more staff, he sent some of them to work with Saul Alinsky, to learn more about conflict organizing. With Hartmire's assumption of the CMM job, all of the people who would have a major influence on the creation of the first successful farm labor union were in place.

One final act was needed to set things in motion: Cesar Chavez had to disengage himself from the cso and focus his full attention on farm workers. Chavez announced his resignation from cso at the organization's 1962 convention in Los Angeles. He explained years later that he was not bitter when he resigned, although he was disappointed because the cso board of directors and the leadership within the urban areas would not allow him to focus his efforts on the organization of farm labor.

Chavez's resignation came as a surprise even to his closest associates. Gil Padilla said, "When Cesar quit, he just said it: 'I resign.' I asked him what he was doing. He never told me he was going to quit. I was on his staff. He said he was leaving because he wanted to do something with farm workers and he said that if I wanted, I could come along with him. That would be fine. I told him I didn't have any money. He said he didn't either, but he could draw unemployment insurance for awhile."

The precipitous action hurt Padilla's feelings. He felt Chavez should, at least, have warned him, but there was no doubt in Padilla's mind that he would follow. Dolores Huerta, who by this time had seven children and had divorced her husband, also decided to follow Chavez into the organizing of farm labor. It was decided both Padilla and Huerta should remain on the cso staff, for the time being, although they would be devoting most of their time to the farm labor efforts.

Chavez moved his family to Delano and began organizing the National Farm Workers Association.

CHAPTER SIX : LA CAUSA

The United Farm Workers of America was born in an era of protest and civil disobedience that began when Mrs. Rosa Parks refused to give up her seat on a bus in Montgomery, Alabama. The prolonged civil rights controversy of the sixties introduced Attorney General Robert F. Kennedy to the cause of ethnic minorities. Bobby Kennedy went into the urban slums and into rural Appalachia. He was moved by what he saw, and it was this concern that led him to *La Causa*. The U.S. Senate Subcommittee on Migratory Labor began a series of hearings that gave voice to the plight of seasonal farm workers; Ed Murrow produced the TV documentary *Harvest of Shame*, and once more the nation was shocked by the living and working conditions down on the farm. Organized labor, liberal church groups, and Mexican American organizations like cso began to pressure Congress to let the *Bracero* program die when Public Law 78 expired December 31, 1963.

As expected, the farmers argued labor shortages required the extension of the law authorizing *Braceros*, but tough old Al Green summed up the prevailing sentiment: "There is no job Americans won't do if they get paid. . . . How many *Braceros* do you find working as roofers? What is worse than working with that hot tar stinking in your face all day? But you find Americans doing that work because they get paid well."

While the political climate was improving for farm workers, they were not in a position to capitalize on it. Chavez told Los Angeles *Times* reporter Ruben Salazar,

Let's face it, most agriculture workers are in the lowest educational levels and don't even understand what unionization means. Many are Mexican immigrants who think joining a union could get them in trouble. We are now in the process of educating them in the importance of organizing.

At the time of the Salazar interview, Chavez was virtually unknown outside the cso circle of influence, and he was purposely maintaining a low profile. When he chose a name for his organization — the National Farm Workers Association — the word *union* was left out because it frightened workers and inflamed growers. The workers lived in fear; they were powerless and they knew it and they expected nothing would change this fact. When a labor union organizer showed up the people felt a cumulative fear generated by the killing of workers in Pixley, the beating and jailing of union leaders from Salinas to El Centro. Many would pack up and leave the field or the camp. One of Chavez's first tasks was to measure the level of this fear; he had to find out what it was the people would tolerate, what it was they wanted for themselves. He felt the nfwa would never succeed unless it met the people where they were, unless it started with their level of expectation.

Chavez said, "I took a three-week tour of the state, crisscrossing the farming areas. I made it a point to stop at every crew and go into the field. I would first ask for the foreman, and if he was there I would ask for a job. But if he wasn't there, I would go around and talk to the workers, to see what they thought about a union.

"In too many cases the people would put their heads down and they wouldn't answer. They'd just work harder. Some of the people didn't even know what the word *union* meant, even when I used various names to indicate in Spanish what it was I was talking about. Some of them understood, though, and they would say 'sure,' they agreed it was a good thing, and I would take their names, if they would give them.

"I went from field to field during the day, and in the evening I would drive into the *barrios* or *colonias* and go around to the grocery stores and the bars, where the people usually were. I had some leaflets with me, which had a cutoff section on the bottom, where people could mark if they were interested and mail them."

Cesar distributed thousands of these leaflets. Less than 100 people responded. Those who did respond had limited expectations: They asked for a nickel or a dime more an hour, for toilets in the fields, for ice water to drink. A few signed their names and some even scribbled a note of encouragement, but response to the questionnaire was disappointing.

Chavez had other resources; ten years of organizing for cso had left a strong network of contacts within the *barrios* and *colonias* in rural California; there were the migrant ministers, and through them, the liberal Protestants in the urban areas; priests like Fathers McCullough and McDonnell provided access to those Catholic churchmen who were working for the emancipation of the farm workers; and there were the liberal and radical youth from the Civil Rights Movement.

Financially, Chavez knew he would have problems, once his meager savings were used up. For this reason he and Helen had moved the family to Delano to be close to both her relatives and Cesar's brother Richard and his family. Richard had a job as a carpenter and was financially able to help out, his sister Rita and her husband mortgaged their house and loaned Cesar and Helen some money. Helen worked in the fields. On weekends Fernando would join her; Cesar worked in the crops only when it was absolutely essential; he was devoting most of his time to organizing NFWA.

Geographically Delano was the heart of Chavez's area of operations. From Delano he ranged as far south as the Imperial Valley and Calexico and as far north as the Sacramento Valley and Marysville. This is an area 550 miles long and 50 to 80 miles wide. It includes all of the San Joaquin, Napa, and Salinas valleys. Laid out on a map this area would extend from New York City south to Columbia, South Carolina. Traveling from Calexico to Marysville would be like driving from Washington, D.C., to Chicago or from St. Louis to Fort Worth.

Delano was a city of 14,000 people at the time Chavez located his NFWA headquarters there. He and Helen rented a small wood-frame house on Kensington Street, a couple of blocks from the center of town, and for a long while his house and the battered old garage out back were the union's headquarters. The city itself was located on Highway 99 and the Southern Pacific Railroad main line, 33 miles north of Bakersfield. There was little to distinguish it from a dozen other towns up and down the highway; the business district was laid out on two streets that paralleled the highway and the railroad tracks; to the east and north were the tree-shaded middle-class residential areas, the high school, city park, and proprietary hospital; to the west, across the tracks, were the honky-tonks, the worker hotels, boardinghouses, and liquor stores; and beyond, still further west, were the worker residential neighborhoods where the Mexican, Filipino, Puerto Rican, and Arab families lived.

Chavez had no base of power here. There was a CSO chapter in Delano but it was dominated by men and women who were the "traditional leaders" within the *barrio*, the storekeepers, barbers, and labor contractors, those who were used to accommodating the dominant agribusiness community. The Delano churches — both Protestant and Catholic — were conservative and offered no promise of help.

Vineyards surround Delano for as far as the eye can see. The land is table flat. Once desert, it was settled early in this century by Yugoslav and Italian immigrants who brought with them a knowledge of vineyards and fruit orchards. They dug deep wells, planted the vines, and prospered. By midcentury the deep wells had sucked the underground water supplies nearly dry, but the federal and state governments agreed to dam the rivers in the nearby mountains and to build canals to import great quantities of irrigation water. This supply of cheap water — it cost less than the energy charges on the deep-well pumps — guaranteed the prosperity of the San Joaquin Valley.

The largest of the Delano area farms was the 5,000-acre Schenley Industries ranch; the next was the DiGiorgio Fruit

Corporation's 4,400-acre Sierra Vista ranch. The remaining 30 or 40 farms were owned by families with names like Zaninovich, Radovich, Pandol, Caratan, Dispoto, Lucich, Caric, Lucas, proud, clannish people. Their prosperous farms range in size from a few hundred acres up to a few thousand acres. Most of the original farmers have retired and turned the operations over to their sons. Financed by huge bank loans, they have built packing and processing plants and cold-storage facilities; most market their own fruit. Together they keep from 2,000 to 5,000 workers employed, depending upon the time of year and crop conditions.

Within this work force are 1,500 Filipino men who were imported into the Delano grape crop in the late 1920s, men who have lived in the farm labor camps on the Delano farms for 30 years. In separate camps the farmers provide room and board for Mexican and Arab male workers. All of these single workers consider Delano their home base, but they move with the grape harvests, starting in the Coachella Valley and moving north into the San Joaquin Valley to Arvin, then in midsummer into Delano. The Delano harvest runs into the fall; during the winter these men work the vines, pruning and tying, and, as the sap begins to run in the spring, they prepare the vines for the coming season.

The Mexican family workers who have established homes in Delano — or in the half dozen small farm worker communities within 15 or 20 miles in any direction — also work the vines and harvest the grapes. These families work in the wine-grape harvest, they prune and harvest tree fruit, drive tractors, irrigate. Most were migrants who had saved enough to settle down, to begin to purchase a home, and to establish work patterns that would allow them to put their children into school and to make a permanent home. These were the people who Chavez hoped would help him build a strong union. With the local farm workers strongly behind the union, in this and other farming areas, then Chavez could hope to organize the migrants. He started holding house meetings, gathering ideas from the people; he called Dolores Huerta and asked her to quit cso and come to Delano.

Dolores said, "When he first asked me to help him organize farm workers I was really honored. I was one of the chosen people and I was really overwhelmed by it, but ever since then he has been fighting with me."

As a CSO staff member Dolores Huerta had become quite prominent within the state; she had been appointed to the state welfare commission and to an AFL-CIO advisory commission. She was flying to meetings in Washington, being courted for her advice on poverty and ethnic problems. The fact that she was very good looking, articulate, and not the least bit bashful added to the attraction she had for the establishment. Chavez asked that she drop all of this and focus her attention on organizing people.

She fought back. "I really misunderstood what he was doing. I thought he was trying to submerge my ego, but he wasn't; he was trying to make me see that all of those things were really bullshit. That the important thing was not trips to Washington, but to stay and work with the people. A lot of times I would misunderstand what he was trying to do, but also maybe it was because I am a woman. Lots of times when I would have an idea, I would have to fight like hell to get him to listen, to get the others to consider it."

Dolores brought her seven children to Delano, established a home, and began working full time with the NFWA. It was decided Padilla, who also had a family, would stay with CSO, but work with them in the union when he could. Padilla recalled, "The plan was we were going to build a union. Charge dues. But in order to do that we had to give the workers something. We decided on a service center approach with something like burial insurance.

"We must have gone to every insurance company in California trying to get something the workers could pay into to give the family $1,000 in burial insurance. I had helped organize a credit union through the CSO in Stockton, and I knew that was a very good thing, so we started to get one set up in Delano."

When Cesar quit CSO and moved to Delano, he maintained close contact with the California Migrant Ministry. In April of 1962, just after Chavez had completed his state tour, Wayne C. Hartmire asked him to speak during a CMM staff retreat up in the mountains, east of Delano. One of the young migrant ministers attending the conference was a big, dour-looking graduate of Union Seminary who exuded Calvinist anger and passion for reform. Years later, after long service as one of Chavez's closest aides, Jim Drake was able to laugh at himself: "I was pretty conservative, pretty paternalistic. I didn't know what a union was, or really want to get involved in one. . . . I had called Chris Hartmire to see if he had anything for me. The United Church of Christ had just agreed to try an experimental program in a place called Goshen [a small, farm worker town, 35 miles north of Delano], and Chris offered me the job. Chris wanted me to have some training and he told me about this guy Cesar Chavez. I met Cesar at the retreat and he agreed I could work with him part time."

Drake started the next day, driving Chavez to meetings, keeping notes. Unofficially he became an administrative assistant. "Cesar and Helen were living in the old house on Kensington Street. It had an old garage out back. The door on the garage was just wired on. We kept the mimeograph machine back there and were worried someone would rip it off. Dolores had got ahold of some paper, and we worked out there. All I remember was that it was so goddamn hot in that little garage all of the ink melted and all that was left was a big, black blob."

Drake, his wife Susan, and their infant son lived in a small house in Goshen, and they began to work in the community. Drake alternated between the Goshen project and Delano, spending three or four days a week in each place. He was convinced Chavez's ideas for a union were sound. "I tried to arrange a union meeting on my own, in Goshen. Manuel Chavez, Cesar's cousin, agreed to come and speak. We rented an old barn dance hall called the Pine Burr, but the meeting was a bust. The people were frightened."

Drake *was* paternalistic. He was also arrogant. Impatient. He was a stern-looking Don Quixote, jousting indiscrimi-

nately with the bureaucratic windmills. The contrast between Drake and Chavez could not have been greater:
Chavez had a quiet patience that was often exasperating; the
key to his success was not rhetoric or bombast or precipitous
action. Where Drake tried to push the workers into something he felt they needed, Chavez let the people lead, and he
followed.

Chavez explained: "I would meet with them, talk to them.
Ask them to bring in some friends. We began to put together
the house-meeting thing, but to do that I had to have
something to get them started, some immediate goal other
than the burial insurance and credit union. It needed to be
something the people could experience right away, something they could work on themselves. We decided to call a
convention of the workers. That would be it. We chose
Fresno, because it was centrally located, and set September
30, 1962, as the date. That left us May, June, July, and
August, five months to get ready."

Using the convention as a planning goal, the NFWA staff
— Cesar, Dolores, Gilbert, Jim Drake, and Julio Hernandez
— spread out through the valley towns, establishing 20 or 30
house meetings. Each house meeting had its own constituency; each met on a regular basis. As one house meeting grew
too large, it was divided into two or three. Chavez, or one of
the staff, tried to attend each meeting; they were on the road
constantly.

Chavez explained, "I ran these house meetings differently
than we did in CSO, because it was important for me to learn
what the workers wanted. They had to teach me what they
needed. I spoke very little in those first meetings, and I
listened to what they had to say."

Drake had a hard time understanding Chavez's willingness
to listen; he didn't understand his ability to blend into a
crowd and move with it. Even years later it was difficult for
him to explain: "Cesar really wasn't a leader, not then. He
would just go work in the fields with them, or he'd be in a
group, but no one really paid much attention to him. He was
the mystical guy who was around, but he was not exerting

113

leadership . . . but it was weird, because things were happening where he was . . ." Drake shook his head as he talked. "I still do not really understand it."

Sylvestre Galvan, a former migrant from Texas, tried to explain Chavez's organizational methods from a worker's point of view: "Cesar Chavez was not well known. Our first impression of him was that he was interested in us. He wanted to help us, and he listened. We were thinning sugar beets and the talk was of the work with the short-handled hoe. It is killing work, bent over like that. It hurts and we can hardly stand straight by the end of the day. Cesar was in sympathy with us, he was interested in learning about the wages and about the work conditions, if there were sanitary facilities. He passed out some cards for us to mark down what it was we desired." The Galvan family — a total of 21 aunts, uncles, cousins, and their children — agreed to hold house meetings in their cabins in the Wasco labor camp, and to bring other interested families into the meetings.

Although Chavez does not remember the specific, original Galvan family meeting, he explained his approach: "First of all I had to get across the idea of what a union was; I tried to describe it as a club, or a cooperative. And I found I had to clearly separate the word 'strike' from the word 'union,' because in their minds those two words were the same. They were frightened of strikes, so I told them this union does not strike, will not strike until we are strong. We had tremendous discussions about economics, about how much the wage should be, how much the rice and beans and flour cost. Then there was the labor contractors. Oh, God. We talked about them. You should have heard the stories of how those people got cheated."

Chavez hates the farm labor contractor system with a special passion he reserves for those men and institutions that prey upon human beings for private profit. The labor contractors feed, house, transport, and work people, all for a fee. Too often these entrepreneurs cheat both the farmer and the worker, charging 50 cents for a canned dog-food sandwich that is passed off as "meatloaf" or $1 for a 35-cent "pony" of wine or 75 cents for a pack of cigarettes or 35 cents for soda pop. The contractor stands between the farmer and the worker, making whatever profits he can.

Galvan recalled, "We didn't know the growers we worked for, only the contractors who pushed us. They pushed us hard and if you didn't work fast, they fired you. Sometimes we were cheated. But what could we do?" He shrugged his shoulders as he asked the question, then changed the subject. "When Chavez came to the house meetings, we talked about raising the wages to $1.10 an hour, and then, in a little while we were getting $1.10 an hour and we felt he had done it for us. He also talked about medical clinics, about a cooperative gasoline station, about service centers to give us help with immigration papers."

Actually Chavez had no effect on the wage structure at that time; it was the AWOC strikes that had driven farm wage rates up all over California, as farmers tried to head off unrest among their own workers. But the effect helped Chavez and the efforts to organize the NFWA. The house meetings were the basic organizational tool; the September 30th convention was the goal. Chavez — with Drake acting as administrative assistant — Huerta, Padilla, and Hernandez drove from Calexico and Coachella to Salinas, and to Santa Rosa and Sacramento and Fresno and back to Marysville and Yuba City and back south to Kingsburg and Visalia. Each house meeting was to elect a delegate and present its ideas for a union at the Fresno convention. On September 30th, between 250 and 300 NFWA members gathered to construct a union, to elect officers, and develop a set of operating rules and regulations.

Cesar Chavez became the first president and the executive officer, Dolores Huerta and Gilbert Padilla were elected vice presidents, and Antonio Orendain, a former illegal alien, former *Bracero*, and green-card immigrant, was elected secretary-treasurer. Manuel Chavez unveiled the union flag he had designed to symbolize the farm worker struggle. It was a huge red banner with a black Aztec eagle on a white circle. Because he was no artist Manuel had used a straight-edge to design a symbolic eagle that could be easily reproduced — even on a typewriter:

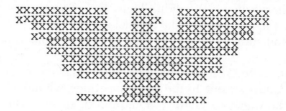

As he unveiled the union's black eagle Manuel commented: "When that damn bird flies the problems of the farm workers will be solved."

The workers were silent; confused by the size, the colors, and the shape of the eagle itself, they were hesitant to endorse such a symbol. The idea of flaunting their newly created union was frightening; the farmers would shoot them or throw them in jail for waving such a flag. They were not ready to display their rebellion.

From 1962 through 1964 the NFWA was virtually invisible to the general public, but the NFWA membership was growing and the $3.50-a-month dues brought in enough income to pay for gasoline, food, and shelter. Chavez and Dolores learned to ask to be fed; they found the sharing of food provided a strong link between them and the workers. At best, theirs was a hand-to-mouth existence. Drake, being paid $500 a month by the CMM, and Gilbert — who quit CSO in 1963 to join the CMM staff at $500 a month — fared better. When the membership approached 1,000 it was decided by the executive board that Cesar and Dolores should be paid a $50 weekly salary; a volunteer, Bill Eisher, who was editor of the union's newspaper *El Malcriado* [The Bad Boy], was paid $25 a week. Helen kept the credit union books and received $50 a week.

Somehow they got by, financially. The CMM and its supporting churches not only contributed the salaries of Drake and Padilla, but also spent a great deal of its own staff's time and effort raising additional support from church and liberal groups. Chris Hartmire was devoting virtually all of his time to *La Causa*. From the outset Chavez steered away from large grants or donations that had any strings attached; he had a feeling that such money would corrupt the learning processes the workers must go through if they were to create a strong union. The struggle itself was important. Any outside helpers would have to join the struggle, would have to suffer the hardships along with the workers.

Within the farm worker movement the word "organized" means "recruited and trained." Cesar Chavez "organized" individual volunteers and entire organizations like the California Migrant Ministry. CMM director Chris Hartmire explained, "At first our idea was to get the Protestant church more involved through specific projects. We tried to do some community organization. We had workers like Drake who were into developing community centers, water projects for communities that had no domestic water supply, things like that. But we began to see more was needed; Jim wanted to spend all of his time organizing, and, bit by bit, the union idea began to take hold."

Hartmire hired a new migrant minister, assigned him to Goshen to finish that project. He moved Drake 35 miles south and west to Porterville, in the heart of the citrus district, assigned another migrant minister, Dave Havens, to Porterville, and then hired Gilbert Padilla to help Havens and Drake build a farm worker organization separate from, but parallel to, the NFWA. The project had Chavez's blessing; any workers the new farm labor project organized would eventually be merged into the NFWA.

First Drake and Havens were sent to Chicago for six weeks to work with Saul Alinsky and observe his methods. Drake said, "Alinsky had a lot of different projects, and we would spend a couple of days at one, then another. We were being used as volunteers, but then we couldn't see what was really happening. I couldn't make any connection between what they were doing and what we were going to try to do in California.

117

"The only thing I think that happened was the experience kind of radicalized us. We were angry, irrational guys at the time. We didn't know what we were doing. Cesar was not giving us much direction because he was up to his ears in survival . . . but the guy who saved us, the guy who kept us from going off the deep end, was Gil Padilla. Gil and I opened an office in Porterville. Someone had decided Dave should try to work with the grower-church establishment side to balance our project, so he worked out of Visalia. Gil and I set up a gas and oil co-op; we were trying to find ways to get services to the people. We were charging them $2 a month dues, for some reason, even though Cesar was charging $3.50. I guess we didn't think about money, much. It was easier for us to give things away, because we were not dependent upon farm worker money. Cesar used to chide the hell out of us for that. He was trying to teach us a lesson, but we didn't know it.

"It was a crazy time. The AWOCS had their thing going, the Longshoremen and the Teamsters both were trying to do something in farm labor, the American Friends had a farm labor project, and there we were trying to organize a union, and, at the same time, we were helping some people in a rent strike in the Woodville and Linnell farm labor camps that were run by the county for the farmers," Drake said.

To finance the new effort in farm labor Hartmire had talked the Porterville United Church of Christ into paying Drake's salary. But it wasn't long before churchmen in this agribusiness-oriented congregation began to question Drake's involvement, and when Drake and Padilla publicly charged that one sugar beet growing member of the congregation was not paying his workers the wages required by law a full-blown controversy developed. Drake and Padilla officially filed a complaint with the U.S. Department of Agriculture on the wage claim, and the Porterville United Church of Christ became the first San Joaquin Valley Protestant church to withdraw its support from the California Migrant Ministry.

But even though the local church withdrew, the parent

denomination's governing board continued to support Drake. This pattern was to continue; local churches would drop out of the CMM as its involvement grew, but the national governing bodies of the Presbyterians, Methodists, Episcopalians, and others continued to provide both funding and a public forum for the farm workers.

The NFWA's first strike was forced upon it. The skilled rose workers who budded and grafted plants on the large commercial rose farms south of Delano were dissatisfied. They had not had an increase in wages for years, their working conditions were getting worse, and they were going to strike. They contacted Chavez, and a strategy session was called. Padilla brought Drake to the meeting with Cesar and Dolores and the leaders of the rose workers. Cesar explained to the rose workers the NFWA was not strong enough to sustain a big strike effort. He pointed out that the growers in the area were already apprehensive because Al Green and the AWOCs were organizing workers nearby, in other crops. Any picket lines, any red-flag waving, might cause more problems than it would solve. The rose workers nodded in understanding, but they pressed their plea for help and that request could not be ignored.

A strategy was worked out: The workers would simply not show up for work; there would be no picket lines, no strike activity; they would just stay away, and their demands would be simple: a small wage increase and a few changes in working conditions. The plan was based on the fact that these workers were so skilled they would be hard to replace, and if they did win, the victory would bolster the NFWA organizing efforts.

Individually, the NFWA staff began visiting the rose workers at home, in the evenings, talking to them, getting them to agree they would stay home, they would boycott their jobs. On the morning set for the work boycott, each NFWA staff member went out before dawn to check on the workers' homes; if they saw lights on, they knocked on the door and asked if the people were going to work. They got embarrassed mumbles, then repeated promises to stay away from the job.

Dolores Huerta knocked on one door, talked briefly to the men inside, and walked away, convinced that all four of them were planning to go to work. She drove her car behind the workers' car, parked so they could not get out of the driveway, took her keys, and walked away.

Drake laughed, "We thought Dolores was really daring as hell."

Near the end of the first day of the work boycott, Chris Hartmire telephoned the president of the rose company at his headquarters in Shenandoah, Iowa, asking that he meet with the union and work out a settlement to the strike. The president hesitated, then refused. The rose workers stayed off the job for three days, but then became apprehensive as labor contractors imported unskilled workers to take their places. The strike was broken. The rose workers went back to work. While the strike was a failure it was also the beginning.

As the NFWA suffered its first defeat and focused its efforts back on the basic job of building a worker constituency, Larry Itliong and Ben Guines moved their AWOC organizing efforts south, into the irrigated deserts of the Coachella Valley. They were with the Filipino table-grape workers, protesting the inequities of the new wage structures set by growers. The problem had its roots in the termination of the *Bracero* program. When Public Law 78 expired, the farmers found another loophole in the Mexican border; Public Law 414 allowed employers to import foreign workers but only on an emergency basis.

Pressured by the farm lobby, Secretary of Labor Willard Wirtz and the U.S. Department of Agriculture agreed that some labor emergencies might exist: If farmers could prove a labor shortage, if they would offer to pay $1.40 an hour to any worker — local or imported — and they still did not turn up enough help, then a limited number of *Braceros* could be brought into the harvest. Only those farmers anticipating filing requests for such imported labor bothered to comply with the $1.40-an-hour order. The grape farmers had not

120

been dependent upon *Braceros;* they used Filipinos and Mexicans who had established residency in the United States or who had documents to allow them to move across the border. The grape growers offered the Filipinos $1.25 an hour and 10 cents a box for field packing. Itliong and Guines called a mass meeting and the workers agreed they would not work for less than $1.40 an hour and 25 cents a box. The growers refused the demand and the Filipinos went out on strike. Because the Coachella season is short and the growers there depend upon the high prices their early marketing brings, they did not want to risk a widespread strike, so they quickly agreed to the Filipino demand. The Filipinos went back into the vineyards.

The success of such strikes was not uncommon. If the farmers were in a critical situation, they would give in; if not, they would hold out. When the grape harvest was completed in Coachella and the workers moved north, into the Arvin area, the grape farmers there offered $1.25 an hour plus 10 cents a box for field packing. The Filipinos again struck, but this time the growers held fast and it was the workers who had to give up. There was little in these AWOC efforts to give any indication that the history of farm labor was about to change, that the maneuverings of the Filipino grape workers were setting the stage for the Delano grape strike.

Chavez was working hard to build a solid foundation under the NFWA. He needed more time to build up the union's strength, to create service centers, medical clinics, and an organizational structure that could sustain the strike battles that would ultimately have to be fought. *La Causa* was attracting volunteers from the Civil Rights Movement, and Chavez put them to work on the staff, much as Alinsky had put Havens and Drake to work in Chicago. The volunteers took care of the routine, they cranked the mimeograph machines, stuffed the envelopes, ran the errands. Cesar and Dolores spent most of their time with the house meetings and with the urban efforts to raise more support for the cause.

Havens, Drake, and Padilla had gotten deeply involved in the Woodville and Linnell farm labor camp rent strikes, and

121

they were using these protests to pull the people together into their farm labor organization. The two labor camps had been built by the U.S. Farm Security Administration late in the 1930s as temporary shelters for the Dust Bowl migrants. The camps were made up of individual 16-foot-by-20-foot tin or wood shelters that had cost $100 each. They were furnished with one electric outlet and one gas outlet; cold water faucets were located at the garbage stand, between every fourth cabin; the toilets and showers were in big, communal buildings that also housed laundry tubs and clotheslines.

In the 1930s and 1940s these camps were an improvement over the ditch-bank shanty camps and hobo jungles under highway bridges; but by the 1960s the shelters were worn-out, dilapidated hovels that were impossibly hot in the summer and bitterly cold in the winter. The federal government had turned the camps over to the Tulare County Housing Authority, and they were operated as "low-rent" projects; if a family had more than four people, it rented two of the huts, large families had three of the one-room cabins; the rents ranged from $18 to $38 a month. At these rental rates the housing authority accumulated an $80,000 surplus between 1958 and 1965. The camps were condemned by the county health department in 1965, but the housing authority not only continued to operate them, it insisted on increasing the rents — the increased revenues were to finance construction of new units. The tenants struck. They withheld their rent, putting it into a trust fund arranged by Drake and Havens. With a poverty lawyer advising them, the rent strikers defied the housing authority, and when the people discovered they could defy the housing authority without being evicted they became more militant. At the time, between 60 and 70 of the Woodville rent strikers were working on the J. D. Martin Ranch, pulling leaves from the vines to expose the young clusters of grapes to the sun. During the rent strike meetings several of these people began to complain about working conditions, about low pay, and about a crew boss.

Drake explained, "There were no toilets in the fields in those days and there was a crew boss who kept peeking under the vines when the women would relieve themselves. The men workers were really mad about it, and the women were embarrassed. It was one of those spontaneous things. They wanted to do something, so we decided to strike.

"We really didn't plan a thing. We just told the workers to wait until they saw us carrying signs and shouting and then to walk out. That was the first time we ever used the word 'huelga.' We [Drake, Padilla, Huerta, Chavez, Eisher, and one or two other volunteers] made up the huelga signs and went out. We still have a picture somewhere of Cesar standing there, by his old Volvo, with the huelga sign. He looked so forlorn, with the cars whizzing by like crazy."

The strike succeeded in pulling all the workers out of the Martin vineyards. But when the workers walked out no one from the NFWA had any idea what to do with them. They were allowed to drift away, to take other jobs, and wait the outcome of the strike. Each morning before dawn the NFWA staff would assemble by the ranch entrances and form its own picket line. Drake said, "It never even occurred to us that it should be the workers doing the picketing."

Strikebreaking crews — including a farm labor co-op started by the American Friends Service Committee — were brought into the vineyards to finish the work. Drake explained: "The service committee had lost control of the co-op; the guy that took over was an ex-labor contractor. He got the crews together and broke the strike. On August 28th we had a meeting and decided we were going to give up. It wasn't very hard to call it off since we never had any of the workers on the picket line to begin with.

"Because the strike had been such a disaster we agreed that we should never hold any more strikes, not for at least two or three years. Cesar got up and said this was a vow. Dolores agreed. We were not going to organize any more strikes."

Cesar does not remember the Martin Ranch failure in quite such dramatic terms. He agreed, "Of course we lost it badly, but we got an awful lot of insight into what happened. It was just a little ol' strike, and we really hadn't put that much into it. You have to remember at the time of the J. D. Martin strike and the rose strike, we still needed about two more years to get ready. We knew that we weren't ready, but the workers had come to us, so what could we do?"

AWOC organizers Itliong and Guines stayed with the grape workers as they moved north from Coachella to Arvin and north again to Delano. Itliong had made Delano the headquarters for the Filipino AWOC Local. By 1965 this local was the only viable group within the AWOC. Even though the Arvin strike was ineffective, the Filipinos didn't give up. When they moved north to Delano they again demanded $1.40 an hour and 25 cents a box. The Delano growers offered $1.20 and 15 cents, take it or leave it. The challenge gave Itliong some problems. The Filipinos were especially vulnerable because they were old, single men who lived in camps on the farms. These Delano camps had been their winter home for 30 years. If they struck, if they walked out and set up a picket line, where would they live?

Itliong finally came up with a strategy: If the Filipinos simply refused to go to work, if they stayed in their camps in what amounted to a sit-down strike, the growers might be shocked into paying the demanded wage. The workers agreed to try the sit-in. The growers retaliated almost immediately, threatening to shut down the camps if the workers did not go back into the vines. The Filipinos refused to leave the camps on 10 ranches. Newspaper headlines on September 10, 1965, read: "Strike Idles 1,000 Workers in Kern Fields."

The farmers under pressure from the AWOC imported Joe Brosmer, manager of the San Joaquin Valley Agriculture Labor Bureau, headquartered in Fresno. Brosmer, a tall, blond, hawk-faced man with an ability to make reporters angry faster than most farmers, began to spread his brand of snake oil on the troubled waters. The farmers were having no trouble in finding workers at $1.20 an hour and 10 cents a box. Brosmer estimated 800 workers were staying in the camps, refusing to go to work; but he said the fact that they had not established a picket line was a sign there was no strike. The growers listened to Brosmer and believed this was a minor incident that would soon pass.

Certainly Itliong and the Filipinos had no real support from the AWOC superstructure; Al Green had a real disinterest in the grapes and was off working behind the scenes in the citrus with Jim Smith, of Joint Council 38 of the International Brotherhood of Teamsters. Smith and Green were from the Stanislaus County labor movement; even if they were technically on the outs because of their affiliations, they had decided to operate a joint AWOC–Teamster drive to organize the citrus groves and packinghouses. The move had a touch of desperation on Green's part; he felt he had to come up with a sizable dues-paying membership to convince Meany and the executive council the AFL-CIO $1-million investment in farm labor was worth while. As far as Green was concerned, the Filipinos were on their own.

The NFWA had had no part in planning the grape strike. Drake said, "I don't know if Cesar knew at the time that the Filipinos were about to go out on strike, but he was making it very clear he did not want any more strikes, not then."

Cesar was apprehensive. Twice in recent months he had found his fledgling organization had been spread too thin; it was far too weak to take on even a small strike. There was no way they could prepare for a major strike with the table-grape growers. He knew the AWOC did not have the unlimited support of the AFL-CIO; since 1959 it had repeatedly demonstrated its inability to sustain a strike and turn it into anything more permanent than a small pay hike. The AWOC had no broad base of support and its parent body — the AFL-CIO Executive Council — had shown all too frequently its willingness to throw in the towel.

Padilla explained: "We were a movement, see. The AFL-CIO tried to organize farm labor, but they couldn't do it because they didn't know what they were doing. They spent a lot of money, they had 17 organizers and cars, the whole thing. But what is a farm worker? Ninety-eight percent are

Chicano. Some are Filipinos. But they couldn't get the Filipinos because the Filipinos had no community. If they left the camps, where the hell were they going to go? The AWOC did not understand that. Hell, the community — even the Chicanos sometimes — didn't really accept the Filipinos then.

"See, you have to have some kind of movement, some kind of solidarity and sense of community. You know? I don't think it had anything to do with the fact that most AWOC organizers were Anglos. I think Anglos can organize better than anyone. I think it was the way they tried it. It was 'gimme the dues' and that was it. The average education of the farm worker was the third grade, and they just didn't understand what the hell the AWOC was all about."

This was the kind of thinking that was running through the NFWA leaders' minds, but there was no question about supporting the AWOC strike. The only issue was "how?" When it became obvious the old Filipinos in the camps were not going to give up, the NFWA made up a flyer listing the struck ranches and detailing some of the demands and grower reactions. *El Malcriado* detailed the AWOC side of the strike, printed Jack London's odious definition of a strike-breaker, and — more to the point — listed some of the writings of Pope Leo XIII on the subject of workingmen's rights to organize into labor unions. The pressure was on Chavez and the NFWA; on September 14th he called his staff together to decide if they should ask the NFWA membership for a strike vote. The staff decided the issue should be put to the membership, and a meeting was scheduled for September 16th, Mexican Independence Day.

The parish hall in Our Lady of Guadalupe Church in Delano was rented; leaflets were written and cranked out on the old mimeograph, an agenda was drafted and refined, press releases were called in to the newspapers, radio, and TV stations. Chavez and Eugene Nelson — one of the college student volunteers — drove south, to Bakersfield, to see if they could talk their way into some free radio spot announcements.

126

The meeting would be a real test of Chavez's leadership. If a large number of farm workers showed up at the meeting it was almost certain they would vote for a strike. The NFWA staff and volunteers went out into a dozen farm worker communities urging workers to come to Delano for the meeting.

On the day of the meeting the parish hall was decorated with posters of Emiliano Zapata, the Mexican revolutionary hero, with Jack London's definition of a strikebreaker, with the huge red *huelga* banner with the black eagle on the white circle. At dusk the crowds began to gather. By various counts, from 1,200 to 1,500 men, women, and children showed up. The parish hall was crowded to overflowing, people packed the doorways and windows and crowded around outside. The people were excited; they wanted to rebel, to rise up in defiance. Gilbert Padilla opened the meeting and introduced the speakers. Antonio Orendain led the crowd in the *"vivas"* — the shouts of *"Viva la Huelga!"* *"Viva la Causa!"* *"Viva Cesar Chavez!"*

The crowd was enthusiastic, eager to learn. And, as each speaker finished, the crowd took up its newfound voice: *"Viva la Causa! Viva la Huelga!"* The history of the AWOC strike was related; Padilla argued that any strike action must be nonviolent. Chavez was introduced. Cries of *"Viva Cesar Chavez!"* filled the hall. He warned the workers of the seriousness of the step they were taking; he reemphasized the practical need for nonviolent action, he reiterated briefly the history of the insurrection 155 years earlier in the Mexican state of Guanajuato that led to Mexican independence from Spain.

The emphasis was on the Mexican workers' history of rebellion against tyranny. Then Chavez began calling on individuals to speak. Who was there from Michoacán? Who from Tamaulipas? From Chihuahua? One after another, men whose roots lay deep in Mexican traditions got up to recite briefly why they felt the strike should be joined. A man of 60 who had been in Pixley in 1933 reminisced about the bitter cotton strikes: "All we wanted was to earn enough money to

127

buy food for our families. I saw two strikers murdered, before my very eyes . . . yet we are still in the same place today, still submerged, still drowned."

The crowd was excited. Angry. Responsive. When Chavez asked for a strike vote, they overwhelmingly raised their hands, and their voices. They chanted: *"Huelga! Huelga! Huelga! Huelga!"* and began to clap in rhythm.

The NFWA would join the AWOC.

When?

Chavez prevailed on the eager workers to wait until the following Monday, September 20th. Several important things had to be done first: Letters had to be mailed to growers, putting them on notice, a meeting with Al Green had to be arranged. Chris Hartmire and others had to be given time to begin the search for support, both in terms of people and in supplies of food, clothing, and gasoline.

The meeting with Al Green was set up for Sunday, September 19th, in the Stardust Motel in Delano. Green came alone. Cesar said, "We told him we would like to have a joint strike, suggesting a joint strike fund. We even offered to work under him, but he turned us down."

Drake also attended the meeting. He said, "Cesar tried to get Al to agree to a joint strike pact, that neither could sign a contract with the growers without the consent of the other. We wanted the money [strike funds] split evenly. Cesar was trying to push Green into some kind of unity caucus between the Chicanos and Filipinos. Green said he thought it was a fine idea, but refused to sign anything."

Chavez added, "He told us that under the AFL-CIO constitution he was not allowed to do anything like this. I asked him for a no-raiding pact — I was afraid that somewhere along the way he would sabotage us — but he wouldn't even go for that."

Green's decision now appears to be one of the turning points in the destiny of the farm workers union. Instead of a single, coordinated strike, financed and directed by the AFL-CIO's own people, the Delano grape strike was really two strikes, the Filipino AWOCS led by Itliong against ten growers and the NFWA led by Chavez against the remaining 30 vineyards.

CHAPTER SEVEN : DELANO
GRAPE STRIKE

At dawn on Monday, September 20, 1965, the National Farm Workers Association joined the Delano grape strike. But it did so slowly and without much of the enthusiasm displayed during the September 16th meeting. From the very beginning it was obvious Cesar Chavez's assessment had been correct: The union was not ready for a major offensive. The NFWA claimed a membership of 2,000 families, but these worker families were scattered all over the farming areas of California and no one knew for sure how many were active, how many would — or could — quit work and walk the picket lines.

For newsmen covering those early days of the strike it was also quite obvious the NFWA was different from either Al Green's AWOC or the AWOC Filipino local in Delano. The AWOC Stockton headquarters staff was a stereotype of the labor movement bumbling through one of its periodic exercises of conscience. The Filipino AWOCS, on the other hand, were using tactics reminiscent of the old IWW anarchist-socialist movement; they struck like guerrillas, sought pay hikes but no union recognition.

Under Chavez's leadership the NFWA was making a radical departure from these farm labor traditions. Instead of drifting with the seasons, calling hit-and-run strikes that sometimes succeeded in pushing wages up, but more often ended in busted heads and jailed pickets, Chavez was attempting to build a permanent, broadly based organization. The NFWA had a credit union with $25,000 of worker funds invested; the union had rented offices in several farming towns and established service centers and a $1,000 burial insurance program.

From the very beginning Chavez made it plain the NFWA was to be a totally independent, service-oriented worker movement, a movement built and controlled by the men and women who worked for wages on the farm.

Months before the grape strike started, the NFWA made application to the Office of Economic Opportunity for $500,000. Little or nothing was known about the OEO grant application outside the NFWA and OEO headquarters in Washington, D.C. The application — written by a beautiful 25-year-old Stanford University graduate named Wendy Goepel — proposed the NFWA as the delegate agency to develop a farm worker cooperative store, a co-op auto repair garage — with resident mechanic instructors — and a full range of consumer protection–money management training courses for worker families. Under the OEO grant the NFWA would also set up community water- and sewer-development projects, citizenship-training classes, and voter-registration efforts. Every project or class was to be staffed by farm workers trained for the work.

Unaware of the NFWA's being drawn into the strike, OEO officials in Washington blue-penciled the co-op store and auto repair projects, but they approved a $267,000 grant to fund the remainder of the proposal. The NFWA staff was both jubilant and perplexed. The OEO-funded programs could be used to help workers to build a strong union but there was little doubt that, once the NFWA was committed to the strike, the OEO funds would be withdrawn.

The problem was an agonizing one. Chavez had learned first in Oxnard — where the *Bracero* issue had welded the workers into a force strong enough to effect change — and then on the J. D. Martin Ranch — where weakness and lack of planning had doomed the strike — that the issue of wages alone was not enough to sustain a strike. Yet wages were the only real issue raised by the Filipinos. Even so, there really was no other choice for the NFWA; not to support the strike was unthinkable.

By relying heavily on the nationalistic feelings generated by September 16th (Mexican Independence Day) and Mexican revolutionary spirit, the NFWA had mustered 1,200 to 1,500 for the strike vote rally. Once there, the workers left no doubt they wanted to join the strike. The staff worked hard to sustain the *huelga* spirit, but, by the following Monday morning, the enthusiasm generated during the strike rally had waned considerably. Jim Drake remembers he arrived at the union's Albany Street headquarters at about 3:30 A.M.: "I guess there were about 100 workers gathered around the office, standing by their cars, waiting, and talking. I know there were a lot fewer than we had said would go out on strike, so we hung around for awhile, hoping more would show up."

The NFWA had rented an old store building in a low-income neighborhood on the extreme southwest corner of the city. The battered old building sat on a corner; the address was 102 Albany. Across the street, to the south, were grape vineyards, to the west a large, open field that was planted seasonally to cotton. The front of the NFWA building had been caved in by a truck and the damage patched with plyboard, but never repaired.

Inside the front third of the building was an open lobby or assembly hall, strewn with folding chairs, a long table loaded with leaflets and cigarette-butt cans. A long counter divided this part of the building from the rabbit-warren offices and cubicles that had been hammered and banged together out of anything rigid enough to hold nails. Every wall was a bulletin board, covered by posters of Zapata and Ché and Pancho Villa, lists of names and phone numbers, a placard noting that industrial workers average $3.50 to $5.50 an hour while farm workers struggle for $1.40 an hour, messages for volunteers who had arrived and gone again without staying long enough for mail to catch up with them.

In the dark before dawn, in the glare of naked, small-watt light bulbs, the place seemed cold, chaotic, a strange blend of

131

Mexican farm workers and long-haired boys and girls dressed in baggy, faded old clothes. They tried to look busy and unworried, but the waiting was not easy. With so few workers showing up it seemed the strike was doomed before it really started for the NFWA. A few minutes before 4 A.M. Chavez suggested they had waited long enough. Staff members were assigned to lead groups of pickets to various geographic areas within the strike zone. They were instructed to stay away from those ten ranches already under strike by the AWOC unless the Filipinos asked for help.

Drake said, "I had the McFarland area with Epifanio Camacho. Camacho knew some more guys that he got out of bed, and we drove south, maybe five or six miles, to a place where he knew they would be picking that morning."

The procedure was simple: The pickets loaded up four or five to a car and formed a caravan behind the picket captain. At the first location, scouted the day before, the picket line was set up at the farm entrances, and as the workers came driving in, they were urged to turn around, to withhold their labor from this one ranch. They could work elsewhere. Some turned away because they supported the strike, some because they wanted no trouble, some drove through the picket lines.

By midmorning the picketing at the entrances had had as much effect as it was going to, so the caravan loaded up and following the leader, they drove the back roads, crisscrossing the flat vineyardlands, searching for another crew at work. When one was spotted, the cars were parked across the road from the vineyard and the picket line was re-formed.

The pickets carried handmade signs, most were black and white with a single word or two: *HUELGA* [strike] or *ESQUIROL AFUERA* [scab, stand aside]. The word *"esquirol"* literally means "strikebreaker" but within the NFWA lexicon it has taken on the pejorative meaning, "scab."

Once on the picket line the *huelgistas* began to chant and shout *"huelga, huelga, huelga"* and *"Hay huelga aqui"* and waved their signs back and forth. If the workers were near the roadway, the *huelgistas* tried to cajole and argue them

132

Mass picketing at White River Farms.
Photo by Ronald B. Taylor

Hiring hall, Selma, California.
Photo by Ronald B. Taylor

Photo by George Ballis

out of the vines, but if the workers were far back in the fields, the pickets yelled the word *"Huelga!"* and tried by motion and short phrases to coax the *esquirols* to come closer, to come and listen to the arguments of the strike.

When a farmer or his foreman discovered the pickets they reacted like nervous sheep dogs, pacing and scurrying about, yipping and nipping, both bossing the sheep and trying to intimidate whatever danger lurked out beyond the flock. The farmer or the foreman drove their pickup trucks furiously up and down farm roads, boiling dust up on the picket lines, nearly running pickets down if they stood their ground. Frequently the farmer would drive up, skid to a stop, jump out of a pickup, and then slowly, menacingly, confront the strikers. Sometimes two or three farmers would stand, arms folded, and glower. Some foremen were verbally insulting. Some of the pickets returned the insults, others seethed in anger; many were intimidated, realizing they had made an aggressive move and the farmer was marking them down in some little blacklist book.

When workers in the vines heard the shouts of the *huelgistas* they would stand up, look, and listen, then talk briefly among themselves, return to work, only to look up again. Obviously the workers were disturbed and uncertain. And such signs were quickly picked up by the strikers, who would increase the pressure and focus on those workers who seemed the most uncertain.

Drake recalled the first day: "We were picketing this place in the wine grapes. I'd never seen them picking for wine before. It was awful. They picked into buckets and pans and dumped them in gondolas that were pulled down the row by tractor. The workers were covered with juice and grime, and the gnats and flies were everywhere. It was really awful work.

"We had just pulled up and started yelling at them when the whole crew just walked out. That was one of the most impressive things I have ever seen. It was like they had been waiting for us. Every single worker came out of the vines, right to us. We were flabbergasted, and we really didn't know what the hell to do with them, there must have been 50 or 60 workers."

As the workers filed out of the vineyard, they were given cards to sign authorizing the NFWA to represent them. Once the cards were signed, and the workers were urged to come to the union office to learn more about the strike, there seemed little else that could be done. The workers began drifting away. Then someone suggested these wine workers should be invited to go along to the next picket line; someone else shouted the idea and the workers cheered and everyone headed for the cars and the search for a new vineyard to picket.

All over the Delano-Earlimart-McFarland strike zone — an area 15 miles long, from north to south, and 20 miles or more wide, from east to west — the pattern was the same. Some of the crews had gone to work that first morning with the intent of walking out, if and when a picket line showed up; most of the workers were indecisive and apprehensive. Often the *huelgistas* would see one or two workers slip away from a field as the picketing started. A few individuals would openly come across to the strike. Some of those who voted for the strike in the parish hall on the 16th became *esquirols* on the 20th. Other workers quietly joined the NFWA at night, but continued to work on ranches where there were no pickets.

Years later Chavez would tell another writer:

> The picket line is where a man makes his commitment, and it is irrevocable; the longer he's on the picket line, the stronger the commitment. A lot of workers make their commitment when nobody sees them; they just leave the job and they don't come back. But you get a guy who in front of the boss, in front of all the other guys, throws down his tools and marches right out to the picket line, that is an exceptional guy, and that's the kind we have out on the strike . . . oh, the picket line is a beautiful thing, because it does something to a human being. People associate strikes with violence, and we've removed the violence. Then people begin to understand what we are doing, you know, and after that they are

136

not afraid. And if you're not afraid of that kind of thing, then you're not afraid of guns. If you have a gun and they [the farmers] do too, then you can be frightened because it becomes a question of who gets shot first. But if you have no gun and they have one, then — well, the guy with the gun has a lot harder decision to make than you. You're just *there*, and it's up to *him* to do something . . .

While nonviolence has always been the avowed policy of the NFWA's strike action, there have been problems in making that policy work. In the heat of confrontation, pickets and strikebreakers find it is not enough to cuss each other so they reach for rocks and clods; a picket loses his temper and wades into a ranch foreman, swinging his picket sign as a club. A farmer carrying a shotgun "disarms" pickets of their strike signs, stacks the signs against a fencepost, and blows them apart with a blast from his shotgun. An old Filipino AWOC walking a picket line sees three farmers standing by the road; he deliberately gets in his old pickup and drives full speed at the farmers, bowling them over, breaking one farmer's leg.

Pablo Espinosa, one of the United Farm Workers' strongest supporters, explained that in those early days of the strike he would not go close to a picket line: "There was no strike where I was working [in September], I usually go for the gondola [wine harvest] where the money comes faster. It is hard work, but the money comes faster. I heard about the union, but I was afraid. I didn't think I could take any crap from the growers. Like I have heard they push you around, from the sheriff and the growers, they spray sulfur on you. I thought I could never take that."

At the time Espinosa was part of a large migrant family living in the Woodville farm labor camp, in the tin shacks owned by the Tulare County Housing Authority. Espinosa was one of the rent strikers. "When Manuel Chavez used to come to our meetings, Gilbert and Jim Drake and those guys would give us reports on what was happening in Delano. I wanted very much to go over there and watch. I had never seen anything like that, you know, because I had come from Texas. I really wanted to come out but I didn't think I could take it. And they told me, 'If you don't think you can take it, then you shouldn't go, you should help the union by collecting food and money or anything you can do, but don't go on the picket line.'

"I didn't know anything about a union, at that moment, even though I had had some experiences, because we were dealing with the power structure of the Tulare County Housing Authority. Even though I had many, many experiences in Texas and Arkansas and Mississippi and Ohio — those places we traveled as migrants — but I never believed that we could win the growers. I just never believed it, not even on a dream.

"I just told myself these people are crazy, what they are doing is a crazy thing. The growers have all the money. And I didn't know then how much power the growers had over the police." Espinosa, who became one of the picket captains who led hundreds of strikers in acts of civil disobedience that landed them all in jail, said that in the fall of 1965, "I started going out but I watched from a distance, I kept my distance from the sheriff and the grower. But then I began to talk to the *esquirols* . . . there was this one guy I had been talking to that was from Texas also, and I was talking about the union, and how it was. He was working in the vines just close to the road and I asked him why he had come all the way from Texas to break our strike. I said that it was a shame for me because he was my *paisano* [countryman]. That is when he told me, 'Shut up, you lazy mother-fucker.' Nobody could call me a mother-fucker. I just exploded, like if you spill gasoline and light a match. I really got hot. You know? I really wanted to go inside and get that bastard, but Ernesto had a hold of me. I challenged that man to come out, but he wouldn't and Ernesto told me to cool it, told me that if I went into the field it would do more harm than good for the union . . .

"It was hard, but little by little I learned how to take that kind of insults. I know that if I challenge them it would be wrong, and that it is good to convince them by talking and since then I have faced many growers and many super scabs and I have challenged them — not physically — but I have challenged them to an argument. I am going to convince them they are wrong."

The picket line is a testing ground where men like Espinosa learn a sense of priorities. The nonviolence of Cesar Chavez is a pragmatic position: If the Pablo Espinosas charged every insult, there would be no picket line, only pitched battles between *huelgistas,* strikebreakers, growers, and sheriff's deputies. Because the farmers have always won this kind of confrontation I asked Chavez if nonviolence was simply a tactic or was it also a philosophy.

"It shouldn't be a tactic . . . no, I shouldn't say that. It is a tactic. Sure. But we are firm believers, you know? I would stake my life on truth. Truth is justice. If you stick to truth, it seems to me, you can overturn mountains . . ."

For the next 30 minutes Chavez delved into the meaning of truth and nonviolence and their relationship to man in general and farm workers in particular. It was a complex mix of pragmatism and philosophy, what started as one line of thought soon tangled with the other: "It all comes down to the question of what we are going to do on earth. Are we here to make money? Are we here just to get what we can for ourselves? Or are we here to do something for our brothers? You really can't help people unless you are willing to sacrifice yourself because first there are always greater demands upon your time than you can take care of and second, everything you do becomes controversial. So you have these attacks against you all the time.

"That is the sacrifice. If you are not prepared for those two things you cannot help people because you cannot take the pressure. So it seems to me that if one understands that it is part of the sacrifice, then you can take it, live with it, and even sometimes accept it . . .

"Then the other issue becomes how you go about your work, violently or nonviolently. It takes a lot not to strike back, not that you don't get the feeling sometimes. The

139

reaction, I guess, is built in us. But if you really understand what it is you are doing, not only being willing to give up your time to help solve an injustice, but also be willing to take all of the abuse that comes with it, and on top of that understand that it has to be done nonviolently, then I think you understand the character of nonviolence . . ."

In one breath he moves on from nonviolence to the subject of truth and justice. "Truth needs another element, and that is time. If you have those two elements, truth and time, and you understand them, then there is no reason why anyone would want to be violent. Number one, sooner or later truth is going to be exposed. It cannot be hidden, you know? Mankind has never been able to deal with the suppression of truth.

"If you understand what time means — and I am speaking of time in terms of not what you have here, today, but in terms of you may lose a strike, but you haven't lost anything. The loss is a temporary condition. As long as you know this, the only thing you have lost is a tiny bit of time, not the main strike itself — if you understand time in these terms then violence is not really that important. Violence really doesn't win anything for you in the long run. So you see, what I am really talking about is the common sense of nonviolence . . ."

Convincing the strikers of this takes constant work. From the beginning Chavez had the volunteers from the Student Nonviolent Coordinating Committee and Congress of Racial Equality conducting classes in the nonviolent tactics they had used in the Civil Rights Movement in the South. Some of the strike action was improvised from the experiences of these volunteers, some of it came from Chavez's experiences in Oxnard.

The strike was traumatic for the NFWA, at first. Drake explained: "Cesar had had a plan, all along, but it was a plan for organizing the NFWA, not a strike. Within 48 hours the events of the strike blew that plan clear to hell. He had planned, for instance, to keep in touch with every house meeting, like clear up to Marysville, because he wanted a

140

statewide organization. That is what he had been working on for years, but now, with the strike, the whole of his life was happening in the Delano-Earlimart-McFarland area and this changed him tremendously.

"We needed support so he began to speak publicly, in places like Berkeley, and he had to begin to rethink and redefine who we were and where we were going. The whole thing began to take on some historical significance so we began to pay attention to speeches, we helped him make notes for his talks."

Through the months of October, November, and December the NFWA began to change, to take on its permanent shape and form. Like an embryo reacting to radical change in its environment, the young organization began to adapt; conflict organizing took on a new kind of meaning. Chaos became normal. The excitement of the first picket-line clashes dulled into repetitive, noisy confrontations. No one will ever know how many thousand farm workers really walked off their jobs in the Delano grape strike within those first few weeks; the pickets would appear, strikers would chant and extol and cajole, and workers would walk out, only to be replaced the next day or the day after that and the picket line would reappear and the process would be repeated. Some of the workers joined the union, some simply went to work elsewhere, others stayed in the vines and strongly opposed the NFWA because it threatened their fragile existence.

Chris Hartmire said at the time: "No one has ever claimed all the farm workers in Delano are out on strike. In addition to the local strikebreakers large numbers of scabs are brought in from the outside. The fact that many farm workers were willing to cross picket lines says nothing about the existence of a strike. Rather it highlights the poverty and insecurity of the people."

The strike itself was taking shape. The NFWA made up lists of struck ranches, and cards signed by workers who had walked out were catalogued and filed, a system of priorities was worked out so that picketing was no longer so haphazard.

The NFWA volunteer legal staff forced the Farm Labor Placement Service to warn workers strikes were underway on specific farms, as the law required. New tactics were developed, strikers sneaked onto the farms at night, going to the labor camp bunkhouses to meet with strikebreaking laborers, trying to argue them into at least quitting, if they would not join the union.

The word *"huelga"* itself became increasingly significant. A Kern County deputy sheriff had asked Chavez to order the NFWA not to use the word because it was not American. While he was talking to Chavez he also suggested that the picketing be stopped, "Because everyone knows you are all out on strike now, so pickets aren't needed anymore." When the deputy's suggestion was not taken seriously the Kern County Sheriff outlawed the use of the word *"Huelga"* and he warned anyone using the word on the picket line would be arrested. Chavez needed a solid public issue and freedom of speech was as good as he would get; it would attract national press coverage and project a David-and-Goliath image that would gain support for the strike.

Drake called Chris Hartmire and asked him to find some volunteers willing to go to jail. Several clergymen from the Los Angeles and San Francisco Bay areas who had been in Delano to see the strike agreed to come back and support the protest. Other urban supporters volunteered and the NFWA notified the sheriff's office that on October 20th it was going to disobey the order against using the word *"huelga."* The press was called. On October 19th one of the ministers, the Rev. Francis Geddes of the United Church of Christ, told me, "We anticipate we might be arrested . . . the sheriff's office will feel foolish for arresting us and abridging our right to free speech."

At 9:30 A.M., on October 20 the sheriff's office, the press, and 44 NFWA pickets — 13 farm workers and 31 volunteers — set out from the NFWA headquarters in one of the strangest farm labor strike caravans of all time. The NFWA cars were followed by reporters from most of the large California dailies, TV crews from the networks, driving rented stationwagons, several sheriff's patrol cars, and a "paddywagon" to carry the arrested to jail.

The caravan had no particular destination; the vineyard selected the night before was vacant when the early morning scouts had gone out, so the search was on for a working crew. The long procession spent nearly an hour driving slowly back and forth along country roads searching for workers in the vineyards. A crew was spotted. Everyone piled out of the cars. The 44 pickets lined up, held their signs up and began chanting the one word: *"HUELGA! HUELGA! HUELGA! HUELGA!"*

Cameramen scrambled around, shooting every possible angle. Uniformed sheriff's deputies, using small snapshot cameras, photographed each picket. A CBS-TV camera crew moved boldly into the vineyards, and, ignoring the foreman's protest, they began filming a father and daughter who were harvesting grapes and trying to ignore all of the fuss swirling around them. The two workers tried unsuccessfully to hide their faces from the camera crew.

After 10 or 15 minutes Sgt. Gerald Dodd switched on the loudspeaker in his patrol car and in both Spanish and English declared the picket line an unlawful assembly. He ordered the pickets to disperse or face arrest. He read the order again. When the pickets did not give up the chant, he ordered them placed under arrest. The pickets quietly lined up as the uniformed officers took their names, and herded them gently into the paddywagon. Among those arrested was Helen Chavez, Cesar's wife. The volunteers included clergymen from the Presbyterian, United Church of Christ, Methodist, and Disciples of Christ churches; there were kids from SNCC and CORE and two runaways from the VISTA War on Poverty program. Bail was set at $276 each, on charges of unlawful assembly. Thirty-three chose to remain in jail, and the following day the NFWA gathered 350 people together to stage a protest on the steps of the Kern County courthouse. They sang "We Shall Overcome" and chanted *"Huelga"* until they were hoarse, but no more arrests were made. The

143

courts ordered the arrested released and eventually the sheriff's order was declared unconstitutional.

Such incidents became part of the theatrics of the strike. The drama of conflict projected *La Causa* into the national conscience. But there was also a need to dramatize the conflict for the workers, and this was done by Luis Valdez, a bouncing, cocky, cigar-smoking revolutionary who created the *Teatro Compesino*, the workers' theater. This was guerrilla theater, street theater; its broad, satirical "actos" brought the bigness of agribusiness down to a ludicrous scale. The *teatro* gave the workers a vent for their anger; they could laugh and cheer and begin to see themselves as something more than helpless *peons* and in the process absorb some of the revolutionary ideas of the strike and the organization of farm worker power.

The need to involve the workers as intimately as possible in all the strike processes was obvious, but the means for doing this was not found until the third week of the strike. Chavez had ordered a big dinner be held for all of the workers, on a Friday night, to pull everyone together, to let them relax and share their experiences. The results were so attractive that another of these Friday night informal meetings was held. The dinner was dropped because of the time and expense involved, but the meetings became a weekly event.

Drake explained, "The Friday night meetings became our platform to the world. We invited people there. It was, for Cesar, the all-important contact with the people, a place to give and take, to share, and to let the outsiders look into what the NFWA was all about."

Chavez did not give up the original ideas or goals he had for the NFWA. Although the strike took most of his time and effort, he told me in one of our first interviews that "win, lose, or draw, we are going to be around. This is just the beginning of a series of attempts to get recognition for farm workers. We will also be active in getting legislation. The industrial unions did not get a start until they had protective legislation [National Labor Relations Act, 1935]."

The interview had started in Chavez's tiny cubicle office,

144

in the midst of the cluttered NFWA storefront headquarters. The phone rang a half dozen times, a volunteer was lost and wanted directions, several pickets were in jail and had to be bailed out, a clergyman wanted Chavez to come speak at his church. There was a constant flow of people in and out of the office, some to do nothing more than grab a handful of aspirin from the big bottle sitting on one corner of Chavez's desk. It appeared as though the strike produced something like a community headache and the one big bottle of remedies was on the Chavez desk.

Chavez hung up the phone and said, "Come on, we'll talk in the car." Driving the battered Volvo from one picket line to another, he explained, "We have the support of Democratic clubs, the American Friends, the migrant ministry, Catholic priests individually, and the Catholic Rural Life Conference. We are also getting support from SNCC and CORE and from the big unions. It's really beautiful . . ."

No one from the press had much background on Chavez, and he was still an obscure figure to most Anglos. How had he gotten such impressive support?

Characteristically he summed up his power base in an understatement: "I know a lot of people because I have been in this kind of work for 15 years."

It wasn't long before Chavez was emerging as the leader of the Delano grape strike, and the Filipino AWOC influence was slipping into a supporting role. The farmers tried to exploit this fact, one farmer putting it this way: "Chavez is an egomaniac on a power trip."

From the beginning the Filipinos kept a low profile; they simply notified their employers they wanted more money and then sat down in their barracks, refusing to go to work. Larry Itliong explained they really had no other choice because they had no place to live if they left the bunkhouses that had been their home for up to 30 years. The Filipinos' fight was essentially a private one, between worker and employer; many of the Filipinos felt a sense of loyalty to their bosses and they only wanted more money, not a big hassle.

The Filipinos and the Mexican workers had never really

mingled on the job, or socially in town. Where ranches employed and housed both Mexican and Filipino workers they lived in separate camps, eating in separate mess halls. Before the strike started there had been little communication between Chavez and Itliong. Each was intent on working with his own ethnic group. Not until September 20th was there any attempt to coordinate the AWOC-NFWA efforts, and then the coordination was more jurisdictional than fraternal. On the surface Al Green and Cesar had met and issued a joint statement avowing cooperation, but underneath they were still at odds. Not only had Green refused to sign any cooperative agreements, but he told the Filipino AWOC leadership not to get too close to Chavez and the NFWA. The Filipinos ignored the "suggestion" and invited the NFWA to share the facilities in the big Filipino Community Hall.

The hall had a huge meeting room, large kitchens, a side dining room, office space, and storage rooms. The Filipino Hall became the scene of the NFWA-AWOC Friday Night Meetings, the kitchen was used to cook at least one hot meal daily for those AWOC-NFWA strikers who were hungry and broke. But this cooperation between the unions carried over into the vineyards only to the extent that each respected the other's picket lines and ranch jurisdictions.

By October the state Farm Labor Placement Service had certified 20 labor disputes in the Delano-Earlimart-McFarland strike area. Because state investigators determined that the workers on these 20 ranches had gone out on strike, the FLPS could not refer workers to these ranches, and any employer under strike had to notify strikebreaking workers a dispute was in progress. The AWOC had strikes against ten ranches, the NFWA had ten "certified" strikes, but it was picketing at least that many more that had not been certified.

Almost from the beginning Chavez and the NFWA faced a problem the AWOC didn't have to contend with: the number of strikes and number of strikers was growing, and this placed increasing demands upon the support facilities of the NFWA. The number of AWOC Filipinos was a constant figure that hovered around 1,000, but the NFWA strike numbers grew from the original 100 to 500 then 1,000 and 1,500 and 2,000. The people represented by these numbers changed constantly as some drifted away, others came in to join the strike. There were no strike benefits other than what the food caravans from Los Angeles and San Francisco and Fresno and Bakersfield brought in; Chris Hartmire and his volunteers worked hard rounding up supplies, and the list of contributors was growing, but there was never enough food, clothing, or money to support the newest batch of strikers. The NFWA had to take their names and send them elsewhere to find work, outside the strike zone.

By this time the farmers were importing strikebreakers in large numbers. They were recruiting from the skid rows of all the major towns, they were busing workers into the Delano area from all over the San Joaquin Valley. Joe Brosmer, manager of the San Joaquin Valley Agriculture Labor Bureau told the U.S. Senate Subcommittee on Migratory Labor, "We [Delano farmers] have never imported labor from the outside, other than the one test of 70 workers to see if the pipeline to Texas was open. Our workers are from this Delano-Earlimart area."

Two of the ranches under strike were the DiGiorgio Fruit Corporation's 4,400-acre Sierra Vista Ranch and Schenley Industries, Inc., with a 5,000-acre operation scattered over Tulare and Kern counties. Both ranches imported Mexican strikebreakers on a large scale. One afternoon, I saw five big buses parked in a DiGiorgio camp. The names of various Texas labor contractors were painted on the sides. One of the buses had just arrived and was unloading 40 or 50 women. The women were carrying cardboard boxes and cheap suitcases, following the directions of camp managers, and filing into the long bunkhouses. There were 250 or 300 women housed here, all of them were citizens of Juarez, Mexico, all carrying "green-card" entry documents, most had been domestic workers in the El Paso area until recruited to work behind the strike lines in Delano. When I told Brosmer of what I had seen and heard he argued that these two companies were the exceptions, that the other growers did not import workers.

Dolores Huerta disagreed. During the Senate hearings she testified that she had been in El Paso, trying to block the farmers' recruiting efforts, and she had watched as one employment agency shipped 60 to 70 workers to Delano every third day. She estimated 2,000 Mexican aliens had been recruited and transported to Delano from the El Paso–Juarez area. During these same hearings Chavez gave the subcommittee affidavits taken from workers who had been recruited by various Delano growers, including, but not limited to, Di Giorgio and Schenley. Three workers from Calexico said a bus from Delano was sent to pick them up; the driver was the brother of a man who operated a camp on one of the family farms. These workers were given papers to sign, including a *"contracto en contra de la huelga"* — an anti-union–no-strike contract — that they signed without knowing what the papers meant. One of the three workers in this affidavit stated:

> The next morning in the field we saw the roving picket line for the first time. Then we understood we were working in a strike area, but since we had no money to leave, we had to stay and work. If we had been told in Calexico before we got on the bus we would not have come . . .

This is the kind of conflicting evidence that kept the exact size and shape of the Delano grape strike obscure. In an early — and quite naïve — effort to measure the strike impact and define the issues I called Brosmer and asked him to set up interviews with some of his growers. He hedged, then told me to call him back the following day.

That same afternoon a Fresno *Bee* editor warned me Brosmer had just gone to the Fresno *Bee* managing editor, Diz Shelton, and asked that I be taken off the story because he said I was prejudiced. When Brosmer could offer no proof of this Shelton asked him to leave. I called Brosmer back on Friday. He said there had been a misunderstanding, he was not trying to influence the Fresno *Bee* or prejudice my reporting. He said that he had been authorized to speak for the growers, so we arranged a Saturday lunch meeting. Before he would talk about Chavez and the NFWA he said he wanted to make sure I knew that the strike had been started by the Filipino AWOCs and that the NFWA did not enter "until it saw an opportunity to further its own goals."

Brosmer felt it was important that I also understand the combined AWOC-NFWA strike had not hampered the harvest of a record crop, and he cited both wine- and table-grape tonnage figures to make his point. The strike he said was "an inconvenience" that required more labor supervision; it caused some farmers to move crews away from picket-line hot spots but nothing more than that. Brosmer said that for the record he was representing the South Central Farmers Committee, and these growers in the Delano-Earlimart-McFarland area did not wish to meet with me personally. It was their opinion, as expressed by Brosmer, that the NFWA was supported from the outside and that "this is more than a strike, it has civil rights overtones, but we do not know the real reason behind this fact, unless the strike is a training ground of some type . . . the minister involvement is the big question. It shocked us the most. Their stated purpose for being here is either false, or based on incorrect information."

From the beginning the NFWA's unorthodox tactics confused and angered the farmers. The AWOC they could understand, but there was no precedent for the influx of ministers, long-haired civil rights workers, and urban liberals. A Farm Bureau spokesman expressed his dismay: "I don't think it is morally right for clergymen to get down in the mud and work with unions."

Chavez fostered the idea that farm workers were looking for civil rights, as well as economic stability and something they called "social justice." He said any nonviolent tactic that furthered these goals would be used, including the boycotting of struck products. Caravans of farm workers drove to San Francisco and Oakland and set picket lines around the docks. Teamsters and Longshoremen refused to load grapes on the freighters. On November 29th the wire services reported 2,500 boxes of DiGiorgio grapes were left on an Oakland pier.

In Delano the NFWA assigned spotters to follow railcars and trucks of grapes to their destinations so boycotters in cities across the nation could gear up picket lines. At first these bird-dog tactics failed, but with the help of SNCC and CORE and Students for a Democratic Society, the market routes into the big Eastern cities were traced and the terminals picketed. Frequently both Teamsters and Longshoremen honored the picket lines.

The principal targets were all of Schenley Industries' liquor labels, the DiGiorgio Fruit Corporation's wines, S and W Fine Foods, and Treesweet juices. The secondary boycott was an old fashioned tactic, unused by organized labor since the National Labor Relations Act was amended in 1947 to outlaw the boycotting of an entire store for carrying a single scab product. But the economic weapon looked promising to Chavez and the farm workers were not covered by the NLRA, so the tactic was legal.

DiGiorgio and other farm interests immediately sought court injunctions ordering the Teamsters and Longshoremen to back out of the dockside support. These unions were covered by the NLRA and their support was an illegal secondary boycott action. The big unions backed off, as required. The NFWA continued boycott pressure when- and wherever it could.

The farmers were not the only ones puzzled and angered by the NFWA tactics. Delano city officials were really steamed because Cesar Chavez and the liberal press were giving Delano a "bad name." The city officials were not only angry but vindictive as well. They wanted an issue to discredit the NFWA. They seized on the NFWA's $267,000 War on Poverty grant as that issue. The Office of Economic Opportunity normally announced such grants through the office of the local congressman, in this case Harlan Hagen. But Hagen didn't announce the OEO grant; he attacked it, arguing his agribusinessmen supporters' tax dollars shouldn't be used to support a strike. The Delano City council, the mayor, and the school board all agreed; this was just another example of that fuzzy-headed, liberal Democratic thinking.

The OEO, taken aback by the fury of the attack, stuck by its guns; the grant would stand. Then Thomas Karter, chief of the OEO migrant division, flew to Delano to confer with Chavez. Karter later wrote,

> During our discussion of the grant it became clear to Chavez that he could not operate a poverty program and organize a strike at the same time. He decided that the strike and the concepts of collective bargaining and union recognition were more important than the $267,000 grant and calmly informed me that he would not accept the OEO grant until the strike was successful.

The OEO grant had been blocked, but "victory" did little to change the mood within the establishment; their feelings were summed up by the Rev. R. B. Moore, pastor of St. Paul's Baptist Church, in testimony before the Senate Subcommittee. Moore, playing heavily on the fact that he was a Negro and therefore understood what civil rights problems were all about, stated,

> Here in Delano, however, these rights, and many more, are ours *already!* They have been granted to us *not* by overt actions such as demonstrations and boycotts, but because this community has always — I repeat, always — been free of bigotry and discrimination.
>
> My point, gentlemen, is that Delano has been marked as an ugly, dirty little town which is callous and indifferent towards its own. That is simply untrue. The professional agitators who have infested our community have branded us a town of starving, ill-clothed, impoverished, suppressed and denied people.

The truth, according to the Rev. Moore, was just the

opposite; the people of Delano, rich and poor, black, brown, or white,

> have a wonderful relationship . . . and any problem we might face can be discussed and resolved. The laborers have been able to do this with their employers on an individual basis, the same as we have been able to discuss racial situations. The result of this harmonious living is that we are happy here.

The conflict and discord between the Chavez-Itliong–led forces and the community — as represented by the Rev. Moores and Joe Brosmers — was to be expected. What was not expected was that the grape strike itself was about to be caught up in a swirl of crosscurrents and inter-union fights that would threaten to suck the farm worker movement back down into oblivion.

Within the labor movement there were no clear policies, no unifying purposes to assist farm workers. At one level the Teamsters were helping the NFWA with its boycott of DiGiorgio products, at another level Teamsters were helping the AWOC organize citrus workers in a move calculated to outflank Chavez. As early as August of 1965 Al Green of the AWOC and Jim Smith of Teamsters Joint Council 38 were planning the move into the citrus areas of Tulare and Kern counties, just to the east of the grape strike area. By December the move had gone far enough to become public: A joint AWOC–Teamsters rally was held in Strathmore on December 14th, and 175 workers were told by Smith, "We stand ready and willing to assist in organizing field workers in every way possible." The Teamsters were to organize the packing sheds where the fruit was processed and shipped; the AWOC was to have the field crews who picked the fruit. In the citrus industry the field labor is hired, dispatched, and supervised by the packinghouse, not by the farmer; and the harvest work is done on a complex, industry-wide "prorate" system that attempts to keep the flow of fruit into the market *below* demand so prices remain profitable.

Through the late winter and early spring the Teamsters

and awocs opened joint offices throughout eastern Tulare and Kern counties; the awoc supplied its rented autos and office equipment. The focus was on the packinghouses; once the Teamsters had the houses organized, the field crews would be easy prey. Teamster vice president George Mock made the Teamster position clear: "The current citrus drive is part of a long-range plan to organize workers in every commodity that is packed and shipped in California . . . this is a long-range program and whether it takes one year or ten years we intend to keep going."

Einar Mohn, the international vice president who ruled the Western Conference of Teamsters, said of the newly merging venture: "We will work out any kind of assistance pact with any afl-cio union that has any right in the field, as long as they recognize our rights."

The Teamsters and the awoc leaders at the local level indicated each union was committing $5,000 a month to the citrus drive. The awoc director Al Green put the whole issue in perspective when he described the citrus effort as "an honest-to-God trade union fight, not a civil rights demonstration. . . . I am relying on union support. The nfwa is administered by ministers. We [awoc] will continue in our own *union* way."

As the Teamsters and the awoc kicked off their joint venture in citrus in mid-December eleven nationally known Protestant, Catholic, and Jewish leaders came to Delano to inspect the grape strike and talk to growers. The growers boycotted a luncheon scheduled by the clergymen and issued a statement angrily attacking the honesty and integrity of the eleven religious leaders. Presbyterian Robert McAfee Brown responded: "We reject the heresy that churches and synagogues are to be concerned only with so-called 'spiritual' matters. The suffering of farm workers and their childrens' cries to heaven demand the attention of men of conscience. . . . [It] is apparent the basic right of collective bargaining is being denied to farm workers in this valley. The workers' only recourse has been to strike. We are satisfied no other avenue of procedure has remained open to them . . ."

At the AFL-CIO midwinter convention, held that year in San Francisco, Paul Schrade of UAW asked the federation delegates to increase the AFL-CIO support for striking farm workers. Schrade got a pledge of $2,500 a month from the delegates and another $2,500 a month from the UAW. Behind the scenes the Reuther forces were organizing a dramatic display of this support. They chartered buses to carry the labor press to Delano to watch Reuther make the presentation.

Reuther flew into the Delano Airport December 16th, accompanied by Schrade and other staff members. They were met by Chavez and Itliong and taken directly to the picket lines around the cold-storage sheds that were strung out along the railroad tracks, through the center of town. Reuther took up one of the round, red picket signs with the large NFWA eagle emblazoned in black, and marched proudly with the farm workers. Flanked by Itliong and Chavez, Reuther was obviously enjoying himself. He told the 60 or 70 newsmen, "I haven't felt anything like this since the old days."

Reuther stopped the march on a street corner and started giving the pickets an impromptu speech: "There is no power in the world like the power of free men working together in a just cause. If General Motors had to change its mind because of the auto workers, then the growers have to change their minds; and the sooner they do the better for them, the better for you, and the better for the community."

That evening, at 6:30, Reuther was the star of an AWOC-NFWA rally in the Filipino Hall. Itliong presided. The hall — which normally holds 300 — was jammed with 500 people. They were out in the halls, out on the porches, crowded into the kitchen and dining room.

Reuther's first words were: "This is not your strike, this is *our* strike."

The crowd roared *"Huelga! Viva Reuther! Viva la Causa!"*

Reuther continued, "When the growers say their workers are not out on strike, they are wrong. The people in this meeting tonight are workers and the only ones who are outsiders are those workers the growers have hauled in here from Texas."

Reuther warmed to the crowd, undaunted by the necessity of having to stop for translation. The crowd responded, and when he announced the AFL-CIO convention had voted $5,000 a month support — half from the United Auto Workers and half from the AFL-CIO's Industrial Union Department — they went wild. He then added a one-time $5,000 Christmas bonus for the farm workers from the membership of the giant federation, and a promise to support the national boycott of grapes.

Rows of TV cameras recorded the event, dozens of reporters from the big dailies in New York, Chicago, Detroit, San Francisco, and Los Angeles filed their stories. *Time* and *Newsweek* took notice of the happenings. The first media event involving a national figure was a success for everyone but the disgruntled farmers. One of the growers, Bruno Dispoto, speaking for all the grape farmers responded with a statement:

We understand the appearance of Walter Reuther in Delano last week commemorated 100 days of a so-called strike. According to the National Farm Workers Association and the Agriculture Workers Organizing Committee, their workers — who include the Student Nonviolent Coordinating Committee, CORE, and migrant ministers — called the strike to attack the "human indignities" and the "poverty" of our working classes . . . the AWOC and NFWA do not represent our workers. Our workers have rejected them for what they are, perpetrators of hate and deceit in order to victimize innocent Filipinos and Mexican American groups . . .

It is without fear of contradiction it can be said Mexican American groups, along with Filipinos, should feel very proud of their standing in our Delano community for their accomplishments individually and collectively. These groups work in an area where the finest labor and management relations have existed for many years and we certainly hope to maintain this basis of communication and agreement for many years to come, without outside harassment.

Dispoto then pointed out California farm wages averaged $1.43 an hour, the highest in the nation, that the Delano-Earlimart-McFarland area grape harvest was the largest in years and that harvest had been accomplished "with our workers. There was no need, with the exception of 70, for outside help to be brought into the area." Dispoto qualified this last statement, acknowledging that "several farming organizations" in the area *traditionally* imported large amounts of labor.

Dispoto concluded,

> The latest action of the NFWA, with the assistance of SNCC and CORE, to nationally boycott products of table grapes from Delano . . . is the wildest kind of vengeance by an irresponsible group. We firmly believe the general public, when the facts are known, will voice their opinion against such deplorable acts as boycotting . . . we are sincerely looking forward to the riddance of these outside agitators and rabble rousers and college kooks and a few migrant ministers and priests . . .

CHAPTER EIGHT : POWER STRUGGLE

In December 1965, just before Walter Reuther made his first trip to the Delano grape strike, AFL-CIO president George Meany asked the federation's executive council to name William Kircher director of organizing, to replace the retiring Jack Livingston. Kircher, a big, bluff 200-pounder who laughs easily and likes to talk tough trade union talk, had been an auto worker, but he was philosophically and politically closer to Meany than Reuther.

Kircher's first task was to deal with the AWOC problems. He explained, "Meany had lost confidence in anyone we had out on the Coast in this thing and he wanted me to do what I could to get things going. We'd never had any major organizational success, yet we'd spent a lot of money out there. Meany told me if we couldn't translate this into some form of organization, then I had better look around for some union that would be willing to take the effort over and make it a part of its operation."

Although Kircher's job was to direct all of the organizational efforts within the federation, Meany had made his primary assignment the farm workers. One of the reasons for this was because of Reuther's maneuvering in the convention and his subsequent trip to Delano. Kircher said, "The Auto Workers took the play from the AFL-CIO. Because of this and other things Reuther had done, Meany saw it as sort of a grandstand play. That one little trip to Delano became Walter's whole stock of pictures for press purposes. He was there for one day and got six years of publicity . . ."

Actually the UAW — and Roy and Walter Reuther — had been strong supporters of the NFWA for some time. Both Reuthers frequently spoke out on behalf of the farm workers and the UAW contributed substantial sums of money to *La Causa*. Paul Schrade, the UAW's western regional director and a Reuther protégé, spent considerable time in Delano, supporting the NFWA cause; and he became one of the farm workers' strongest allies in Los Angeles. While there was no doubt about the UAW's support, Walter Reuther's feud with Meany did cause the farm workers some embarrassment. The UAW president on several occasions attacked Meany and the AFL-CIO, charging among other things that the federation was not supporting the farm workers as it should. The comments infuriated Meany and put Chavez in a position where he had to walk a tightrope between the two.

While the Meany-Reuther feud simmered, both Kircher and Schrade moved among the farm workers. From a public relations point of view, Schrade and the UAW had the easier time of it because they were openly on the side of Chavez and his followers. Kircher, on the other hand, was saddled with the AWOC and the responsibility of either getting it moving or abolishing it. Kircher traveled to the AWOC headquarters in Stockton; he drove south to Delano to meet with Larry Itliong and the Filipinos; he felt his way around the labor movement in California, trying to size up the situation. He did not know Chavez, and the various attitudes and opinions he picked up in his travels were confusing. Some called Chavez a communist and/or a civil rights leader; others swore Chavez was the only man who could pull the farm workers together into a meaningful organization.

Kircher took a closer look at the Delano grape strike, met Chavez, and observed, "It was obvious Cesar had taken over the strike and that he had a lot of charisma and ability to work. But I didn't get a chance to really see him in action until those Senate hearings Pete Williams held in California."

U.S. Senator Harrison (Pete) Williams, Jr., chairman of the Senate Subcommittee on Migratory Labor, had once again introduced bills to provide farm workers with minimum wage protections, collective bargaining under the National Labor Relations Act, regulations preventing the exploitation of child labor, and tighter controls over the grower-dominated Farm Labor Placement Service. The drama of the Delano grape strike was attracting national press, and Chavez supporters suggested to Williams that hearings in California might help bring attention to both the bills and the cause of the farm worker. Williams agreed, and scheduled hearings March 14, 15, and 16, 1966, in Sacramento, Visalia, and Delano.

Kircher's first strong impression of Chavez came during the opening day of hearings in Sacramento. Congressman Harlan Hagen, allowed to sit with the committee because Delano was in his district, questioned Chavez about communist influence within the NFWA. Hagen was a Dixiecrat Democrat, and he said he had information that a member of the NFWA had been to Cuba under the sponsorship of the Progressive Labor Party "which is a Trotskyite organization at a minimum and maybe it is borderline Stalinist or Marxist . . ."

Kircher recalled: "It was direct red baiting. But I was very impressed with the way Chavez handled himself. He easily came out ahead of Hagen. He gave direct, courageous answers to the 'Have you quit beating your wife?' kind of questions and he passed deftly between the horns. He was good."

Chavez had been one of the first witnesses called by Williams. During his testimony Chavez summed up the case for the farm workers this way: "I hope everybody here agrees that a man who works on a farm is made just like a factory worker, that his children like to eat just as much as the factory worker's, and that his wife does not like to live in a substandard house . . . [The] average farm worker in Delano has seven children, lives in a house which he rents for $55 a month, makes payments on a car, furniture, and to a finance company. Before the strike he worked eight months of the year at $1.10 an hour and his wife worked four months beside him, and on weekends and in the summer, his children worked too. . . . This man buys food at the same stores at the same prices that the farmer does. . . . [If] the farm workers are equal, then they deserve the same protection of the law that other men enjoy, and the Williams bills which confer this equality must be passed . . ."

The farmers opposed all of the Williams bills, but the proposal to include farm workers in the NLRA drew special attention. Allan Grant, a spokesman for the California Farm Bureau, contended: "Statutory collective bargaining would mean the strangulation of our food supply by a relatively few persons. . . . [We] in Farm Bureau support the right of workers to organize voluntarily . . . [but] we are opposed to forced unionism as it is now being advocated in the Delano area . . ."

Martin Zaninovich, a Delano grower and president of the South Central Farmers Committee, made it clear the farmers still maintained their position: "There is no strike among the Delano farm workers. The so-called strike is pure myth, manufactured out of nothing by outside agitators who are

159

more interested in creating trouble in the United States than in the welfare of farm workers."

It was during these hearings that the first of the grower-sponsored company unions — the Tulare-Kern Independent Farm Workers — appeared, and was exposed. Led by labor contractor Frank Arrero, six Delano residents had asked to testify during the last day of the hearings, in Delano. They were listed as farm worker witnesses. When Senator Williams called them to the witness stand, Arrero explained he was acting as interpreter for those in the group who could not speak English.

Williams told him to proceed. One of the workers began explaining in Spanish — with Arrero translating in English — that he had worked for one rancher for ten years, that he lived in Delano and was raising his family here. The testimony rambled on, without relating to the bills before the committee. Williams interrupted, suggesting the committee might learn more if it asked questions.

Williams: Are you all field workers?

Arrero: Yes, sir, all field workers.

Williams asked their opinion of the bills before the committee. They had little knowledge of minimum wages or child labor laws. A question about collective bargaining brought a demonstration from a group in the audience. After order was restored, Senator George Murphy took up the questioning: "First, would you establish exactly who you people represent?"

Arrero: Well, I for one am a member of the Tulare-Kern Independent Farm Workers . . . now we are not supporting the strike.

Arrero explained the TKIFW could see "nothing wrong" with legislation that would better the working conditions and wages of farm workers, but voluntarily added, "I for one think that unionism should not be shoved down our throats."

Arrero, under questioning by Senator Robert F. Kennedy, admitted he was not a picker "right now."

Kennedy: Is that what you ordinarily do? You do picking?

Arrero: Ordinarily I do contracting and farm work also.

Kennedy: Are you registered with the state as a contractor?
Arrero: Yes, sir, I am a licensed contractor.
Kennedy: Aren't you therefore an employer?

Arrero said, "Yes," he was an employer, but that he was attending the hearings as an interpreter. Kennedy established that Arrero was in fact, acting as spokesman for the group, that another labor contractor was "acting chairman" of TKIFW, that the TKIFW board of directors was dominated by foremen and crew leaders, the TKIFW secretary was a woman who operated a downtown business. Arrero also admitted that some farmers were "honorary" members, paying the $1 a month dues.

During a recess newsmen questioned farmers who appeared to be with a large group of the TKIFW supporters. The farmers admitted they had brought the group to the hearing because they were the "real workers" of Delano and they wanted to express their support for those TKIFW members who were testifying. Some of this group *were* field workers, most were crew bosses or crew pushers or foremen, others were labor contractors.

These were the Mexican American or Filipino farm workers who had "made it" in Delano, in the only way a brown- or black-skinned man or woman can make it in the dominant, conservative agribusiness society. They had worked hard, done what they were told, never complained, and had been willing to exploit others and to be exploited themselves. Traditionally, in the San Joaquin Valley agribusiness scene, the best job a field laborer can aspire to is that of foreman; to get to this position he or she must learn to push crews — make them work faster — then to boss crews. The crew leader's job security and his prestige in the community depends upon his ability to act as a middle man between the employer and the worker. When the foreman says "the boss needs 50 plum pickers the day after tomorrow," the crew boss's job and hope for advancement depends upon his ability to bring in 50 plum pickers; he works through aunts and uncles and cousins and friends, the word is spread through the *barrios* and *colonias* and with it, the crew boss's reputation in the community. He becomes a man who can provide work, someone to know. At this juncture some men branch off and become labor contractors, others stay on, doing irrigation work and tractor driving, and finally they achieve the pinnacle: foreman.

In 1965 Cono Macias was the number one foreman for the Bianco Fruit Company; he supervised the labor contractors who brought in crews, and he bossed the workers himself, using a network of sub-foremen and crew leaders he had developed. Macias worked as many as 500 people in his grape crews from Lodi in the north to Coachella in the south. The Bianco headquarters was in Delano. Macias is a big, good looking, aggressive man, who takes pride in his ability to feed, clothe, and house his family and provide for the education of his children. He is also proud of the fact that when Cesar Chavez put an NFWA picket line around the Bianco vineyards "not one of my workers walked out. Not one."

Macias was a migrant, the son of migrants. He remembers going to grammar school in Mercedes, Texas, where the school principal gave boys five swats with a paddle if they were caught speaking Spanish. He added, "And if you straightened up before he was done, it was ten instead of five. I hate Texas, I'll never go back. If you do *anything* to protest there, they will kill you."

Macias is conservative; he has made it the "*gabacho* way," the establishment way. He admits it, and tells how his father, a migrant turned labor contractor, instructed him in the art of getting along. "My dad told me that if I agreed with *The Man,* to say so, but if I disagreed, I should keep my mouth shut and walk away. Sometimes you get mad inside, but you have to learn to take it. If you fight, they will kill you or you go to jail."

Cono Macias is smart, and he learned to "take it" and keep quiet; he advanced and became recognized as a trusted Mexican American. Because he was articulate and understood the agribusiness system, he was singled out as a leader. He could express the workers' desires, sense their moods, interpret their reactions for his employers. It was Macias's contention the Bianco workers did not walk out on strike because of the labor relations policies he, as a foreman, was able to effect on their behalf. He was paternalistic.

Who were the Bianco workers? Were they local Delano area residents, as the Delano growers contended? Macias said that at least half were migrants from Texas or Mexico who moved in large family groups, traveling with the seasons. He laughed, "You had to be good to these people, because they were close. If you fired one, you lost 25 or 30 people. They would all quit and go off to work somewhere else."

In 1964 and 1965 Macias said he favored the idea of a union for farm workers. He praised Cesar Chavez, but contended those working in the NFWA under Chavez — the *Chavistas* — were mad for power or were vindictive. He said NFWA organizers singled out the crew leaders and foremen and picketed their homes, intimidated their families, threatened their children. He said, "Chavez had great ideas, but then those commies came in, now he says one thing, and his organizers do another . . ."

In his own way Cono Macias wants to be a leader of farm workers, but he also covets the middle-class existence of a supervisor earning $15,000 to $20,000 a year. At the time I interviewed him, in the early summer of 1974, he, his wife, and their 8 children lived in a neat, well-furnished suburban home. He had been a leader in several grower-dominated "worker associations" that were fronted by crew bosses and labor contractors to counter the Chavez-led movement. For the past year and a half Macias had been a Teamster organizer and then an area supervisor in charge of 20 to 30 other organizers. Like Macias, most of these men were Anglocized, but they gave a Mexican appearance to the Teamster effort.

The Teamsters used Macias and his followers for six months more, then sacked them in an internal power play that reestablished the Anglo power structure. Although he was angered and hurt by the move, Macias seemed to accept such "internal politics," and his resolve to work within the established agribusiness system seemed unshaken. When I observed that Macias was obviously being used by this system because he was trying so hard to make it the "*gabacho* way" he shrugged, nodded agreement, and said, "But there is no other way for us to make it."

Obviously Chavez disagrees. The NFWA would replace the labor contractor; it would restrict the power of the foremen and crew bosses by contractual agreements that give the workers a real voice in determining wages and working conditions. Chavez's plans would eliminate the agribusiness power structures that dominate men like Macias. The labor contractor lies at the heart of this system; most large growers use labor contractors, or they turn their own foremen and crew bosses into unlicensed labor contractors, forcing them to recruit gangs of workers.

Within the six San Joaquin Valley counties that make up the primary organizing area of the NFWA there are 360 licensed labor contractors. Chavez testified:

> One must first understand that a farm labor contractor does not contract work in the full sense of the word . . . he buys and sells, human beings. His profit is based on the sweat and toil of the workers. . . . All the farm labor contractor does is to promise hourly workers at the lowest rate he can find men to work at . . .
>
> What is happening in Delano on this strike, the farm labor contractor becomes the professional strikebreaker. You see, the grower does not know the work force. He will know those who are employed by him year round, which amounts to about 2 or 3 percent of the total work force. Now the labor contractor, being that he was a worker once upon a time, does know the work force and so in Delano we have the farm labor contractor being the biggest recruiter of scab labor or strikebreakers, with one exception, DiGiorgio Fruit Corporation. They do their own recruitment.

During his testimony, Chavez brought up a complaint about law enforcement agency tactics that opened up a whole unplanned look at the kind of frontier justice that still

164

prevails in many rural areas. Chavez told the senators that Kern County sheriff's deputies were photographing individual pickets and interrogating them as they marched peacefully along public roadways.

Senator Williams: I don't understand by what authority you have to go through the inquisition and questioning and all of that. Is there fingerprinting?

Chavez: Unless you are arrested, no. At one point we made up our minds we had been harassed enough, and we refused to give them any information and refused to let them take our pictures, we told the inquiring officer from the Kern County Sheriff's Office that if he wanted more information from us or wanted to take our picture, he would first have to arrest us . . .

Senator Murphy, the conservative, was shocked frequently during this series of hearings, often expressing his dismay at what he saw and heard. On this occasion he suggested, "We ought to invite the Kern County Sheriff in and find out his explanation of this."

The invitation was issued, and accepted by Sheriff Roy Galyen. Galyen was an old Kern County lawman; as a captain in the highway patrol he had helped quell the violent cotton strikes in 1933 and he had participated in policing most of the farm labor struggles since that time. Galyen appeared at the final session of the subcommittee hearings in Delano, two days later. The sheriff explained his deputies were taking pictures on the peaceful picket lines so that, if trouble did occur, they would have the means to identify the troublemakers.

Senator Robert Kennedy had joined the hearings a day late, and had not heard Chavez testimony about the picture taking. Now it was his turn for dismay. Galyen tried to make Kennedy understand the need to identify potential troublemakers. The photos — and field interrogation information — were just for the use of the Kern County Sheriff's Office and were kept in confidential files. The file contained the names and photos of 5,000 people.

Kennedy: Do you take pictures of everyone in the city?

Galyen: Well, if he is on strike, or something like that.

By this time Kennedy was pressing hard, and Galyen was becoming more and more defensive. The old Kern County lawman was not used to being questioned like this; this was his county, and he knew from experience what was likely to occur when workers rebelled.

Sheriff Galyen saw his job as one of keeping the peace, by preventive measures if necessary. This was the first time anyone other than the farm workers had publicly raised the issues of civil rights and constitutional guarantees. Kennedy asked the sheriff if fingerprints had been taken. Galyen said that some pickets had been fingerprinted after they had been arrested for unlawful assembly. The sheriff explained the arrest: ". . . we had news from the inside, there was going to be some cutting done if they didn't stop saying certain things, so I'm responsible to arrest them as well as anyone else."

Kennedy: What did you arrest them for?

Galyen: Why, if they got into a riot and started cutting up the people . . .

Kennedy: I'm not talking about that. Once you got into a riot, I understand that, but before, when they're just walking along, what did you arrest them for?

Galyen: Well, if I have reason to believe that there's going to be a riot started and somebody tells me that there's going to be trouble if you don't stop them, it's my duty to stop them.

Galyen explained that it had been the strikebreakers working in the vineyards who had threatened to cut up the pickets: "The men right out there in the field said 'If you don't get them out of here, we're going to cut their hearts out.' So rather than let them get cut, we removed the cause."

The NFWA pickets were arrested. Senator Murphy asked, "Do I understand you, sheriff, that it is your opinion that it is better to take precautionary moves before the trouble starts, that this is in the best interest of the community?"

Galyen: Who wants a big riot?

Kennedy: How can you arrest somebody if they haven't violated the law? . . . Can I just suggest that the sheriff reconsider his procedures in connection with these matters. . . . [Can] I suggest that the sheriff read the Constitution of the United States.

One of the most significant things to come out of the hearings was the position taken openly and unanimously by the Catholic Bishops of California. Until Bishop Hugh Donohoe of Stockton took the witness stand representing the California bishops, the Church as an institution had remained quietly neutral. Most farm workers and most Delano growers were Catholic, but, in the San Joaquin Valley, the growers dominated the Church. Bishop Aloysius J. Willinger of the Monterey-Fresno Diocese, which included Delano, was theologically conservative and he was considered pro-grower. When liberals like Father James Vizzard, of the National Catholic Rural Life Conference, came to Delano to support the striking farm workers they were sharply reprimanded by Bishop Willinger. Despite this, a few individual priests made the pilgrimage for a day or a week, and several young Jesuits remained in Delano as chaplains to the farm workers. One priest, who had a pilot's license, rigged a loudspeaker on a plane and flew Chavez low over the vineyards so he could try to talk the workers out of the vines. The priest's superiors read news accounts of his flight and ordered him grounded.

While some Catholic churches and individuals helped as they could, there was no overall operating policy until Bishop Donohoe testified. He made it plain that the bishops were not addressing themselves to the narrow issues of the Delano grape strike, but to the broader "farm labor problem as a moral problem." The bishops built their statement on Papal and Vatican Council doctrines; they gave careful consideration to the rights of the employers, then established their position in support of the farm workers' right to form a union of their own choosing. The bishops made two points that put them in direct conflict with the growers: First, they said the role of the labor organizer was vital to the formation of any union; and, second, they recognized that the workers had an absolute right to strike, if all other recourse had failed.

In conclusion, the Catholic Bishops of California said they saw "no compelling reason for excluding farm management-labor relations from the National Labor Relations Act."

It was a strong statement, placing the Church squarely behind the workers. For Chavez and his followers it was a good sign. The Catholic Church is an important part of *La Causa*. Our Lady of Guadalupe, the "Dark Virgin," the protector of the poor Mexican working people, is one of *La Causa*'s important icons. The traditions of the *peregrinación* [pilgrimage] and of fasting and penance have been woven into the traditions of the striking grape workers. The Mass itself is celebrated on truck beds parked in the fields, by priests wearing great red *huelga* flags as vestments.

Nowhere was this involvement of the Catholic Church more obvious than on the March to Sacramento, in March of 1966. A few days after the Harrison Williams hearings closed, Chavez announced he would lead a Lenten *peregrinación* from Delano 300 miles north to the state capital in Sacramento, where, on Easter Sunday, the farm workers would lay their case before Governor Edmund G. Brown.

Chavez recalled, "We began with 75 workers, and we carried the Virgin of Guadalupe, the union flags, and the flags of Mexico and the United States. All through the towns of the Central Valley we marched, singing union songs and workers songs and songs of joy. Each night we held a rally for farm workers in nearby towns and each morning there was a joyful Mass."

Kircher was back out on the West Coast. He joined the march. "I got some old clothes, and I figured the best goddamn way to find out what was going on was to avoid the experts and live with the people, so I walked with them, and I talked with them. . . . I happen to be a practicing Catholic and I go to Mass on a daily basis if I can, and here we were, going to Mass every morning, meeting every night, and Cesar began to talk [to Kircher] more. . . . [The] march was obviously an organizing tool. New. Radical. Different. A crew of people walking along the highway carrying the banner of Our Lady, calling meetings at night which attracted farm workers out of the fields and towns, opening with "De Colores" [a song about the colors of spring in the fields], maybe a prayer. The whole thing had a strong cultural, religious thing, yet it was organizing people.

"Chavez knew more than anybody else, he knew more about where the thing had to go, he knew more about what problems the workers faced and he knew that to approach the organization of these people like an organizer going into an auto plant some place, was ridiculous. They had no frame of reference, they were people who had been born in Mexico and had lived most of their lives working in Mexico and the United States. While Chavez directed their attention to the economic needs, he pulled them together through this common denominator, the cultural religious form.

"I'll never forget one night, we were talking. It was toward the end of the march. He held his two hands in fists, like they were holding something, palms up, fingers closed. He looked at one closed hand and said 'Today we must have the Eagle and Our Lady of Guadalupe; when we get the contracts we won't need Our Lady' and he opened one hand. It wasn't that he was taking advantage of the Church, it's as if he knew that to get from where the farm workers were to where they had to go, they needed help. He is a guy who knows what he ultimately wants and he knows he can't get there in the traditional ways. Radical? Sure, in the sense of being different."

But the march was not a radical departure for Chavez; rather, it was a synthesis of organizing techniques he had used before. The grape strike had forced his attention away from the creation of a statewide organization; he had all but abandoned the small cadres he had developed in other areas; and now, through the march to Sacramento, he would reestablish contact with some of these people. The march became a mobile house meeting, a way of involving farm workers outside the strike area in the primary battle.

The route of the march lay up through the San Joaquin Valley, past Stockton and the San Joaquin River delta country, and into the Sacramento Valley, passing through 30 *barrios* and *colonias.* Each night the marchers would stop, and local farm workers would feed and care for them. This simple act of asking the local people for food and shelter was one of the fastest ways to get them involved in *La Causa*; whether people believed or not, the traditions of hospitality were strong, when the people on the *peregrinación* asked for help, it was usually forthcoming, but not always.

The appearance of the *huelgistas* was sometimes an embarrassment to the shopkeeper-leaders within a *barrio* or *colonia* because it strained their relationship with the agribusiness community. In Cutler, a small Tulare County community, the Latin American Club did not want to become part of the controversy, not just at that time, because the growers who supported the club's annual Tomato Harvest Festival would withdraw that support. The charities benefiting from the event would suffer. So, when the *huelgistas* asked if they could use the club's large hall, the request was denied.

As the march progressed, it took on a pattern: The original group of marchers endured the long, painful miles between communities, then, as they approached a town, the supporters would come out and take up the march. On weekends entire families would turn out and walk for a day or two. The ranks filled and thinned and swelled again. Usually at night there was food and shelter of some kind; occasionally they were forced to camp out. The march was supported by a truck carrying supplies, a makeshift ambulance, and mobile first-aid station.

Bill Kircher marched with the *huelgistas*, a day or two at a time, alternating between the march and his Washington, D.C., office. He was already thinking of ways to abolish the AWOC efforts in Stockton; he wanted to salvage what he could and, hopefully, merge that with the NFWA operations, but there was a catch. Chavez was notoriously independent. Kircher needed time to talk to Chavez, privately, quietly, to feel him out on the AWOC problems.

As the march neared Fresno the big AFL-CIO director of organizing made his move: "Someplace close to Fresno, I forget the town, I could see Cesar was really beat. He was tired, he was limping from some problem with one foot. He'd been sleeping in the park, or wherever, and I said to him, 'How about if I go over to that big motel over there and I rent us some nice big rooms, with some double beds, some nice cool sheets and some showers?'

"I'll never forget. He said, 'Oh, God, that'd be great!' And that's what we did. I rented four rooms, for Cesar and I and Jim Drake and somebody else, I don't remember who . . ."

That night, as they talked, Chavez explained that Al Green had opposed the idea of the march, that Larry Itliong and the Filipinos had defied Green. Some of the NFWA membership had objected to taking the Filipinos into the march, but Chavez said he had "laid the law down: I told them Filipino brothers would be with us, if they chose, and their AWOC banner would be up front, beside our Black Eagle. And that I would hear no arguments about that."

Kircher was having a hard time understanding Green and the Stockton operations. He explained to me years later: "As I got into the AWOC picture I found the most ridiculous kind of structure. The principal AWOC office was in Stockton, and that was where Green was, but the strike was in Delano. Stockton to Delano is probably 175 miles. The AWOC leadership in Delano told me if they even wanted to print a leaflet they had to draw it up and send it in to Stockton.

"My first judgment was the AWOC was crazy . . . but as I got talking to Green, it was obvious the problem was jealousy, the whole identity of the cause had gone over to Chavez and the NFWA . . ."

One of the most disturbing things to Kircher was the AWOC–Teamster relationship in the citrus industry. While the Teamsters had organized eight or nine citrus packinghouses and had won NLRA elections (packinghouses are covered by the NLRA), the AWOC seemed to receive no benefits from the partnership. Kircher said, "As I dug deeper, I found that all of the organizing the AWOC had been doing had been done with labor contractors. They said they had over 100 signed contracts between the AWOC and labor contractors."

Although his talks with Chavez produced no commitment, Kircher continued to look for an excuse to move against the AWOC. It came unexpectedly, in the middle of the march. He recalled: "We were about 30 miles from Modesto, and somebody walks up with this Turlock newspaper; there was a front page story about the march, and right in the middle of it there's a subhead that says 'AFL-CIO Boycotts March.' Well Jeeze-us Christ. Here I am, director of organizing for the whole goddamn federation reading in the Turlock paper that the AFL-CIO is boycotting the goddamn march. Not only that, but AFL-CIO leaders are charging the NFWA is not really a union, that it is some kind of a civil rights organization, you know, that kind of crap. This was Green, it was his line, so I waited until we finished the meeting that night and I had one of my staff guys come with me and we drove to Stockton . . ."

The next morning Kircher met with the AWOC staff. "I told them I was talking as their goddamn boss, and it was an either/or situation. They had been telling me what big shots they were in the Stanislaus County labor movement, well I told them: 'The march reaches Modesto tomorrow, and I'm going to judge how goddamn important you guys are on the basis of how many AFL-CIO unions you turn out to welcome the farm workers as they come marching in.' Well, sir, they turned them out. There were the carpenters and the building trades, waving homemade *Huelga* signs."

Chavez recalled the blowup in slightly different perspective. He said, "There was an article in some paper, about how Green wasn't sure we were a union, and that whole shit about civil rights movement . . . so when Bill Kircher came on the march, he was talking about the NFWA coming into the AFL-CIO. I gave him the clipping and I asked 'How can we trust you guys?' You know? So he called on Green and he really chewed him out. He told Green to show how much he could turn out when we came into Modesto. So when we got there we had all the building trades, the laborers, the carpenters, the guys that put the putty on the glass," he paused, thinking, "the glazers . . . they were all there."

172

Why had the AWOC failed in its five-year efforts?

Chavez said, "They weren't organizing . . . they were mostly up in Stockton. One of the things they would do would be like get up early, about 4:30 in the morning and go to skid row where the buses load. By that time AWOC had signed a whole series of contracts with labor contractors. Before the guy could get on the bus he had to pay a dollar dues, or he had to sign an authorization card and get the dollar deducted from his pay. When the buses left, the AWOC guys went home. That was it. Ah, but the workers were pissed off about it, having to pay a dollar to ride the bus . . ."

Kircher ordered Green to fade into the background; he shut down the citrus operations, transferred AWOC funds to Delano, and gave Larry Itliong direct control over his end of the Delano grape strike. Kircher explained, "Within a week, for all practical purposes, the AWOC was reduced to what Larry was doing in Delano. Larry was the real inspirational leader of the AWOC operation. He and Chavez started working together as a team . . ."

The maneuvering had been effective, from Kircher's point of view, but Chavez was still resisting a full merger. Chavez explained, "See, I was worried that it would curb our style, you know? I was worried we wouldn't be able to do the secondary boycott. I knew we couldn't really have two unions; on our part I knew we weren't going to make any deals with the growers, but I didn't know what Green would do; I was afraid he might make deals behind our backs. After Kircher shut the door on him, I was most concerned about the boycott. . . . Of course what we really wanted was to have the status of a small, national union."

The boycott was a far more important tool to Chavez than most observers realized. "We had started talking about a boycott as a tactic way back before we had started organizing, when we were laying plans for the union. We talked boycott, we knew what the word meant, but we really didn't know, you know? We didn't know a primary boycott from a secondary boycott.

"Then in December 1965 things were really going pretty bad for us. We had all those damn court injunctions against us. They really restricted our picketing; they limited the number of people we could have on a picket line, and one time they wouldn't even let us say the word 'huelga.' We wondered how in the hell would we win the strike if all of that was against us, if the growers could just go into court and get orders against us. So we turned to the boycott.

"But it wasn't only that, you see, we also knew we had to get people involved, a lot of people, if we were going to win. We were asking how, and somebody pointed out the boycott would really involve people, and it would carry the farm worker story to the cities. At that time the farm workers were the 'new cause' for the college kids and what was left of the civil rights groups, and we knew they would help us."

The DiGiorgio Fruit Corporation and Schenley Industries were both ideal boycott targets. These conglomerates had from $250 million to $500 million in income; they had contracts with a half dozen other labor unions and therefore understood labor relations; each had dozens of highly visible product labels that were easily identified on the supermarket and liquor store shelves, and, perhaps most important, farming was only a small part of the total corporate picture for each company.

The march and the boycott were coordinated; for the first time the NFWA staff began to use a "media event," the march, to project their boycott tactic into the public conscience. College volunteers and a few farm workers were sent out as the "boycott staff"; they were assigned to all the major cities from San Francisco to New York and told to work up boycott support committees. These volunteers were given little resources beyond the travel money; once they arrived in their assigned city they had to scrounge their own living, and build a boycott structure. The news of the march to Sacramento was the tool that gained them access; it was their selling point.

Date line New York: The National Council of Churches supports the Delano Grape Strikers.

174

Dateline Boston: Grape boycotters stage a Boston Grape Party.

Dateline Fresno: Tired Marchers pass through the city, on their way to Madera. Of the original 75 only 60 are left.

The march was to end Easter Sunday on the steps of the state capitol in Sacramento. Chavez invited Governor Edmund G. Brown to be there to meet with the workers, but the governor's appointments secretary politely declined the invitation. The governor would be in Palm Springs with his family on Easter Sunday. Brown was suspicious of the farm worker movement led by Chavez, and he favored a quiet, private meeting, not a public speech that might be construed by agribusiness as an unfriendly gesture. The governor's refusal to meet with the workers earned more headlines, and sent a ripple of anger through the marchers.

Behind the scenes Chavez was urging all of his supporters to apply pressures on both DiGiorgio and Schenley Industries. In cities like Los Angeles and Chicago NFWA supporters approached everybody who might have some influence. During the Senate hearings, one of the NFWA volunteers, Wendy Goepel, rode in the car carrying Senator Robert Kennedy to the airport. She talked with the senator, trying to enlist his support for the Schenley boycott, and there are people in the farm workers union who believe the Kennedy influence was exerted.

Whether or not Kennedy's influence was applied, Schenley was beginning to feel the sandpaper effect of the boycott on its public image; the company was completely organized, except for the 5,000 acres of vineyards, and it had a good labor relations reputation. Corporate officers worked hard to maintain this good relationship with labor unions. The Schenley corporation retained labor relations expert Sidney Korshak; he was asked to handle the farm labor problem, but things were not coming together for him. Then a chain of circumstances, and a rumor that turned out to be a hoax, got talks started between the NFWA and the corporation.

The rumor had it that union bartenders, led by Herman (Blackie) Leavitt, were going to boycott Schenley liquors if the company did not recognize the farm workers. Leavitt, then head of Bartenders Local 284 of the Hotel and Restaurant Employees and Bartenders International Union, explained that one of his secretaries was active in various causes. She had gone to a coffee klatch to hear Cesar Chavez explain the strike and the boycott. When she returned to the office she was concerned. Leavitt recalled, "She was telling me about this nice little guy, Cesar Chavez, who was trying to organize farm workers. She said he was awfully naïve and that he needed help learning what labor organizing was all about."

Leavitt agreed to talk with Chavez, and the secretary arranged a meeting. Chavez brought Gilbert Padilla and Dolores Huerta along. Leavitt was moved by the talk with the farm workers leaders and agreed to help them. A secondary boycott by the bartenders would obviously be a violation of the NLRA's regulations against such an "unfair labor practice." But Leavitt said that he and his secretary, acting entirely on their own, without any approval from the international union, prepared a phony memo suggesting the bartenders might be considering such a boycott.

Leavitt said his secretary, through her contacts with other militant secretaries, arranged to have copies of the memo fall into Schenley hands. The reaction was swift. The company stormed at Leavitt; he agreed to a meeting, the company pointed out the bartenders' use of the secondary boycott was outlawed and suits would be filed. Leavitt explained that what individual bartenders did was their own business. According to Leavitt he and Korshak had been "friendly adversaries" for many years and they talked some more. Korshak telephoned Lewis Rosensteil, chairman of the Schenley board of directors, and explained what was happening. After learning about the bartenders' threat and that the problem involved only 5,000 acres of vineyards, Rosensteil ordered the farm sold. Korshak suggested that remedy was a bit drastic and countered with the idea of recognizing the NFWA, pointing out it was a sound public relations move. Rosensteil agreed, and told Korshak to settle the issue.

Korshak told Leavitt to set up a meeting with Chavez. Leavitt said, "Chavez was very suspicious of Anglos at that time. And he particularly didn't trust outside labor leaders, so I worked through Bill Kircher."

Kircher was speaking to the Louisiana state AFL-CIO convention in New Orleans. Leavitt reached him by phone around midnight, and they worked on the phone most of the night, arranging the meeting for the following afternoon at Korshak's palatial Los Angeles home. Kircher caught a 6 A.M. flight into Los Angeles. Leavitt said, "Chavez came in from the march and he brought Chris Hartmire and 4 or 5 farm workers with him, and announced the worker committee would make the decisions. That set Korshak back a bit; he had been hoping for a quiet, one-to-one meeting."

In the end Chavez settled for four people: Kircher, Leavitt, Hartmire, and himself. The recognition agreement and negotiation procedures took all afternoon and evening to work out. Then the two sides set up a press conference for the following day. On April 6, 1966, Schenley officially recognized the NFWA. The news sent an electric shock through the farm workers and the Delano grape growers. The march to Sacramento picked up its tempo. Kircher used the news to push his own efforts to get Chavez to agree to bring the NFWA into the federation. Kircher issued a statement:

The role of the AFL-CIO in the Schenley agreement indicates our respect for the NFWA. We look forward to the day when the movement is part of the great mainstream of organized labor, the AFL-CIO. The needs of farm workers, so long forgotten, demand the total strength and solidarity of all of organized labor.

Council of California Growers executive director O. W. Fillerup trumpeted agribusiness's displeasure:

While the NFWA and its religious cohorts were righteously preaching democratic processes and marching on Sacramento, the leaders were closeted elsewhere, working out a

177

deal that denied workers any voice in the proceedings. . . .
Schenley Industries, whose farm operations are incidental to
their basic whiskey-making business, is not representative of
California Agriculture, where growers steadfastly refuse to
sell out their employes and force them into a union which
does not represent them.

The next day, on April 7, the DiGiorgio public relations
staff cranked out a new corporate position: While the
company wouldn't arbitrarily recognize the NFWA it would
ask the California state mediation and conciliation service to
conduct secret-ballot elections on the DiGiorgio properties to
determine which union, if any, the workers preferred. The
company also suggested it was time the farm workers were
brought under the National Labor Relations Act. DiGiorgio
— to the chagrin of the remainder of California agribusiness
— was beginning to realize the NLRA has some protections for
the employer that were very desirable.

The DiGiorgio suggestion had some barbed hooks fixed
within its text; the corporation wanted a "no strike–no
boycott" guarantee, backed by binding arbitration procedures. Chavez and Kircher were reserved in their responses;
they congratulated the company on its stand favoring NLRA
coverage, but the "no strike–no boycott" clause was unacceptable. The unions wanted election procedures, but not at
that price. Growers around the state were furious with
Schenley, and now DiGiorgio. The rest of agribusiness found
the DiGiorgio NLRA position untenable.

Some growers were alleging the AFL-CIO had taken Chavez
and the NFWA over, that a merger had been transacted
without the knowledge of the farm workers. Chavez, in a San
Francisco press conference, responded: "The NFWA is as
independent now as it was when it was founded. We have
the support of the AFL-CIO and good relationships with the
Teamsters Union and the rest of organized labor, but there
has been no merger."

Then Chavez added: "Delano is where we must win. It is

the cornerstone for organizing all farm workers all over the nation. The AFL-CIO approves and supports this position."

Merger was still some months away, but there was little doubt the big federation — through the offices of Bill Kircher — was backing the radical independent movement. The 25-day march from Delano to Sacramento became the vehicle for projecting this support into the national media; the march that had started in desperation with 75 people, had now swelled to 4,000 people as it approached the outskirts of Sacramento. The marchers were jubilant, and this mood carried through the television and printed news accounts. Thousands more waited on the steps of the state capitol to welcome them.

In the happy pandemonium of Easter Sunday, as the marchers and the congregated farm worker supporters milled about, the 57 *"originales"* — the men and women who had marched the entire 300-mile distance — were escorted to the seats of honor. Chorusing shouts of *"Viva la Huelga!"* and *"Viva la Causa!"* rent the air.

Dolores Huerta, in the principal address of the day, warned the Democrats to be wary for they "do not have us in their hip pockets. . . . We will be counted as your supporters only when we can count you among ours. . . . We are no longer interested in listening to the excuses the governor has to give in defense of the growers, or to his apologies for them not paying us decent wages or why the governor can't dignify the workers as individuals with the right to place the price of their own labor through collective bargaining. The workers are on the rise. There will be strikes all over the state, and throughout the nation, because Delano has shown what can be done, and the workers know now, they are no longer alone . . ."

With the end of the march, the NFWA and the subsidiary AWOC had passed successfully through the first trial by fire. The recognition by Schenley, the shift by DiGiorgio to new positions on elections, and the inclusion of farm labor under the NLRA were the outward symbols of something deeper; farm workers were beginning to realize that a union was

179

possible. The farm workers were stepping from the shadows of the Wheatland Riot and the Pixley massacre into the full glare of the sun. They were just beginning to sense the meaning of Walter Reuther's words: "There is no power like the power of free men working together in a just cause . . ."

CHAPTER NINE : FIRST SUCCESSES

What had started six months earlier as an unplanned, ill-prepared farm labor dispute over wages in an obscure part of the San Joaquin Valley had developed into a burgeoning worker movement that was creating a momentum of its own. *La Causa* was like a runaway freight train rolling down a steep grade into a complex switching yard filled with alternative routes and blind sidings.

As the speed built up there was less and less time to contemplate or deliberate; long-range plans had to be brushed aside as each new crisis rushed into view; once a decision was made, it irrevocably altered the route; the onrush of the next crisis arose out of the last decision. There was no time for picking and choosing, no time for right and wrong, but only fleeting impressions of what seemed best.

This lack of control, this necessity to react to events, did not paralyze Cesar Chavez and his followers; rather, they seemed to thrive on the conflict and the result was that the movement developed a unique character, a character consistent with the life and environment of the seasonal farm worker. Cesar Chavez, as the son of a migrant farm worker, had learned to adapt to a life that had to be met day to day, a life that was chaotic and beyond the control of his parents.

But Chavez's life hadn't always been rootless. His highly romanticized memories of living on the family farm in the north Gila Valley gave him feeling for the land and — like the Mexican revolutionary, Emiliano Zapata — a feeling for land reform. The worker's destiny should be linked to the idea of owning a small plot of land on which he could develop an idyllic lifestyle. The land should be used to bring dignity to people who suffered a mean existence.

Such thoughts came from Chavez's feeling of being uprooted from a warm, loving, secure atmosphere on the farm and being cast adrift in the harsh environment of migrant life. On the farm the family had a sense of purpose and direction, they had some control over their lives, but once on the road this sense of purpose and control disappeared. Such feelings shaped Chavez's unique leadership. He is a guerrilla leader, in the tradition of Zapata, who has adapted the aggressive nonviolent philosophies of Gandhi to the farm worker cause.

Jim Drake said, "Cesar is a reaction. Whatever the opposition forces him to be at the time, that is what he is. . . . If there is a big strike, Cesar *is* the picket line, he is there, with the people, reacting. He is at his best when there is a lot of pressure, he is at his worst when there isn't much happening. When not much is happening, he goes off on tangents. At first, you know, I felt he was kind of godlike, that he didn't make mistakes, that he had some kind of uncanny ability to see through everything.

"Now I know he makes mistakes. . . . I don't think he is so much the strategist as I think he embodies his strategy. You don't have to be right on target with your strategy, it's just that every strategy you decide on, you die with it, carry it to the ultimate. It isn't strategy that wins, it is commitment. Cesar can make a mistake in strategy and no one will know because he will adhere to it . . ."

Talking about the first days of the strike and the development of strategy, Chavez said, "In the beginning we *were* doing it from day to day. We were reacting, you know. We had like a general idea, but that was all; you have to understand there were about four or five things we had to deal with, and the biggest of these was not the strike. The most time was spent keeping the people going, disciplining them, training them, making sure there was no violence, keeping up their morale. Then we had to decide how to take the bad turns by the police or the government or the growers and exploit them to our own advantage. We had to deal with rumors because we had no real intelligence unit then. We would hear something from a crew boss or a foreman about what the farmers were doing, and we'd react. Another thing was raising money. And we had to get the news out to the public; we were no good without that."

Chavez spent much of his time dealing with the press, learning how to handle the various sides of the media. "There's a great difference between TV and the printed media. TV is the easiest, they want facts, fast, on the spot, and they eat up so much material but it isn't lasting and they need more. Newspapers are the hardest. TV will take anything, but newspapers are more skeptical, and the valley papers are so conservative. The national press tried to fit us into a traditional union mold, but we didn't fit. They didn't understand us."

As a result of Chavez's brand of leadership, the farm workers' cause became more than a local labor dispute over wages and working conditions. *La Causa* became a struggle to radically shift the balance of power from the agribusiness managers to the union of farm workers; but it was even more than a power struggle, it was a social revolution as well, because of the emphasis on social services, on land reforms, and community-development projects. *La Causa* involved the churches and the radical and liberal communities in its struggles. Because of this, the leaders of the AFL-CIO and the Teamsters were hard put to understand the farm worker movement. George Meany and Frank Fitzsimmons — with their posh offices, six-figure salaries, and fat expense accounts — are Catholics, but their Church leaders don't come out into the brawling world of plumbers and truck drivers on strike. Men like Meany and Fitzsimmons are from *organized* labor, where the emphasis is on structure and formalized conduct. They meet management on an equal footing; they play golf at the same clubs, dine at the same expensive restaurants, send their children to the same schools. Management and labor are "friendly adversaries" — using Blackie Leavitt's words — who understand the use of power and politics. The farm workers' cause was too different, too disorganized, too ethnic and uncouth, too wrapped up in the mysticism of Mexico and Mexican Catholicism.

As distasteful as this may have been for leaders like Meany and Fitzsimmons, it was this very set of characteristics that projected both Chavez and *La Causa* into the national consciousness. Neither the AFL-CIO nor the Teamsters had ever made a move that seriously threatened California agribusiness. Yet in less than one year after Chavez led the NFWA into the strike, the farm workers had gained enough strength to give the farmers a healthy push. Individually the giants of agribusiness were beginning to shift position, to search for new tactics to counter this growing worker power. The DiGiorgio offer to let its employees vote in union recognition elections signaled the beginning of this move from right to left. When Robert DiGiorgio suggested Congress should amend the National Labor Relations Act to include agricultural workers, he flew in the face of agribusiness's historic position, a position that had kept farm workers powerless while auto workers and plumbers and steel workers created strong unions.

The DiGiorgio corporate managers were indifferent to the traditions of farm politics; their motives, like those of all corporations, were dictated by maximization of profits. When the DiGiorgio Sierra Vista Farms were struck by the NFWA, the company tried the traditional anti-union tactics, but when these did not work, they tried an end run on the NFWA flank. Kircher, assisting Chavez in dealing with DiGiorgio, pointed out the election proposal was a neat public relations move for the company that put the NFWA at a disadvantage. The company pressed its advantage in a letter to employees:

We have been trying to arrange an election through officials of the State of California to allow you to tell us if you want to be represented by one of three unions now active in the area, AWOC, NFWA, or the Tulare-Kern IFWU, or if you want no

183

union, as it has been in the past. So far only the IFWU [referring to the Tulare-Kern Independent Farm Workers, exposed as a company-dominated group during the U.S. Senate hearings] has agreed to an election. . . . NFWA has thus far refused to have an election . . . because it knows it does not represent you . . .

Chavez said that in addition to the unacceptable language prohibiting boycotts and strikes at harvest, the NFWA found the suggestion that the TKIFW be on the ballot intolerable: "We will have nothing to do with the Tulare-Kern Independent Farm Workers; it is a company union, controlled by growers. . . . [Ours] is the only union that has had a dispute with DiGiorgio. . . ." Kircher acknowledged the NFWA jurisdiction in the DiGiorgio strike and pledged full AWOC and AFL-CIO support for the strike and boycott.

While the company and the NFWA positions were miles apart, the door was left open for election negotiations. In the meantime there were other problems to deal with. Cesar had assigned Dolores Huerta to work up a basic NFWA contract position in preparation for the Schenley negotiations; he called off the Schenley boycott and issued orders to step up the DiGiorgio boycott; Christian Brothers Winery, after some behind-the-scenes pressures, recognized that its workers wanted to be represented by the NFWA and negotiations were begun; Kircher was pressuring for the AWOC-NFWA merger and had to be stalled; the union was short of funds and Chavez had to travel to the boycott cities to stimulate fund-raising efforts.

In the Rio Grande Valley, Texas melon pickers had gone out on strike and then turned to Chavez and the NFWA for help. Chavez was not ready for a second front, especially one so far away. With the fight at DiGiorgio shaping up, he told the Texas workers they would have to wait. Meetings were arranged quietly with DiGiorgio officials to explore the possibility of establishing election procedures acceptable to both labor and management.

The most important problem was designing a contract that

would give the workers some control over their working conditions. Chavez said the new contracts would provide union-run hiring halls and have grievance procedures and job protections. Dolores pored over other union's contracts, working out language that would fit farm labor. The workers themselves would be directly. involved in the day-to-day enforcement of the contracts. The concept of ranch committees began to emerge as the NFWA leaders talked about how to deal with the existing labor contractor–crew boss system.

Chavez declared, "To fire a worker they must prove to the union that the worker is not keeping up his part of the responsibility to the contract."

The NFWA was still operating out of the old storefront at 102 Albany Street; as the movement grew, more room was needed. The union rented a pink house directly behind the storefront, and then a gray house on the next street over. The pink house became Chavez's administrative headquarters; his office was a small corner bedroom, down a dark narrow hallway, past the bathroom. The house was crowded. There was never enough room; phones were always ringing; long-haired volunteers and dark-skinned farm workers were jamming in and out; there was the constant yammer of voices talking, laughing, swearing in Spanish and English. There were always people coming and going; some were sleeping on the couches or the floor, eating out of brown bags and paper cartons.

Jim Drake was running the offices, trying to keep the bills paid, juggling Cesar's schedule and keeping track of decisions coming out of the incessant meetings between Chavez and the staff. A car had broken down. Repair? Replace it? Twenty more workers walked out on strike; where was the money coming from to feed and house not only the strikers but their families, too? Tell them to seek work elsewhere? Go on welfare? What?

Whenever a major issue arose, Chavez called Huerta, Padilla, Antonio Orendain, and Julio Hernandez into consultation. These were the NFWA executive board members, and their policy meetings often lasted far into the night, as they argued, talked, fought, and talked some more. Dolores and Cesar fought, frequently yelling at each other. She explained, "You know what happens? The people working under Cesar were overwhelmed by him. They found it hard to make a decision, or they wouldn't fight with him. When I think he's wrong, or when I think my way is better, I fight with him. You know? We've had some bloody fights . . . he is stubborn . . . he has a tremendous amount of personal strength, and people are overwhelmed by it . . ."

When arguments were resolved, when issues were finally voted into policy, Chavez considered that policy a mandate. All decisions on the subject then flowed from the mandate. For example, the board set a budget policy on telephone bills; the ceiling was $1,600 a month and the staff was admonished to keep within these limits. If there is one special area of concern that receives more attention from Chavez than any other, it is the expenditure of money. Drake recalled that once he came to work to find all the phones were dead. Without saying anything to anyone Chavez had ordered the phone company to shut them off. For a few days the office was in chaos, work came to a standstill. Finally, Chavez called a staff meeting to explain that he had shut the phones off because the $1,600 limit had been grossly exceeded. He made it clear the staff could write letters, or use pay phones at their own expense, or make collect calls, but they could not exceed the budget limits the board had set. The phones were turned back on.

Sometime not long afterward the phone bill was again over $1,600. Some of the staff complained the constraints were too limiting, that coordinating a boycott in 50 cities across the country required more phone money. Drake, knowing Chavez's attitudes, told them "No" and put locks on the phones. Someone broke a phone lock, and, when Chavez saw this, he took the phone, yanked it out of the wall, and wryly commented that particular staff person would have no more trouble with going over phone budgets.

Money was always a problem. Chris Hartmire was moving about the state, giving talks to churches and civic groups, urging more support for the farm worker cause. He led caravans of volunteers, carrying food and clothing to the farm workers. Cesar traveled to the colleges and labor conventions, seeking more aid. The AFL-CIO and the UAW contributions were the backbone of the budget, but the muscle and flesh of the union came in the $5, $10, and $20 donations, as hundreds of groups and individuals responded.

The talks at DiGiorgio sputtered through late April and early May without progress. Chavez focused all of the boycott efforts on DiGiorgio's highly visible line of products: S and W Fine Foods and Treesweet fruit juices. Kircher put the full weight of the AFL-CIO behind the primary boycott, saying, "The company took the union on; it did not recognize the NFWA and it asked for this head-to-head fight."

Cesar asked Fred Ross to come to Delano and help organize the campaign against DiGiorgio. Ross started putting together worker meetings; he, Hartmire, and Drake worked to get Catholic, Protestant, and Jewish religious leaders and laymen to exert pressure directly on the company. Robert DiGiorgio said the company would be willing to allow an outside observer to come in to expedite the stalemated NFWA–DiGiorgio talks, and he suggested Bishop Aloysius Willinger of the Monterey-Fresno Catholic Diocese for the job. Bishop Willinger accepted the offer, and sent Monsignor Roger Mahoney as his observer. Chavez objected. Bishop Willinger's conservative posture and agribusiness bias made him unacceptable. Mahoney was asked to leave the meetings.

At the time Mrs. Ophelia Diaz was a crew boss on the DiGiorgio Sierra Vista Ranch. She had been employed by DiGiorgio for twenty-five years, working her way up from seasonal harvester to the full-time job of bossing crews. Her husband had a similar job on a nearby ranch; they had a large family and had recently moved into a modest new home. All their children were in school. They had "made it," but Mrs. Diaz was not satisfied. She listened to the *huelgistas*. The talk about Chavez stirred her curiosity, but she made no move toward the NFWA until her foreman handed her some cards and ordered her to have her crew sign them. The cards authorized the International Brotherhood of Teamsters to represent the undersigned worker.

With her husband's consent, she took the cards to the NFWA office and asked to meet with Chavez. Fred Ross recalled, "She had been told to sign a card and to have her crew each sign one and she didn't think that was right. She said most of her crew was sympathetic to the NFWA and they probably would sign with us, if we could get cards to them. We gave her some NFWA authorization cards."

Mrs. Diaz explained she carefully placed some Teamster cards on top of the NFWA cards and took the stack of cards into the field the next day. She started signing workers up in the NFWA; when the foreman came around he saw the Teamster cards on top, and thought she was following his orders. The ruse worked for a while, but then she was discovered and fired. She said, "We had decided to sign up with the Chavez union and the farmer found out about us, and he fired me. My husband got fired from his job, too. Because my picture had been in *El Malcriado,* I found it hard to get another job, so I went to work with contractors."

When Chavez heard Mrs. Diaz had been fired, he walked out of the DiGiorgio talks, saying, "We are breaking off negotiations with DiGiorgio until this company agrees to rehire this woman and agrees no more pressure will be brought against their workers who are sympathetic to the NFWA."

The Teamsters' move into the vineyards surprised most observers. Some Teamster locals, especially those in San Francisco, Los Angeles, and New York, had been supporting the grape strike. Teamsters frequently had refused to load or haul shipments of grapes until the growers went into court and got injunctions against such secondary boycott actions. Such support had come from union locals; the move against the NFWA at DiGiorgio was being directed by Joint Council 38, headquartered in Modesto, the same group that had been in partnership with the AWOC in the citrus. Teamster president James Hoffa, in a telephone interview, told me the

International was supporting Joint Council 38's move. He said the Teamsters, with the support of the International Longshoremen and Warehousemen's Union, were moving in to organize field labor on a major scale. For more details, he suggested I talk to Einar Mohn, the international vice president in charge of the Western Conference of Teamsters. Both Hoffa and Mohn argued that the Teamster move was logical because the Teamsters were already representing workers in the canneries, the packing sheds, and cold-storage plants that processed the fresh fruits and vegetables. They said the Teamsters were merely protecting their jurisdictional flank by organizing field labor.

Taken in historical perspective, the Teamster move was just one of a long series of jurisdictional raids that occur periodically in the push and shove of organized labor in the United States. The big unions — and the federations — have never been content to stay within the confines of their own territory. But why did the Teamsters pick DiGiorgio to launch this major move into the fields? Why did they show up just at the critical point in the NFWA–DiGiorgio election talks? Both Kircher and Chavez suggested the company invited the Teamsters in, to head off the NFWA, and that by jumping into bed with the grower the Teamsters were warming up for a "sweetheart contract."

Kircher told Mohn he thought the Teamster move against an employer already under strike by another union was unethical, even in the hurly-burly political atmosphere of American organized labor. Mohn, disturbed by Kircher's allegations, agreed to a secret meeting with Chavez and Kircher. Mohn came away from the meeting saying the Teamster plans were "indefinite," adding, "This is a complex issue. The old AWOC — how alive it is I don't know. The NFWA is there, it gets a lot of publicity, but little is known of its real goals, whether it will shape up into a trade union, or a civil rights movement."

The ILWU's interests were never explained; although the Longshoremen have farm labor contracts blanketing Hawaii agribusiness, they had never made a move toward mainland farm workers. No one on the ILWU staff would explain Hoffa's reference to their help.

Chavez and Kircher began the counterattack by rounding up as much Catholic and Protestant church support as they could; churchmen from all over the nation, led by Father James Vizzard, director of the National Catholic Rural Life Conference, and Archbishop John Cody of Chicago, leaned directly on Mohn. He waffled, then agreed to pull back out of the DiGiorgio Vineyards. While Chavez met with Mohn to work out some jurisdictional guidelines, Teamster organizers from Joint Council 38 continued to work the DiGiorgio Vineyards.

The Teamsters are a difficult organization to understand; apparently, when it suits the overall purpose, the orders issued from the top never get to the operating level, or if they do they are ignored. Publicly, the orders were given to withdraw, but quietly, Joint Council 38 may have been told to steal as much as they could while talks were under way. In an attempt to clarify the issue, I called Hoffa again. He acknowledged that the Teamsters were pulling out of DiGiorgio, but Hoffa added, "We are going to continue our campaign to organize farm workers."

The Teamsters' apparent willingness to withdraw from DiGiorgio's ranches set the Chavez-DiGiorgio talks in motion again. But the Teamsters were having second thoughts. Einar Mohn met with Bishop Willinger, then Mohn announced he had a petition from 400 DiGiorgio workers on the Sierra Vista and Borrego Springs ranches, asking that the Teamsters not abandon the farm workers. Bishop Willinger called for free elections, supervised by a disinterested outside body. Of course his office was available if anyone should ask.

The Teamsters were back in the race. Kircher and Chavez were meeting with DiGiorgio officials in San Francisco, working out an election proposal; they decided to meet the Teamster threat head on, the combined NFWA-AWOC forces would agree to oppose the Teamsters in an election, winner take all. The new NFWA-AWOC position was put on the table, and the talks were recessed temporarily. Chavez had to leave because the second round of Schenley contract talks was scheduled to start the next day, June 21, in Los Angeles. While Dolores Huerta was the chief negotiator, Chavez wanted to be on hand, so he had accepted an engagement to speak to the Retail Clerks' regional convention that same day. Kircher was to represent Meany at the same convention.

Kircher explained, "We had agreed to an election at DiGiorgio, agreed on procedures. We had 12 points and we were down to the last three or four. The next day we had to fly to Los Angeles, but we told DiGiorgio we wanted to keep things going."

Chavez indicated the negotiations had not progressed quite that far. "We had agreed we wanted elections, we were trying to work out the rules for the elections, but we were miles apart. When we left San Francisco we agreed we would be meeting the next Monday. They had kept a straight face through almost three hours of negotiations. . . .[We] thought they were on the up and up, you know. But they had already made a secret deal."

The exact time and place of the Monday meeting had not been fixed. When Kircher and Chavez arrived in Los Angeles, Kircher called the DiGiorgio offices in San Francisco to set the meeting schedule. He was told there would be no meeting and that a telegram was on its way explaining why.

Kircher said, "We drove out to East L.A. without knowing what DiGiorgio had up his sleeve. We had a little office, Dolores met us there, and there was the telegram announcing an election [June 24] to be supervised by an accounting firm. The AWOC, the NFWA, that so-called independent [TKIFW], and the Teamsters were all on the ballot. We were had. This was rigged. All the cards were in DiGiorgio's hand.

"They had a good public relations position on us because most people don't know the protections you must have. It looked good on the surface. They had called a press conference for the next day to announce the election publicly. We were depressed. I said I was going to San Francisco and break up that goddamn press conference."

After a brief huddle, it was decided a two-pronged attack

on the DiGiorgio elections was needed. Chavez was committed to stay in Los Angeles; Kircher and Huerta were sent
back to San Francisco to break up the press conference and
to get AFL-CIO lawyers to file suit in court to prevent
DiGiorgio from putting the AWOC and NFWA names on the
ballots. To file suit they had to put up $25,000 bond. The
money was raised from San Francisco Bay Area AFL-CIO
unions.

When Kircher and Huerta arrived at the San Francisco
Press Club, they were met at the door of the meeting room
by DiGiorgio officials who tried to prevent their entry.
Kircher recalled, "They said it was a private press conference, and I told them it didn't look very private to me. They
told me they would call the police and I told them they damn
sure better get enough cops, and we just went in. Up on the
stage stood Robert DiGiorgio. All three networks were there,
the radio guys, newspaper guys, and I stood right in the line
with them, . . . when DiGiorgio finished reading his statement, I jumped up there and told him I could prove he was a
damn liar. And we started talking and the news guys listened.
The cameras were running. We broke it up. We cast an aura
of suspicion and doubt. Then we went immediately into court
and got the AWOC and NFWA names ordered off the ballot . . ."

DiGiorgio went ahead with plans for the June 24th
elections. Chavez countered by calling on all DiGiorgio
workers to boycott the elections. The elections were to
involve workers on both the Sierra Vista Ranch near Delano
and the Borrego Springs Ranch in San Diego County. There
were 732 workers eligible to vote on both ranches, by
DiGiorgio rules. On the day of the election the NFWA put
picket lines around both ranches.

Cesar personally directed the Borrego Springs operation.
He said, "We were out there, on the end of the road, asking
people not to vote. We were pretty successful. Most of the
people refused to vote the first time, so they the [DiGiorgio
supervisors] went back out to the crews and told them they
had to vote and vote for the Teamsters, so we had the stuff to

get them legally, because we had people inside who told us what had happened."

Cecil Hoffman, Jr., a Presbyterian minister from Los Angeles, was with Chavez at Borrego Springs. He reported: "The election was obviously planned to confirm what the company had already decided, that those who went out on strike should have no opportunity to vote, and that the vote should give the nod to the union of the company's choice."

At both the Borrego Springs and Sierra Vista ranches many DiGiorgio workers did refuse to vote, even though they were bused into the polling places by the company. Of the 732 eligible to vote, 385 cast ballots; 284 voted in favor of a union, 60 voted against any unionization, and 41 cast blank ballots. Of those favoring the idea of a union, 201 voted for the Teamsters, nine voted for the NFWA, three for the AWOC, and the remainder named other unions.

The election was claimed as a success by the Teamsters and the company. But Chavez countered, saying the NFWA-AWOC call to boycott the election was successful because nearly half the 732 workers eligible to vote refused to do so. Monsignor Roger Mahoney, assigned by Bishop Willinger as an observer, said in an interview seven years later that he did not think this first DiGiorgio election was fair because the company had set it up and had established all the rules. He said the Teamsters participated in the establishment of election rules, but obviously the AWOC and NFWA had not. Mahoney said the results of the election were not valid if for no other reason than the fact that Chavez-led forces boycotted the balloting.

To wrest the initiative from the DiGiorgio-Teamster faction, Chavez, Kircher, and Huerta with the help of Chris Hartmire set out on a flanking attack. Their goal was to pressure Governor Edmund G. "Pat" Brown into calling for an official investigation of the company-dominated elections. Brown had just narrowly won the Democratic nomination in the June primaries and, facing an aggressive Ronald Reagan in the fall, felt he was politically vulnerable. Kircher went directly to Brown, suggesting the governor take a "statesmanlike position" by inviting a nationally recognized arbitrator to conduct an unbiased investigation and make recommendations on how to settle the dispute.

Coincidentally, the Mexican American Political Association was meeting in Fresno. MAPA had been considered a safe source of support by most Democrats, and its recommendations commanded respect in the *barrios* and *colonias* of the state. Huerta was dispatched to the MAPA convention to generate some heat on the governor. Huerta, in addition to being a tough negotiator, is one of the most effective lobbyists the farm workers have. She worked behind the scenes, getting the MAPA leaders to agree to meet with the governor to ask that new elections be called.

Governor Brown had been avoiding a meeting with Chavez for months. While he was considered liberal, and generally sympathetic to the causes of the poor, Brown was suspicious of the farm worker controversy, sensing it could pull him into political quicksand because the conservative wing of the state's Democratic Party was heavily influenced by agribusiness. Because he needed Mexican American support, Brown agreed to meet with the MAPA leadership, unaware that they were bringing Chavez with them. When he was introduced to Chavez the surprised governor recovered quickly, proclaiming so the press could hear, "This meeting is two months overdue."

In the end Brown agreed that, if the farm workers could show him the elections had been unfair, he would act. Chris Hartmire recalled that he, Cesar, and other union officials met again with the governor to present statements by farm workers who had gone through the first elections. Hartmire said the statements clearly established the lopsided nature of the balloting processes. Brown, also a Catholic, was being pressured by liberal churchmen, as well as by the MAPA leadership. He agreed to intervene and appointed Ronald W. Houghton, co-director of the Institute of Labor and Industrial Relations, Wayne State University, to investigate and make recommendations. Both the Teamsters and DiGiorgio were caught in this flanking maneuver and could do little but wait. Houghton's reputation was beyond attack. Within two weeks Houghton suggested new elections be held, under the direction of the American Arbitration Association. The company and the Teamsters had little choice but to agree, and negotiations were started to establish ground rules acceptable to the NFWA, the AWOC, the Teamsters, and DiGiorgio. The TKIFW company union had disappeared and no one mentioned it again. Tentatively, all three sides agreed on an August 30 election day and to allow any worker to vote who had worked 15 days for DiGiorgio at any time since the day before the strike started in September 1965. The number totaled almost 2,000.

When asked how such an agreement was reached, Fred Ross suggested: "Well, they made the mistake that powerful groups usually make. They underestimated the strength of the opposition. They thought with the powerful organization of the Teamsters and the fact they [DiGiorgio] would be able to throw their weight around, that they would beat us. They actually thought they had enough power and enough friends among the workers to swing it . . . [They believed the migrants had scattered like the sands of the desert, that we'd never be able to round them up. . . . [They] underestimated our willingness to work and to win . . ."

Chavez took the election proposal back to the membership for approval, Kircher swung the AWOC members into line, and the Teamsters and the company all agreed. The election was set, the rules adopted, but not before a big flare-up over the company's dismissal of 192 workers. Within the group were a large number of suspected NFWA sympathizers. Chavez cried, "foul," the company shrugged and explained that such layoffs were normal for that time of year. Chavez was trying to keep workers in the area. He needed their votes, but he could not come up with 192 jobs, and there wasn't enough left in the NFWA stockpile to support them until the election. A compromise was reached: These workers could vote by mail.

As the unions and DiGiorgio were working out the election procedures, disgruntled California agribusiness leaders were trying to create a public forum of their own from which to launch a counterattack. They had been badly stung by the U.S. Senate Subcommittee hearings and, to counter the liberal slant of those hearings, the farmers prevailed upon California State Senator Vernon Sturgeon, chairman of the senate's agriculture fact-finding committee, to schedule Delano hearings.

Sturgeon tried to build up interest in the hearings by sending a subpoena to Albert J. (Mickey) Lima, head of the Communist Party's Northern California operations, and Saul Alinsky, director of the Industrial Areas Foundation and one-time employer of Cesar Chavez. Sturgeon said Mickey Lima's car had been seen at the NFWA headquarters.

Lima refused to testify, but told reporters later he had given his daughter the car so she could bring loads of food and clothing to Delano to help strikers. Saul Alinsky obviously wanted to testify; the crusty old radical loved matching wits with farmer politicians. When they asked the ultimate question — "Are you now or have you ever been a member of the Communist Party?" — Alinsky smiled slightly, impishly, and replied: "I am not now, nor have I ever been a member of the John Birch Society, the Minute Men, the DiGiorgio Corporation, *or* the Communist Party." He then countered the committee questions, making it evident they had done no homework, that they were reacting to rumors handed them by agribusiness. It was an uneven contest, and the committee disengaged in awkward retreat.

The red baiting got nowhere, so the committee turned to the Delano farmers, to hear their side of the struggle. Growers Jack Pandol, Bruno Dispoto, and Dudley Steele took the stand. They were obviously angered by the Schenley and DiGiorgio actions, and they swore there were no labor disputes on their ranches. Pandol told the senators his workers had told him they wanted no part of a union, especially the Chavez union. Later, Pandol told me the smaller Delano growers felt trapped: "We're pawns in a big game, the big guys are using us and we're caught between

196

the Teamsters, who control the markets and transportation, and the AFL-CIO."

Two days after the state senate hearings ended, Chavez and Kircher announced the merger of the NFWA and the AWOC into the United Farm Workers Organizing Committee, of the AFL-CIO. Although Chavez had dreamed of a totally independent farm workers union, the announcement was no surprise. Fred Ross explained, "Cesar learned as he went along; he knew he had to have money, and he had to have more strength. Such a [merger] would bring him both money and strength . . . so he had to do it."

Chavez explained the merger this way: "We couldn't have two unions, I knew that, but see, I was worried that it would curb our style. You know? I was worried we wouldn't be able to boycott. . . . I told them I didn't mind joining, as long as we got a good deal, but we had to have the right to boycott. . . . [We] negotiated with Bill for, gee, well from March all the way through August, and then I had to do a lot of selling with the people in our union to get them to accept the idea. They were suspicious."

One of Chavez's first moves as director of the new UFWOC was to order all of the AWOC offices closed out. The activity of the handful of AWOC organizers still operating outside the Delano area was terminated, the credit cards and cars were collected, the offices vacated, the files brought to Delano. Not long after that Green retired. Two of the AWOC organizers caught up in the merger quit and went over to the Teamsters. Itliong was named second in command of the UFWOC, Padilla, Huerta, Tony Orendain, and Filipinos Phillip Vera Cruz and Andy Imutan were named Vice Presidents.

Mohn denounced the merger as a "desperate attempt of the AFL-CIO to revive its AWOC effort," and the raucous donnybrook was on. The DiGiorgio election campaign ground rules allowed both the Teamster and UFWOC organizers onto DiGiorgio property only during the noon hour and after work.

The elections involved the workers on both the Sierra Vista

197

Ranch and the smaller Borrego Springs Ranch. The UFWOC assigned 25 farm worker organizers and 15 or 20 of its Anglo volunteers to the election campaigns. Kircher imported a dozen AFL-CIO organizers to help out. Fred Ross bossed the Sierra Vista campaign; Chavez and Gil Padilla were in charge at Borrego Springs. The Teamsters brought in their professional organizers from all over the Western Conference, and Bill Grami, director of organizing for the Western Conference, supervised the campaigns on both ranches. He set up a Teamsters' headquarters in a two-room suite in a Delano motel.

Both sides cranked out reams of printed material. The UFWOC pamphleteering leaned heavily on the Robert Kennedy–Jimmy Hoffa feud and Kennedy's allegations that the Teamsters were a corrupt, gangster-ridden union that routinely sold out the workers' interests. The Teamsters relied on the John Birch–agribusiness red-baiting materials, charging the UFWOC effort was riddled with subversives, pinkos, and long-haired freaks from the New Left. The campaign materials and styles used on both the Sierra Vista and Borrego Springs ranches were quite similar. At noon and again after work the Teamsters and the UFWOC forces would gather where the workers ate lunch and where they parked their cars; a raucous battle of words would begin as soon as the workers appeared, each union trying through insult and slander to discredit the other in the eyes of those not yet committed.

On the Sierra Vista Ranch this daily confrontation took place in the "bull ring," a large open area between the company dining hall for permanent employees and the packing sheds. On one side of the bull ring a grove of large trees offered shade. This was where the seasonal field and shed workers went to eat their lunches. Out behind the grove were the big, ethnically segregated labor camps maintained by the company for single workers.

Each day the Teamsters had a big load of beer and soda pop waiting beside the grove of trees, when the lunch whistle blew. As the workers poured out of the packing sheds, and as truckloads of workers were driven in from the fields, the Teamster public-address truck began driving slowly through the bull ring, around the grove, through the camps, and back out into the bull ring. A carnival barker of a man named Art Chevaria drove and kept up constant chatter that was filled with humor, biting insults, and the cajoling banter used to pull suckers into the sideshows. Chevaria singled out Luis Valdez, the director of the *Teatro Compesino,* asking everyone in earshot if they knew Valdez had been to Castro's Cuba for training. And Chevaria delighted in picking on longhaired, bearded Anglos; he would attack their old clothes, their sandals, and ask if their rich parents were too stingy to buy decent clothing. He would call for volunteers to donate clothing and funds for a haircut and shave.

The Teamsters weren't the only ones bothered by the unkempt look of some of the New Left volunteers. Fred Ross finally put it to the youngsters straight: "I told them they were obviously out for their own liberation, not the liberation of the farm workers. That here the work was liberation of the farm workers. I told them we couldn't afford to lose them [workers] because of their [volunteers'] looks and that the farm workers didn't like their looks."

Nick Jones, a former member of SNCC at North Dakota State University, a college dropout who joined Students for a Democratic Society in Chicago and worked the UFWOC boycott efforts there and in Seattle, disagreed with Ross. Jones argued that he had seen no hostility shown by farm workers toward the volunteers — Nick was one of the scruffiest looking at the time — and Ross just laughed.

Ross said, "I told him the workers would let him know their feelings by simply ignoring him."

Two days later Nick Jones shaved, and eight years later laughed at himself, "You know, Fred was right. And I thought they were put off because I didn't speak Spanish well."

Ross had organized the DiGiorgio election campaign around the fact that every worker with two weeks of time at DiGiorgio since the previous September was eligible to vote.

The more voters turned out, the better the UFWOC chances. The company had been required to turn over the total list of eligible employees. Ross set the staff to cataloguing these names and addresses, letters were written to the migrants, and staff members in the boycott cities were given lists of names to contact in their areas. Every worker on the list still living within a 50-mile radius of the union headquarters was contacted personally.

Each day, Ross would hold three meetings for those working the Sierra Vista Ranch itself. Just before the noon break, the staff would meet to discuss strategy, how to confront the free sodas, the raucous voice of Art Chevaria, how to avoid anger and fighting at the insults that that man could generate. After the noon hour there was a critique, then preparation for talking to the workers in the evening in the camps. A final late-evening session finished the day. Administratively, a big election map was created, a car pool organized, schedules worked out. Every eligible worker would be taken to the edge of the ranch property, where American Arbitration Association–controlled buses would carry them to the polling place.

Two weeks before the election the DiGiorgio corporation sent another mailing to its employees: this time the company questioned the "good faith" of the NFWA and endorsed the Teamsters. No mention was made of the merger. William Grami, commenting on the company endorsement of his union: "We could imagine they [DiGiorgio] liked the businesslike approach of the Teamsters as compared to the revolutionary, vicious, irresponsible approach of the NFWA."

Reacting to the DiGiorgio endorsement of the Teamsters, Chavez told a magazine writer:

> We shook the tree, and now they are trying to pick the fruit. That's how they operate. And if they get away with it we'll never get them off our backs. Just when we get a grower softened up, they'll come in and try to make a deal with them. That's how they do it, through the bosses.

As the August sun sent temperatures rising above the 100-degree mark, the campaigning took on a fury and excitement that was confusing. With the Teamsters and UFWOC organizers screaming insults at each other, no one could predict what effect the campaigning was having on the workers, they had never been subjected to this kind of pressure before. The Teamsters claimed they had 1,000 signed authorization cards, the UFWOC confidently predicted most, if not all, farm workers supported *La Causa*.

On election eve the American Arbitration Association closed the ranch to campaigning and sealed off the exits. The next morning, only election officials, official observers, and the press were allowed into the voting area. The balloting was to take place in a wood-frame office on the ranch. The press was allowed to view the polls before they were opened, then was confined behind a rope barrier just outside the building entrances.

Although there were approximately 600 to 700 workers at Sierra Vista and half that many at Borrego Springs, nearly 2,000 were eligible to vote. This total included all of the original strikers. By nightfall, 1,317 farm workers cast votes. This was viewed as a testament to the UFWOC efforts to get the voters back from wherever they were currently working. Some of the voters were bused in by the UFWOC from the El Paso–Juarez area, some drove from the interior of Mexico to Delano for the voting. One man came all the way from the Mexican state of Jalisco, a journey of nearly 3,000 miles.

On the day of the election the UFWOC plans did not go smoothly. Fred Ross explained, "That morning we had the cars lined up around the block, near union headquarters, and we were dispatching them one at a time to pick up voters and drive them to the ranch. As one car would leave, another was coming back.

"The only problem we had was the eagerness of the workers themselves. Those who had not been picked up yet wouldn't wait at home, they came down to union headquarters, and this screwed things up. So we had to start hauling some from the office, but we could never be sure after that if we'd left somebody at home."

The balloting itself lasted 15 hours. And the AAA announced the count would take at least two days. The DiGiorgio elections contained two kinds of ballots, one for the packinghouse workers, the other for the field workers. A total of 1,317 ballots were cast, and the AAA reported just over 300 of them were challenged, but this had no effect on the outcome of the elections:

The packinghouse workers voted 94 to 43 in favor of the Teamsters.

The field worker vote: UFWOC 530, Teamsters 331.

Less than 20 workers voted "no union."

Donald Connors, DiGiorgio chief counsel, said the "results are inescapable." The field workers preferred the Chavez-led UFWOC.

Einar Mohn acknowledged the defeat in the fields, but he said the Teamsters were not giving up; they would contest the next scheduled vote at the big DiGiorgio Arvin Ranch. Mohn added the Teamsters would also continue to organize field labor whenever and wherever they chose.

Fred Ross recalled: "The morning after the election I was really tired, I don't think I've ever been that tired. The results weren't in yet, but already Cesar was talking about the Lamont-Arvin [DiGiorgio] elections. I just slipped out of the chair and went to sleep on the floor as Cesar and Jim planned what should be done down there. Cesar let us all have two or three days off before we started again, so I drove over to the beach and went to sleep for three days."

While the troops rested, Cesar and Kircher flew off to Texas to join the last miles of a march by the striking melon workers; they were walking from Rio Grande City 450 miles to the state capital in Austin. Chavez, buoyed by the DiGiorgio victory, spent a week with the Texas strikers before flying to Miami Beach to talk to the electrical workers' convention there, and to lobby for support from Joe Keenan's union. On the return trip, Chavez detoured to Mexico City to seek out the assistance of the Mexican unions; he asked them to help halt the flow of strikebreaking labor coming into both the Rio Grande Valley and California.

The expected battle at the DiGiorgio Arvin Ranch — the same ranch defended by Congressman Richard Nixon in 1952 — never really developed. At first the Teamsters began to campaign, but soon realized the UFWOC had the advantage. At the last moment the Teamsters attempted to pull out of the election. Of the 377 workers voting — the number was small this time because the grape season in the Arvin-Lamont area was long past — 285 favored the UFWOC. *La Causa* was very much like a freight train picking up speed as it worked its way through the track maze.

But the Teamsters did not give up. Their next chance came as UFWOC workers struck the Perelli-Minetti Vineyards. The Perelli-Minetti family crushes its own grapes and produces a number of good wines and a vermouth that has a large demand in specific markets. All during the Delano strikes, the union had left P-M alone because, in Chavez's words: "We wanted to have a place where we could recycle pickets, where we could put them to work, after they had been on the picket lines for a while and they needed a rest or to earn some money. . . . We had a lot of our people in there [P-M Vineyards] and one day they just decided to strike, so we had to take care of the strike."

Chavez said that within a week the company was asking to recognize the union and negotiate. Dolores Huerta, a volunteer named Marshall Ganz, and one of the union's volunteer attorneys met with the P-M officials and started negotiations. P-M asked that the picket lines be pulled off, but the UFWOC refused until agreement was reached and a contract signed.

Chavez said, "The next Monday, about 6:30 A.M., three buses came through the picket lines with scabs from other ranches, some were waving papers. We thought it was a leaflet, but they dropped one and it was a copy of a contract between the Teamsters and Perelli-Minetti.

"The Teamsters had been around since DiGiorgio, so we decided to really teach those bastards a lesson. We came that close [he held up his hand, measuring a quarter-inch between thumb and forefinger] to making Perelli-Minetti go bankrupt. We really put the squeeze on them with the boycott, we combed the United States, we were out with a vengeance. We would follow the product whenever it went; we knew by then, because of the Schenley boycott, where the wines went. . . . We finally found out where he was selling his bulk vermouth [wholesale quantities to bottlers of other labels] and we began to boycott the bulk buyer labels. We told them 'we are boycotting your whole line, even though only one label is scab.' . . . Perelli-Minetti's vermouth was very popular in New York and this bulk buyer was handling it, so he called Perelli-Minetti and told him no more. . . . There was one section of the winery that was devoted to kosher wines, and the workers told us when the rabbi used to come to consecrate the wine, so we followed him, we found out what was happening, then we got the Jewish groups behind us and we put the squeeze on."

Once the p-m boycott was well established, Chavez turned his attention back to the Texas strikes. The Texas Rangers and local lawmen were protecting the agribusiness interests; strikers were being arrested and worked over, picket lines were broken up. Chavez sent Jim Drake and Gil Padilla down to the Rio Grande Valley to reconnoiter and help out, if they could. Both Drake and Padilla ended up in a Texas jail. Drake explained, "When we got there we found they had arrested three guys for picketing down by the river, on La Caseda Farms. In that country, when they arrest you, they take you to another county so your friends can't find you. We knew that, so we put up a picket line around the county courthouse in Rio Grande City. We were going to march all night, so they couldn't take the pickets to another county. The sheriff came out with his deputies and told us if we didn't quit marching, he was going to arrest us, so we quit marching and stood on the steps of the courthouse. There were about 30 of us. The deputies ordered us off.

"Gilbert told us all to kneel, and he turned to me and told me to start praying.

"So I did.

"The cops said they'd count to ten and then arrest us, and Gil told me to pray for the sheriff.

"So I did: 'Oh, God, help this poor, ignorant sheriff!'

"That did it. He says to me, 'Hey, you. Come with me,' and he took me inside, but he didn't arrest me. A bunch of his deputies — they all had fat bellies hanging over their belts and 45s hanging on them and saps [blackjacks] — started asking questions. But when they saw a card in my wallet identifying me as a preacher, they just took me back and locked me up with the three pickets. An hour later Padilla was thrown in the same cell."

The next morning they were brought before the judge, a man who, it turned out, had proper respect for religion and preachers. He offered to let Drake go free because he was a minister. Drake said, "I told him I didn't want to go free, I wanted them to arrest me formally, and book me, I wanted a record to show they had arrested me while I was praying. . . . Gil was standing beside me, and when I refused to be released, he raised his hand and told the judge that although he was not a preacher, he was a social worker and he would certainly like to go free. The judge couldn't figure out what to do with us, so they turned us both loose."

The strike in Texas, the P-M boycott, the faltering negotiations with DiGiorgio, the attempts to get Christian Brothers from backing away from its recognition of the UFWOC, the strikes against the Delano grape growers, all were producing problems that needed attention. And always there was the need for money, for food, for supplies. In Los Angeles a former Christian Brother, Leroy Chatfield, was staging fund-raising events; folk singer Joan Baez did two performances in concert and brought in $20,000; a Beverly Hills lawyer opened his home for a $100-a-couple champagne party and raised $13,000.

In Bakersfield, a P-M boycott picket line around a Mayfair market produced an interesting side effect. Drake was running this particular line, but the store and the cops made the farm workers stay out on public property, away from the store. The store manager let a group of conservative old ladies set up a counter picket line in front of the store's front doorway. A brash young attorney, just out of law school, walked onto the scene, without knowing anyone. His name was Jerry Cohen, and at the time he was working for an OEO-funded firm called California Rural Legal Assistance, in McFarland, 30 miles to the north.

Cohen said, "These old Bircher ladies were right next to the door and that pissed me off; so I went to the manager and said either the Bircher ladies go out to the sidewalk, or the union pickets come into the door, and so we negotiated and all the pickets got to be by the door . . . okay? So I forgot about it, it wasn't a big deal, except Carol Silver [his boss at CRLA] called me in and accused me of being on the picket line . . ."

Cohen had come to the CRLA McFarland office because he thought he was going to be able to help the farm workers. McFarland was the scene of the first rose strike. It was only five miles south of Delano, and should have located him in a position to aid farm workers. Silver said no, CRLA rules prevented him from being involved with UFWOC. In the meantime, Drake reported to Cesar and others that a CRLA attorney had helped them. The union's legal staff had all been volunteers; the latest, Alex Hoffman, had worked himself into a state of physical and nervous exhaustion. A new lawyer was needed, and Cohen was recruited by Leroy Chatfield. After a brief meeting with Chavez, Jerry Cohen quit CRLA and became the UFWOC chief counsel.

Christian Brothers winery was still dragging its feet, contending it had agreed only to hold recognition elections. An election was scheduled by the state conciliation service, but Chavez backed out when he learned labor contractors were working the crews over to prejudice the vote. Chavez charged: "We know Christian Brothers are anti-union and their operation is a commercial venture like any other; they are separated from the Church and its social policies. We expected Christian Brothers to live up to the social pronouncements of the Church, but they have not."

A Christian Brothers boycott was threatened.

By early March of 1967 the confrontation between the UFWOC and the Teamsters over jurisdiction in P-M vineyards was moving toward a settlement. The boycott had hurt the company badly, and all the signs indicated the Perelli-Minetti family was willing to settle, if the Teamsters and the UFWOC could reach an agreement. Labor negotiator Sidney Korshak was brought in by the company and he served as go-between in some secret talks between the Teamsters and the Chavez forces.

In the midst of all this, Chavez got a call from 30 families of hungry farm workers. Rains had kept them out of the fields in Sutter County, north of Sacramento, and they were without funds. Because they were not residents of the county, the welfare department would not help them; because they could not pay rent, the low-rent housing authority was evicting the 150 men, women, and children. In desperation they rebelled, and turned to the UFWOC for help. Cesar Chavez and his ubiquitous cousin Manuel dropped everything and drove 275 miles north to Yuba City to help in the futile protest. Such interruptions were common, but one by one the various issues were resolved; Christian Brothers agreed to a "card-check" election, conducted by the state conciliation service, and learned its workers did, in fact, prefer the UFWOC. Negotiations were started. The DiGiorgio contract negotiations were submitted to binding arbitration, and arbitrators set a $1.65 minimum wage, a nickel less than the Schenley contract. The same basic fringe benefits and the establishment of the hiring hall were allowed. Almadén Vineyard and then the E. and J. Gallo Company, the world's largest vintners, recognized the UFWOC, after card-check elections.

By mid-June the talks between Teamsters and the UFWOC reached the critical stage. Rabbi Joseph Glazer, head of an interfaith committee that had been acting as a mediator during the talks, announced agreement was near and scheduled a press conference in San Francisco. Then something went wrong and he had to back off and cancel the press conference. While Cohen and Huerta carried on the talks,

Cesar flew back to Texas to help focus attention on the growers' importation of Mexican nationals to break the strike. At the same time UFWOC supporters in Washington, D.C., were pressuring Secretary of Labor Willard Wirtz to close off the inflow of strikebreaking Mexican workers. Wirtz, after sending investigators into Texas, certified there were six farms under strike, and he invoked the regulations prohibiting the importation of alien workers into a strike.

Chavez flew back to California for more talks with the Teamsters, and to center the UFWOC attack on one table-grape grower, the 11,000-acre Giumarra Vineyards. He warned the Giumarras that if they did not agree to union recognition elections, the company would become the target of the union's next boycott. The UFWOC contended it had had a strike at Giumarra since September of 1965; the company emphatically denied this, saying there were no strikes at any of the Giumarra's vineyard locations in Tulare and Kern counties. As the long fight with Giumarra began, the battle over the P-M vineyards ended.

On July 21, 1967, Rabbi Glazer presided over a press conference in the Veterans of Foreign Wars Hall in Delano: Perelli-Minetti Company had agreed to turn its Teamster contract over to the UFWOC, the Teamsters had agreed to withdraw from the vineyards, and a jurisdictional agreement was worked out. The UFWOC recognized the Teamsters' rights to the canneries, packinghouses, and freezers; the Teamsters recognized the UFWOC's jurisdiction over all field labor.

CHAPTER TEN : THE FAST

The farmers made ideal adversaries. Their tactics were predictable, their public relations efforts dull and unimaginative. None of their moribund maneuvers worked . . . for long. Agribusiness was entrenched and defensive, the Chavez forces were mobile and aggressive; time and again the issues created by the farmers were turned by Chavez to the advantage of the farm workers.

The farmers controlled most of the local press, and in the past that — and their rough tactics — had been enough. The small daily and weekly newspapers told the farmers' side of the conflict without reservation, and the small-town editors had offered their opinions about what should be done with "outside agitators" and old-style communists and the newer variety of long-haired radicals. But Chavez sidestepped the small-town media and took *La Causa* out into the national arena, where the big influential metropolitan newspapers and network news departments were attracted to the farm workers' struggle. Agribusiness had no economic leverage over the big-city press, and farm spokesmen were soon complaining that the metropolitan labor writers, network news crews, and magazine journalists were biased, that they reported with a left-leaning tilt that obscured the truth about Delano. Despite what the liberal journalists reported, the farmers insisted *there was no strike*.

Never before had a strike been worked to the lasting advantage of the farm laborers. In the past they had been kept voiceless and powerless because they had no access to a public forum and they were unable to shut off the growers' inexhaustible supplies of cheap labor imported from China, Japan, the Philippines, Puerto Rico, Yemen, and Mexico, always Mexico. As Chavez studied the lessons of farm labor history it became obvious the UFWOC's only route to power had to come through alternative tactics, tactics that developed from a power base outside agribusiness's sphere of influence.

Over the years, Chavez had assiduously developed an ever-increasing number of contacts with men and women who were sympathetic to the causes of the CSO (Community Services Organization) and then the farm workers. These contacts formed a constituency that could be developed into a power base within the urban churches, labor unions, civic organizations, and political bodies. The national press was the conduit through which this power base could be energized and expanded. The Chavez plan was to develop and harness the power of public opinion; once stimulated, such power could make itself felt either politically or economically. Because economic pressure appeared to be the fastest and the most direct route to agribusiness collective bargaining agreements, Chavez launched the consumer boycotts. By using both the primary boycott — informational picketing urging customers to shun specific products within a market — and the secondary boycott — the picketing of a whole store, urging customers to boycott the entire market because it carried the offensive product — the farm workers increased their pressures.

In 1965 the farmers had underestimated Chavez and the NFWA. They had economic control over Delano, and the power that went with it; and they foresaw no problems they could not handle in the traditional ways. When the grape pickers walked out of the vineyards, the farmers declared there was no strike and shouted their warnings about communist agitators stirring up trouble within the work force.

The red-hunting California State Senate Subcommittee on Un-American Activities responded. Its investigators snooped around the grape strike, followed up John Birch Society innuendoes, pored over the 5,000 photos and background dossiers in the sheriff's office files, and came away frustrated. When the 1967 subcommittee report was finally issued it didn't even make good reading. The report writers waltzed all the way around Farmer Brown's red barn, poked under the haystacks, recounted the communist horror stories of the 1930s, dropped in the names of kids from SDS, SNCC, CORE, and the W.E.B. Du Bois Club, mentioned three or four real live communists seen in Delano, and after all of the stalling and padding, the staff reported on page 77:

We are certain that the 500 members of the AWOC and a large majority of the members of the NFWA were in no way connected with any of the New Left or subversive organiza-

210

tions that swarmed into Delano. The concern of the membership unions, and after they merged of the resulting union, was and is to obtain better wages and working conditions.

The farmers were angry. They hadn't expected the report to say the Chavez-led movement was a legitimate union bent on normal union business. But that was the case; the UFWOC was a union, albeit a new one just taking permanent shape and form. As contracts were signed, its operations were becoming structured into hiring halls, social service centers, medical clinics, and administrative offices. More and more, the striking of ranches and the conflict with lawmen over restrictive court injunctions limiting picket activities became the instruments of confrontation. Rather than exerting economic pressure on the growers by depriving them of workers, the strikers were using the confrontations to provoke issues that could be exploited by boycotters in the metropolitan areas.

Magazines like *Saturday Evening Post, Look, The New Yorker,* and *Business Week* joined with the metropolitan dailies and television news programs in recording the strike and boycott. *Time* devoted its July 4th cover story to the "Grapes of Wrath, 1969: Mexican Americans on the March." According to *Time*:

> The welfare of agricultural workers has rarely captured US attention in the past, but the grape strike — la huelga — and the boycott accompanying it have clearly engaged a large part of the nation. . . . As if on a holy crusade, the strikers stage marches that resemble religious pilgrimages, bearing aloft their own stylized black Aztec eagle on a red field along with the images of the Virgin of Guadalupe, patroness of Mexicans and particularly those who work the soil. . . . La Causa's magnetic champion and the country's most prominent Mexican American leader is Cesar Estrada Chavez, 42, a one-time grape picker who combines a mystical mien with peasant earthiness. La Causa is Chavez's whole life; for it he has impoverished himself and endangered his health fasting.

In soft, slow speech, he urges his people — nearly 5,000,000 in the US — to rescue themselves from society's cellar. As he sees it, the first step is to win the battle of the grapes.

Conservative columnists William Buckley and James Kilpatrick were attracted to the subject. After a trip to Delano, Kilpatrick wrote about, "Hippies, yippies, priests, professors, political figures, and housewives with time on their hands — all of them whooping it up for the downtrodden grape pickers of Kern County, California . . ." Kilpatrick called the farm worker movement "a hoax, a fantasy, a charade, a tissue of half truths and whole fabrications. . . . [To] swallow the Chavez line you must believe grape workers in the Delano area are miserably paid, wretchedly housed, and cruelly treated . . ."

While the total media exposure was invaluable to the boycott of California table grapes, Chavez did not — and still does not — enjoy the public role. When asked about his notoriety, Chavez physically winced and turned away, shaking his head. He acknowledged such things had to be endured, because they were necessary to build the union, but he added, "There is a tremendous price you pay for this notoriety. It has an effect on your family, and on you, yourself. It is very sad that it should happen this way, but it does. We are in a society where people want to know who is the head of a movement, there is a tremendous demand for that identification. I am talking about the outside public now. But there is also a demand within the movement to have someone who can tell the grower, who can tell the judge, who can speak out on TV. You know when some of the workers see me on TV they come up later and say 'We were on TV last night and I heard you . . .' They use the word 'we' just like they were there with me . . ."

As Cesar talks about the union, and its demands on his time, it is obvious he is actually operating on four separate levels: He is the figurehead who must keep a high public profile; a tough administrator who can be something of a tyrant; an able organizer who relates to the field workers on a personal level; and a family man, a husband, and father of eight. For most men there is not enough time in the day to take on all four of these roles. Chavez manages by working incredibly long hours, and by focusing his entire attention on one subject at a time.

Chris Hartmire, after watching Chavez for a dozen years, observed: "The public does not see Cesar as a hard-nosed leader, but he is. He has a rare combination of organizational skill and toughness and a deep religious conviction, coupled with a healthy personality. He takes this healthy personality with this organizational experience and toughness and religious conviction and pours it 100 percent into the struggle. At some point in history he and Helen decided this is what he had to do and that he would be with her and the kids when the struggle allowed that to happen."

Commenting on the Chavez family, Dolores Huerta said, "Helen is the strength that holds the family together; she and Cesar agreed in the beginning that if he was working with the people, the people had the priority, and the family must understand."

But Helen Chavez and the children have played a far more important role than just understanding. They are the great levelers; they bring a sense of reality to Chavez's life. Chavez explained, "Don't let the public part fool you. Me, here, I am just a plain human being, and I get reminded of this constantly at home. My wife sees me just as the same old guy, you know. She has the advantage, she is removed from the public part and she lets me know very definitely who I am. I think that sometimes, although I don't enjoy being taken down, it is a good thing, that reminder at home . . .

"My kids don't like the public stuff either. I don't think the kids resent my being away. Maybe some but not much. Generally they don't go to public functions with me. If they saw what happens there, I think they might resent it. I remember taking them to a performance of the Ballet Folklorico, and they let me know they didn't want to go again because the people, the reporters, and photographers wouldn't let us alone and the kids said they felt like freaks.

They didn't like it and I didn't like it either. I still don't like it, when they point a camera at me I have this tremendous battle inside. I want to say, 'Don't take my picture!' but I have had to decide that the best thing to do is just submit, and try to act normal, to forget it."

As a public figure, on tour, campaigning for the boycott, for a political ally or against a farmer-sponsored legislative proposal, Chavez has learned to submit to those around him who plan the meetings, speeches, and tours each day. As an administrator, he runs the union; and, frequently he will dominate the union's board of directors. It is the board that is supposed to set the policies for Cesar and the staff to follow, but his feelings are so strong in some subject areas, Chavez frequently rides over objections and overwhelms any arguments.

Bill Kircher gave an example: "In 1967 the UFWOC had won contracts with Schenley, DiGiorgio, Perelli-Minetti, Christian Brothers, Almadén, Paul Masson, and a few other wineries. We had a meeting in Delano, 10 or 12 of us. I wanted to go after the rest of the winery operations because they were the most vulnerable to boycotts; I wanted to go after everything that was in a bottle until we had 100 percent of that part of the grape industry.

"Cesar wanted to go after the table-grape guys. . . . [He] saw them as the dirty sons-of-bitches that had shit on the workers for so many years. Cesar said the farm workers would never be men until they could prove themselves by taking on that segment of the grape industry. He was so aggressive on his side of the argument, I found myself alone, and that's when they set out after the table grapes . . ." Kircher, a big, forceful man, used to dominating the scene, laughed a bit as he told the story, but it was obvious he was still awed by the strength of Chavez's determination.

Chavez has very strong ideas, based in part on his own experiences and prejudices, and in part on his feel for what "the people" want. He likes to be close to the farm workers, to keep in touch with their feelings, but as the union began to grow, he found the NFWA and then the UFWOC bureaucracy insulating him. On several occasions as we talked about the union's bureaucratic problems he would stop, sigh, and say he wished he was back, in the beginning, back with the house meetings and the close contact with the people.

Pablo Espinosa, a migrant farm worker from the Rio Grande Valley of Texas and now a union organizer, explained: "Cesar gave me attention that I had never had before; I don't know how to describe it. I wanted somebody to listen to me. You know, you never shake hands with the labor contractor, you never shake hands with a foreman, you never shake hands with your boss. I wanted somebody to pay attention to me, as a man, as a person.

"Cesar had the direct attention for us, not like the politician that shakes your hand, says 'how are you?' and pats you on the back and is gone . . . Cesar gave his attention to me. We didn't have much to say, you know. He asked about the strike. What I thought. What did I want to do? He ask about my interest in the union." As Espinosa talked it became apparent he was not talking about a personal meeting with Chavez, but a group meeting. Espinosa had been one of a dozen workers from Woodville who had come to Delano one evening to meet with Chavez.

Espinosa said, "Cesar made me feel like nobody made me feel. Manuel and Jim and Gilbert used to tell us about Cesar this and Cesar that, and I really didn't pay all that much attention, not until I met him."

But there was more to Espinosa's feelings than just the meeting with Chavez. Even in the middle of a strike, the union was paying attention to the tiny problems that are important to a worker's life. Espinosa and his family were living in a 10-by-16 tin shack in the Woodville farm labor camp, and he was interested in learning to repair his own car to save money. A door-to-door magazine salesman talked him into making a down payment on an $80 set of books that he thought would be instruction manuals. Instead he began receiving do-it-yourself magazines on boating and other hobbies. There had been a language confusion and the salesman had used a lot of flimflam, so one of the UFWOC's

215

volunteer lawyers had little trouble in breaking the contract and frightening the salesman off.

It is this kind of service that is one of the founding stones in the Chavez movement. Within weeks after the first union contracts were signed, Chavez asked Leroy Chatfield to establish a network of service centers throughout the farming areas of California and Arizona. Chatfield, a former Christian Brother who gave up his vows to join *La Causa*, raised $25,000 from a foundation, AFL-CIO's Industrial Union Department contributed $50,000 more to the project.

The union purchased 40 acres of alkali land west of Delano, near the city dump, and began to construct its service center–union headquarters complex. Under Chatfield's direction the service center became the organizational umbrella under which the union developed its medical clinics and its cooperative auto supply and service station. Richard Chavez constructed an adobe gasoline station, complete with lubrication racks and shops for mechanical repairs on the 40-acre site. The credit union — still managed by Helen Chavez — was brought into the service center jurisdiction, and Chatfield later developed the health and welfare programs that were to give the farm workers their first medical insurance.

The union's land was named "The Forty Acres," and it became something special to Chavez; he had trees planted and talked of a cooperative farm; an irrigation system was built and pasture was planted for a few head of cattle to graze. The United Auto Workers donated $50,000 for the construction of an administrative building, and it was dedicated by the UFWOC to the memory of Roy Reuther. The union staff moved from the two old houses and the storefront at 102 Albany out to the Forty Acres. The new building had offices, a reception area, and a big meeting room that doubled as the hiring hall for the dispatch of workers to ranches under contract.

Chavez had an office in the northeast corner of the building; Larry Itliong moved his old AWOC operations from the Filipino Community Hall to the Forty Acres, and he took up offices just down the hall from Chavez. Administratively the UFWOC was run by a board of directors weighted four to three between the old NFWA and AWOC; the board members were Chavez, Huerta, Padilla, and Julio Hernandez on the Mexican side, and Itliong, Phil Vera Cruz, and Andy Imutan on the Filipino side.

From 1967 through 1968 the union not only was fighting its guerrilla warfare against the table-grape growers, but it was also feinting toward the wine grapes. Kircher had been right, the vintners were very susceptible to boycott pressures; even the threat of a boycott produced results, and, one by one, Almadén, Paul Masson, Gallo, Novitiate, and Franzia recognized that the UFWOC did represent the vineyard workers and began negotiating labor contracts. Chavez left the negotiations up to Dolores Huerta.

She explained, "Our first contract language came right out of the ILWU (Longshoremen) pineapple-worker contracts in Hawaii. I met with our workers to see what they wanted, and I put their ideas into contract language. If the grower wanted to negotiate, things moved pretty fast, but if they didn't want to negotiate, then the talks dragged out like Christian Brothers. They were very difficult, and this is where persistence pays off, you just have to keep hammering away. You may have to have five meetings to change two words . . . this is where Cesar gets uptight. He never really quite trusted what I did until he started to negotiate himself; then he found it was pretty hard to get the kind of language that I had gotten, and he started respecting what I had done.

"When I am negotiating, I go by my instincts, and I guess that is what is hard for people to understand. I think my instincts are really good, and I know what we want. Where Cesar is the head of the union and is forced into compromising, I'm not, and he can always override me, if I go too far."

The wine-grape victories were heady stuff, but the primary fight was with the table-grape industry in general and the Giumarra Vineyards particularly. Six thousand of the Giumarra's 11,000 acres were in vines, the payroll fluctuated

217

from 200 permanent workers up to 2,000 at the peak of harvest.

The Giumarras were tough, aggressive opponents; they were well financed, and they had solid political connections. Giumarra lawyers went into court frequently and argued successfully that they needed protection for their workers; understanding judges issued injunctions restricting the number of pickets the UFWOC could place around the various ranches; the judges also banned, or severely limited, the use of portable voice amplifiers called "bullhorns." No matter that higher courts later were to find such injunctions were an abridgment of free assembly and free speech; the court orders had their intended effect, to restrict and inhibit union activities.

With the strike line activity limited, the growers could continue to import strikebreaking labor without major confrontations. Secretary of Labor Willard Wirtz had ordered the flow of Mexican aliens north, across the border to the struck ranches, shut off, but the order had little effect. The farmers continued to use alien labor, legal and illegal. The workers with entry documents artfully dodged Wirtz's orders, and those without documents sought out a coyote — a smuggler. These operators charged the alien $250 to $300 to bring him across and find him a job.

Through the early spring of 1968 the union focused its attention on fighting the flow of strikebreakers. UFWOC members sought out the farms using illegal alien workers and reported them to the U.S. Border Patrol. Patrol apprehension rates soared, but not as fast as the flow of illegal aliens coming through the border; and the alien returned to Mexico frequently slipped back across and returned to work within a few days.

On May 30th, U.S. Attorney General Ramsey Clark flew into San Francisco to address a convention; as he drove up to the hotel he was confronted by 200 UFWOC pickets protesting that the Justice Department's Immigration and Naturalization Service was not doing enough to enforce the laws. Six days later Clark issued orders to crack down on the flow of illegal strikebreakers. The order was dramatic, and it put the administration on record in opposition to the use of illegal aliens, but it had little practical effect, so Chavez switched tactics. He ordered Manuel Chavez to the border area, to begin a concerted drive to organize the thousands of alien workers living in Mexicali and Calexico. He asked the Mexican government for permission to establish a medical clinic in Mexicali's *Colonia Nueva*. Permission was granted. The clinic, in addition to providing medical care, was an attractive organizing tool.

Simultaneously with the fight over the green-card and illegal alien strikebreakers, the union cranked up its boycott efforts against Giumarra. But the decision to single out just one table-grape grower was causing too many problems. There was no practical way to boycott just one grower. The table grapes on the supermarket counters were seldom identified by producer, and, when they were, labels could be switched. Chavez changed tactics, ordering an all-out effort against all table grapes not carrying the union's black Aztec eagle imprint. The UFWOC had been depending a great deal upon volunteers from the Civil Rights Movement to staff the boycott efforts in the major cities. These volunteers complained their efforts were hampered by the fact that they were obviously not farm workers. They asked that some farm workers be sent out on the boycott. Chavez agreed and asked for farm workers to volunteer. The AFL-CIO unions were asked to help supply transportation, food, and shelter for these farm worker boycotters. An alliance of Colorado unions donated enough money to buy a new 60-passenger bus that was given to the UFWOC to transport boycotters across the country. The group of farm workers was dispatched to New York City, where the central labor council endorsed the boycott and offered the help of its member unions. Paul Hall's Seafarers' Union housed and fed the boycotters while they were in New York City.

But the boycott wasn't going anywhere; there was no emotional steam in it, no dramatic issues to exploit. The whole UFWOC effort was turning dull — there was no spark, no new confrontation. A restlessness was setting in among the young Chicanos, they wanted action. They had watched the civil rights protest grow, they had seen the Watts riots in Los Angeles on television, they had heard the cry of Black Nationalism from Malcolm X, and watched as the ghettos of Newark and Detroit were burned and sacked by rioting blacks. In Denver, tough-talking Rodolfo (Corky) Gonzales was leading a move toward Brown Nationalism and Chicano Power; in Crystal City, Texas, José Angel Gutierrez led Chicano activists in verbal and political attacks on the *gringo* establishment; in northern New Mexico, Reies Tijerina and his followers gained notoriety when they seized a federal forest campground, took rangers hostage, then raided the Rio Arriba County Courthouse in a violent shootout. Tijerina proclaimed the land belonged to the Indian and Mexican populations, not to the *gabachos* who had stolen it.

For some within the farm worker movement, the nonviolence of Cesar Chavez was a tactic that had been tried, and found wanting; these young men and women felt it was time to return to the tactics of Pancho Villa and Emiliano Zapata. The Mexican revolution had been violent and romantic, and they wanted the struggle of the farm workers to follow the same course. Older people began to listen to the talk, and to nod their heads. Such undercurrents worried Chavez, and, in late February of 1968, he called an unexpected meeting of the membership to announce that he had started on a personal fast February 15th. The fast was an act of penance, because the union was moving toward violence; but the fast was also an act of militancy on Chavez's part, started in the hope that it would counter the violent rhetoric.

Chavez said, "You reap what you sow; if we become violent with others, then we will become violent among ourselves. Social justice for the dignity of man cannot be won at the price of human life. You cannot justify what you want for *La Raza*, for the people, and in the same breath destroy one life. . . . I will not compromise. Racism is wrong, racism is not the way, nationalism is not the way."

For his fast, Chavez walked to the Forty Acres. He had a

220

Helen and Cesar Chavez during fast.
Photo by Ronald B. Taylor

Chavez attends farm worker Mass during fast.
Photo by Ronald B. Taylor

cot installed in a small storage room within the adobe service station building. The room became a monastic cell; just outside, and across a narrow breezeway, there was a larger room that was turned into a combination chapel and administrative office. From this room Chatfield directed the logistics of the fast; he created a tent city outside the service station to house the hundreds of farm worker families that came to spend a day or two to meet with Chavez and show their solidarity.

In the second week of the fast, news of what was happening was leaked to reporters from the Los Angeles *Times, Time* magazine, and TV newsmen. Overnight the fast became a national news event. For 25 days Chavez drank only water. As word of the fast spread through the farm worker communities of California and Arizona, the people started coming to Delano. They stood in line for hours waiting for their turn to meet and talk to this man who, by the act of religious fasting, became a symbol of their suffering. The fast became a powerful organizing tool. Chatfield explained, "Cesar would talk about the workers' home area, he would ask about the conditions there, and then he'd suggest they should try to help themselves, to help form a coordinated effort among the workers, and they would agree. It was like the march [to Sacramento] only different, instead of his going to the people as he did on the march, they came to him."

Jerry Cohen said, "The fast meant a lot of different things to different people. I could see the fast really molded the union for the first time. We had nine different contracts at the time, but we had nine separate ranch committees, working separately. That fast gave us an opportunity to bring all the ranch committees together on a project, and it was Giumarra that gave us the project we needed."

Giumarra had court injunctions against mass picketing, and the union had refused to obey these court-imposed restrictions. Giumarra had gone back into court and argued the union had violated the injunction on 12 occasions and asked for contempt citations. The judge ordered Chavez to appear in court to determine if the farm labor leader and his union were in contempt of the court. A media event within a media event was in the making. On February 26th, Chavez appeared, weak and disheveled; assisted by Chatfield and Cohen, he walked to the courthouse between lines of kneeling farm workers. The workers — their numbers were estimated between 800 and 1,000 — were absolutely silent. The line of silent, kneeling workers extended from the courthouse steps, through the main doors, into the hallways, up the stairs to the courtroom itself.

Cohen explained, "The ranch committees organized the protest, they led the workers to the courthouse, and ordered them to kneel and pray. It was the first time they had worked together. It shook everybody. Johnny Giumarra, Jr., and about four others walked into the judge's chambers. They wanted to kick all the farm workers out of the courthouse. I had some cases about peaceful demonstrations near public buildings that I was going to argue . . . but the judge looked at Giumarra and said, 'Kick the workers out of here? If I did that it would be just another example of *gringo* justice.' To hear that coming from a Kern County judge was something . . ."

It was obvious the fasting Chavez was in no shape for a protracted court appearance, so the judge postponed the hearing until April 22nd. (A few weeks later the Giumarra attorneys quietly asked the judge to dismiss the case; the kind of mileage Chavez worked out of the initial court appearance gave the boycotters something they could use for months and the Giumarras weren't about to repeat the performance.) Much of the strategy for this particular demonstration was developed by Cohen; while he was without experience when he came to the union, he was bright and aggressive and he soon developed the kind of law practice that might be described as legal karate. He learned to use the law — and lawsuits — to expose grower tactics and enhance worker power positions.

Chavez allowed him the room to try and fail and try again. Cohen said, "Cesar has a really good ability to instill confidence in people. You go and get the shit kicked out of you, say in court, and you tell him and he says 'That's great' and turns whatever happened into something good. You soon learn that there isn't a hell of a lot that can happen that can't be turned around into some good. He has a lot of guts, and you can sense his guts and people get a lot of strength from the positions he takes or the things he does."

I asked Cohen why he thought Chavez had fasted. He answered, "Cesar was mad. There had been a lot of loose talk about violence. He had told them the life of one man or woman was worth more than the success of the cause, but they were not listening, so he decided he had to teach them a lesson. They had to find out who had the balls, and he showed them. *He scared the hell out of them.* He didn't say, 'I'm not going to eat until you guys shut your mouths about violence,' he just said the union was committed to nonviolence, then started fasting. The people responded like 'God, what is this guy doing?' The people were scared and frustrated, they didn't know what the hell to do with him.

"Then, too, it was the third year of the strike and there wasn't much happening. So Cesar gave them something, he sort of spent himself. He talked to them privately and attended the Mass each night. What I liked about the Masses was the spirit of the farm workers. People came from all over the valley. I know that Cesar could feel it too; he saw what a fantastic cement that fast was . . . it was an amazing organizing tool."

The 25-day fast came to an end on March 11, 1968, in the public park in Delano. Senator Robert Kennedy was there to break bread with Chavez, and to lend his support to the farm worker cause. No man in American politics had so stirred the poor people in this nation, no one had responded to the white poverty in Appalachia, the black poverty of the south and the urban ghettos and now the brown poverty of the farm worker like "Bobby." There were 4,000 farm workers in the Delano park that day, and when Kennedy arrived he found them on both sides of a mile-long processional path, waiting for him. He walked through the entire group, flanked by three aides.

Every farm worker there tried to touch him, to kiss him, to shake his hand. In the press of the mob, Kennedy staff men and Dolores Huerta tried to form a human shield around him. The crowds, the photographers, and TV crews were swept up in the turmoil.

All the newsmen were up close, moving, backing along in front of Kennedy. I was blocking for Fresno *Bee* photographer Carl Crawford, trying to force enough room for him to get his pictures. He would get swept away in the ebb and flow and have to fight his way back.

Dolores spotted me and yelled, "Ron, help us."

She held her hand out, and I grabbed it and was pulled into the shielding circle around Kennedy. It was hard to keep your feet as the crowds pushed hard to look, to touch. Kennedy, reaching over our arms, smiling, moved hand over hand, left then right, touching, shaking hands. Finally, we were before the truck trailer platform and someone got Kennedy into a small roped-off area in front that was reserved for Chavez, Helen, Cesar's mother and father, Librado and Juana Chavez. Kennedy sat next to Cesar.

There was an ecumenical Mass — ministers, rabbis, and priests participated — then speeches and the ceremonial breaking of the bread ended the fast. After Chavez and Kennedy had broken bread the senator mounted the platform and talked to the workers. He advocated inclusion of farm labor under the NLRA, he urged a crackdown on the use of green-card aliens and illegal aliens as strikebreaking workers, and he brought cheers when he said, "Farm workers need equal rights under the laws."

Several times Kennedy attempted to speak in Spanish, but his Boston Irish accent was too strong. Dolores Huerta, peering over his shoulder to see his text, translated his Boston Irish Spanish into the much softer Mexican version, and everyone laughed. Kennedy, obviously enjoying the moment, looked down at Cesar, and asked: "Am I destroying the Spanish language?"

Chavez had prepared a statement, but was too weak to read it himself. An aide read:

Catholic Worker leader Dorothy Day on UFW picket line.
Photo by Bob Fitch, Black Star

Chavez and Robert F. Kennedy.
Photo by Ronald B. Taylor

Chavez and Walter Reuther. Larry Itliong at left of Reuther.
Photo by Ronald B. Taylor

Our lives are really all that belong to us . . . only by giving our lives do we find life. I am convinced that the truest act of courage, the strongest act of manliness, is to sacrifice ourselves for others in a totally nonviolent struggle for justice. To be a man is to suffer for others. God help us be men.

Months later, in an open letter to an agribusiness association, Chavez tried to explain the fast and the movement's nonviolent philosophies:

Knowing of Gandhi's admonition that fasting is the last resort in place of the sword, during a most critical time in our movement last February, I undertook a 25-day fast. I repeat to you the principle enunciated to the membership at the start of the fast: "If to build our union required the deliberate taking of life, either the life of a grower or his child or the life of a farm worker or his child then I would choose not to see the union built."

We advocate militant nonviolence as our means for social revolution and to achieve justice for our people, but we are not blind or deaf to the desperate and moody winds of human frustration, impatience, and rage that blow among us. Gandhi himself admitted that if his only choices were cowardice or violence, he would choose violence. Men are not angels and the time and tides wait for no man. Precisely because of these powerful human emotions, we have tried to involve the masses of people in their own struggle. Participation and self-determination remain the best experience of freedom; and free men instinctively prefer democratic change . . . only the enslaved in despair have need of violent overthrow. . . . We hate the agribusiness system that seeks to keep us enslaved, and we shall overcome and change it not by retaliation or bloodshed, but by a determined nonviolent struggle carried on by those masses of farm workers who intend to be free and human.

The union's primary nonviolent tactic is the boycott. Dolores Huerta explained, "The whole thrust of our boycott is to get as many supporters involved as you can. You have to get organizers who can go out to the unions, to the churches, to the students and get that support. You divide an area up — in New York we split it up into eight sections — and each organizer is responsible for an area. We get supporters to help us picket and leaflet; we go after one chain at a time, telling the shoppers where they can find other stores."

From 1968 through 1969 the UFWOC maintained boycott structures in 40 to 50 cities. One or two farm worker families were assigned to each city to work with the Anglo staff volunteers. It had been decided the union could not support salaried people, and everyone — brown, black, or white, from Chavez on down — was paid $5 a week and expenses. Even so the cost of the strikes, the boycotts, and setting up the union administration was running from $30,000 to $40,000 a month. The boycotters were supposed to find room and board wherever they could and to seek out financial support. In New York and Los Angeles they got good support from liberal entertainers, like Pete Seeger and Peter, Paul, and Mary. Their concerts brought in from $5,000 to $15,000 each. Dolores Huerta traveled the liberal cocktail circuit speaking and lobbying.

For each volunteer the boycott is a trial-and-error learning process. Nick Jones, who has coordinated the boycotts in eight metropolitan areas in eight years, explained, "At first, you don't have any idea what the hell you are doing, but after a while you get a feeling for how it's done. It takes six months to crank up a boycott in any city; it takes time to get the churches and the unions and students organized into work- able units."

As he talked we were driving back to Boston from a small upper New England town where an interfaith committee had been meeting to discuss the boycott. Two of the liberal Protestant ministers — both outfitted in corduroy sport coats and turtleneck sweaters and puffing on smelly pipes — were concerned about the "moral implications of taking sides in a labor issue," and there was a practical problem: if they became involved they might lose a $500 movie projector donated to a church youth project by local Kiwanians. They and their parishioners were concerned Christians who wanted to help, but was the boycott the way to do it? Was it fair to picket a store, asking customers to turn away just because grapes were being sold?

The interfaith meeting was not a failure. Nick pointed out: "We go to a meeting like this for several reasons. First, did you notice there was a nun and a priest who looked like they might become strong supporters? And one or two of the others, especially the rabbi, may turn out to help us. You can pick out individuals in these meetings. Then I wanted to see how our volunteers were going to handle it, that's why I let them run the meeting, even though they let it get out of hand. They're learning."

The interfaith meeting had taken place in late afternoon of what turned out to be an incredibly, long day. I had started out with Nick Jones and a half dozen volunteers picketing the vegetable and fruit produce terminal market in the Chelsea district before dawn. Long lines of trucks rumbled and bounced through the industrial back streets, past crumbling, dingy warehouses, their drivers cranking the big steering wheels around tight corners, as they came in with loads of fresh vegetables and fruit from as far away as California. As they neared the produce market the trucks queued up, starting, stopping, starting again, they crawled along the narrow, rutted roadways leading into the market's front gate. All you could hear was the clashing gears, the honking horns, roaring diesel engines, swearing drivers, and the shouting UFWOC pickets as they waved their homemade boycott signs and pushed leaflets at the passing drivers.

It was late fall and the weather was cold; the air stank, and the mood was bustling foul. When the sun was up far enough to turn the smog to iodine yellow, the pickets called it quits, gathered up their picket signs, and climbed into the UFWOC van. After taxiing his passengers home, Nick drove to a morning meeting with a state AFL-CIO official, drove to another meeting with the director of the Massachusetts Council of Churches; after a quick bite at a donut shop, he was off to look at a picket line, then to another meeting. In between meetings he made a half dozen phone calls, borrowing the use of a phone here, another there. He kept up the pace all day. By 10:30 P.M. we ended up in a tavern off Harvard Square, meeting with law professor Gary Bellow, who was helping the UFWOC with boycott legal problems. At the time, supermarkets had filed suit to prevent UFWOC boycott pickets from entering the public parking lots maintained by the markets. As we sipped beer, Bellow explained his legal theories on the case to Nick and a young lawyer who was donating his time to the union. By midnight we were driving back through the dark streets, headed home to the boycott house. Nick was proud of the fact the Boston boycott was raising $3,000 a month more than it spent, and this was being sent to the union's general fund.

The Boston boycott house was a big, old, gray three-story rectory that once served a Catholic church next door. It is in the heart of a black ghetto, and the building has had little care since it was abandoned by the church and donated to the union cause. The house has seven bedrooms and three bathrooms, in various states of disrepair. What formerly was the front sitting room has been converted into a workroom and print shop, while the large dining room and kitchen have retained their original functions. The 10 to 15 boycott people living in the house rotate the cooking and housekeeping chores. Because of the racial tension in Boston everyone who was white was warned about walking the streets alone at night. Two of the volunteers had been robbed at knife point a few days before I arrived.

The boycott house in Jersey City is almost a duplicate of the one in Boston, except it is located on the dividing line between the Puerto Rican and black neighborhoods. Violence and burglary are common occurrences; the Jersey City boycotters have lost duplicating machines, movie projectors, and tape recorders in a series of thefts. The burglars come in over the rooftops, and drop down the fire escapes to gain entry.

In New York City and Washington, D.C., the boycott

houses are in comfortable, older neighborhoods; and in sprawling Los Angeles the boycott people live in a number of rented, single-family tract houses scattered over a wide area.

Over the years, the boycott tactics have jelled into recognizable patterns. As the grape season starts with the Coachella harvest in late May or early June, the union sets up its intelligence operations to track the fruit from the farm to the eastern supermarkets. Experience has shown that if pickets can be on hand when a railcar or truckload of grapes arrives in the big terminal market-produce dock in Boston or New York or Chicago, all kinds of things can happen. An intimidated broker may simply refuse the shipment, a sympathetic Teamster working on the loading dock may accidentally mess up the delivery orders, a warehouseman may misplace the non-union fruit.

The picketing of terminal markets ends by midmorning, and the boycott crews head back to their house, or to a nearby cafe for some breakfast and a planning session. Some of the volunteers will picket supermarkets, some of the farm workers will give talks to civic groups or women's clubs, urging support for the boycott. In addition to the boycotters living in the boycott houses, there are local volunteers who agree to come out and form the picket lines when they are called.

In Baldwin, on Long Island, three housewife pickets were working Hill's Market. Ann, the most outspoken of the trio, explained, "We belong to a Christian-family movement and my husband and I are leaders in the group. We had about six couples and we decided to take the farm worker boycott on as a project. At least we've informed a lot of people, we've written letters to the market presidents, we've gone from store to store and asked the managers not to sell grapes, we've asked them to support the farm workers."

Whenever the farm workers themselves appear on the picket lines the morale of the volunteers soars, and the effect on the customers flowing in and out of the supermarkets is noticeable. In Toronto, Mrs. Ophelia Diaz, one of the workers fired by DiGiorgio for her UFWOC sympathies,

233

explained why she and her husband closed up their Earlimart home and brought their family out into the boycott: "We've got to fight until we win. If we stayed home we couldn't picket anymore without looking down the gun barrels, so we came over here to ask the people not to buy the grape."

In New York City, Mrs. Maria Colon swore she would live in this city until the boycott was won, until the contracts were signed, even if it took two or three years. Speaking rapidly in Spanish, she said, "Cesar Chavez is a miracle for the workers, he has taken the blindfold off our eyes so we can see what needs to be done. We see the people in the union must work to bring about change in the fields and that is why we are here in this big city."

The volunteer housewives and farm workers were having negative effects on the grape markets. Some supermarket chains and independent stores did withdraw grapes from the shelves; market managers complained that boycotters were telling shoppers the grapes were poisoned with pesticide, that boycotters staged sit-ins and shop-ins in the stores, harassing the customers. While the boycott caused the shippers to divert truck and train carloads of grapes from one terminal to another in search of open markets, California agribusiness spokesmen were not admitting the union tactics were having any effect.

Allan Grant, president of the California Farm Bureau Federation and former Governor Reagan's appointee to chair the state board of agriculture, categorically stated, "The boycott has been unsuccessful." But in almost the next breath, Grant said the boycott was "the most serious crisis that California agriculture has ever faced. It has developed into the ultimate confrontation. . . . [It is] immoral, unethical, and reprehensible. . . . [The UFWOC] is trying to blackmail California."

The boycott was an indiscriminate weapon; it shut some markets off to everyone, including the small grape growers of Fresno County who were then outside the strike area. Although the UFWOC attempted to coordinate boycotts, the efforts in each city were quite autonomous and were frequently chaotic. The boycott staff people were shifted from city to city; men like Eliseo Madina and Nick Jones became experts at applying the boycott pressures effectively, but some of the volunteers who were put in charge could never get things together. In some places individuals used the farm worker cause to work out their own hostilities toward society.

Through 1968 and 1969, the boycott stirred the farmers as nothing else had for years; the American Farm Bureau Federation and its state affiliates began to push union-busting legislation that would outlaw boycotts and strikes at harvest time and place control of all farm labor relations securely in the hands of agribusiness. U.S. Senator George Murphy agreed to carry the legislation in Congress. A coalition of California agribusiness organizations joined in the hiring of a high-priced San Francisco–based public relations firm, Whitaker and Baxter, to help Murphy push his bill and to generally polish the farmers' sagging image. While no figures were ever released, the cost of such a move must have totaled more than $1 million.

Whitaker and Baxter had a solid, conservative reputation; the firm had been hired by the American Medical Association in the late 1940s to defeat President Harry Truman's National Health Insurance legislation. W and B coined the phrase "socialized medicine" and built a successful campaign around slogans using those two words. Year by year, the firm built its reputation, using the same sloganeering techniques. For the agribusiness anti-boycott effort, W and B came up with "consumer rights" and established Consumer Rights Committee offices across the country to protest the withholding of grapes from the marketplace. Supermarkets had no right to withhold grapes; the public had the right to choose what it would and would not purchase.

Whether by coincidence or not, Richard M. Nixon began his 1968 presidential campaign in San Francisco that fall, and one of his first concerns was for the farmers who he felt were being unfairly used by the Chavez forces. Nixon ate some grapes to show his support, then he made a surprising statement that was clearly out of touch with legal reality. He said, "We have laws on the books to protect workers who wish to organize. We have a National Labor Relations Board to impartially supervise the elections of collective bargaining agents. . . . The secondary boycott of California grapes is clearly illegal. . . . [It] is to be condemned . . . with the same firmness we condemn any other form of law breaking."

Somebody on the Nixon staff had goofed. Politicians like Nixon, acting on behalf of their agribusiness constituents, had opposed the inclusion of farm labor under the NLRA for 33 years. At the time Nixon made the San Francisco statement the National Labor Relations Board had no jurisdiction over farm workers. The UFWOC's secondary boycott actions were clearly legal.

In the San Joaquin Valley, some Delano grape growers and Californians For Right to Work were attempting to come up with a public relations campaign of their own based on a new variation of their old company union routine; the new "worker" organization was called the Agriculture Workers Freedom to Work Association (AWFWA). Among its officers were some of the same labor contractor–crew boss names that had appeared in the old TKIFW group. The AWFWA was headed by a general secretary named José Mendoza, a former shoe salesman, who once worked as an OEO poverty fighter in Kern County. He was a man who carried a passionate hatred for Cesar Chavez and the UFWOC. This hatred was never explained. Investigation revealed the AWFWA was financed in part by Californians For Right to Work. One member of CRW's board of directors was Delano grape grower Jack Pandol. A suit brought by UFWOC attorney Jerry Cohen alleged AWFWA was a company union. The suit alleged Pandol and the Giumarras were among those farmers who supported the AWFWA financially.

A firm called Public Research Institute also supported AWFWA. Officials of PRI, a private Southern California publishing company, acknowledged Mendoza had been paid for some investigative work in connection with a booklet it was producing on the grape strike. The editor of the booklet,

Donald Gazzaniga, wrote in the foreword: "What he [Chavez] espouses is as Un-American as Karl Marx. . . . The Cesar Chavez stories are lies . . . the Chavez movement is a fraud."

The UFWOC suit brought the AWFWA to the attention of the U.S. Department of Labor, and, after an investigation, the labor department declared the Mendoza organization was required by law to file a Form LM-20, an annual report disclosing its internal structure and financial resources. The LM-20, dated February 22, 1969, revealed a list of 14 growers who had either contributed funds or worked for the AWFWA cause. Pandol, John Giumarra, Jr., and John Giumarra, Sr., were named as principal organizers of the AWFWA. Gazzaniga and PRI were an integral part of the AWFWA operation.

The LM-20, signed by both the AWFWA president and secretary, contained a statement that explained that AWFWA was the outgrowth of an untitled group led by growers and its function was "to tell workers not to be afraid of Chavez, to be united and we [AWFWA] as an organization would support and protect the workers; we were to oppose the UFWOC efforts to organize and to boycott. . . . [we were to] try to enlist workers and to obtain information on UFWOC's plans . . ."

Cono Macias's name appeared on the AWFWA forms filed with the labor department. Macias, the Bianco Ranch foreman who opposed the Chavez movement, said he had been unaware of the grower influence on the AWFWA until Mendoza started traveling and giving speeches. "I didn't like that, because he was being paid by the right-to-work people, and then a [Department of] Labor investigator came around and asked me some questions and showed me some canceled checks from the growers. After that I didn't want anything more to do with the AWFWA."

One of Mendoza's primary functions was to travel — at CRW expense — across the country denouncing Chavez and telling the audiences that the vineyard workers were not on strike, and that the farm workers did not support the UFWOC boycott. In December 1968, Mendoza appeared before the

50th annual American Farm Bureau Federation Convention in Kansas City. A writer for the *California Farm Bureau Monthly* reported Mendoza was "the spokesman for the bona fide farm workers" and as such he received "a standing ovation at the conclusion of his talk."

Mendoza's words were just what Farm Bureau wanted to hear and read. Allan Grant — writing in *Presbyterian Life* (December 1968) and his own *California Farm Bureau Monthly* (January 1969) — used Mendoza and the AWFWA as proof of the farmers' story, contending the AWFWA "has the greatest following among farm workers and their families." But all was not going well within the AWFWA. It had little or no membership, its farmer-oriented constituency had been exposed, and José Mendoza had disassociated himself from the organization sometime during the fall of 1968, weeks before he spoke to the Farm Bureau convention and weeks before he had been the subject of Grant's articles. Mendoza continued to travel and speak out against Chavez.

During much of 1968 Cesar Chavez was confined to a hospital bed at home. The fast had left him weak, and he began to suffer severe back pains. Doctors suggested these muscle spasms may have been caused by the fact that one of Chavez's legs was shorter than the other, resulting in a twist in the spinal alignment; or the problem might have been muscle deterioration, or a degenerating spinal disc. Helen was worried because her husband refused to stop work. She called Bill Kircher to help get proper care for him. Dolores Huerta flew in from New York and refused to go back out on boycott assignment until Chavez paid attention to what the doctors said and began to take care of himself. Chavez continued working from his hospital bed, or from the rocking chair beside it.

During this time I used to drop in, to visit, to ask a few questions, and to listen to Cesar talk about his childhood. One afternoon he began to talk about the 1935 National Labor Relations Act and the Taft-Hartley amendment made in 1947. I paid little attention at first, because I knew he favored passage of a Senator Harrison Williams proposed amendment that would place farm workers under the act's jurisdiction. But then it dawned on me he was saying just the opposite. He had changed his mind; the NLRA — as amended — was no good for farm workers: it would take away the right to the secondary boycott and would provide farmers with the legal machinery to stall strikes at harvest. Chavez pointed out that the original Wagner Act was pro-union and allowed workers to build strong organizations; but the Taft-Hartley amendment, passed over President Truman's veto, was anti-union.

Chavez had never made such statements publicly, and I asked if I could quote him directly. He said that I should not quote him directly, but I could attribute the story to an unnamed source. The story caught the growers and the AFL-CIO by surprise. No one in the federation, with the exception of Bill Kircher, really understood farm workers or Chavez, and for him to switch positions without informing federation leaders was a breech of protocol. Top AFL-CIO leaders were angry. Kircher, acting as a go-between, managed to smooth George Meany's ruffled feathers and patch together a workable agreement: the AFL-CIO would maintain its position that farm workers should be brought in under the NLRA, but it would do so quietly, without confronting the new Chavez position.

The years from 1967 through 1968 were slow for the UFWOC. The death of Robert Kennedy and Martin Luther King, Jr., cast a pall over the whole movement; the Murphy bill, the Whitaker and Baxter consumer-rights campaign, the continued marketing of grapes, despite the increasing boycott pressures, all had a deadening effect. The Chavez fast had buoyed the campaigns, but Cesar's back troubles, the fact that he was bedridden and not able to move among the union people, had its effect.

By 1969 the union's fortunes began to improve. Chavez's back began to mend, the boycott structures began to build the kinds of pressures they were designed to produce, and the tempo quickened once more.

A dozen grape growers in the Coachella Valley quietly began talks with the union. These farmers, because of their desert location, are the first into the marketplace with fresh fruit; their farming costs are higher than those in Arvin or Delano, but their early-market position gives them higher prices. The Coachella growers admitted the boycott was driving them to the bargaining table. But the talks never got very far. After some bitter arguments, only one of the growers, Lionel Steinberg, indicated he would continue to try to patch together an agreement. The other growers withdrew, vowing to fight Chavez as long as they could hold out.

Never content with the issues at hand, the UFWOC leadership was casting about for a new, dramatic controversy. They found it, almost by accident, as the result of Jerry Cohen's aggressive legal tactics. Some grape workers had complained to the UFWOC that they thought they had been poisoned by pesticides as they worked. They felt sick. They had serious skin rashes. Cohen asked them what kinds of chemicals they had been around. They did not know and they could not find out. Cohen looked up the law; in California farmers and commercial pesticide applicators must file a total disclosure of what they intend to use with the county agriculture commissioner when they apply for an applicator use permit. Cohen went to the agriculture commissioner's office to find out what had been used in the vines where his clients worked. He was told such information was confidential; applicators' chemical trade secrets were protected and the county agriculture commissioner — with his investigative staff — was the sole judge and protector of the public interest and the workers' safety.

Cohen filed suit, and, during the course of his investigations, he came up with some astounding facts. Despite California's restrictive pesticide-application safety regulations, hundreds of workers were being poisoned. The problem had grown to alarming proportions as the use of DDT-type chlorinated hydrocarbons was outlawed because of their long-lasting impact on the environment. The substitutes for the DDT-type pesticides were the short-lived phosphate-base poisons that attack the central nervous system. These highly toxic materials — a single drop of concentrated poison applied to the skin can be fatal within seconds — were diluted and sprayed onto the vines and leaves. Cohen discovered that the California State Department of Public Health had done occupational safety studies and found hundreds of workers adversely affected by a spray called parathion, even though farmers had followed all of the stringent safety regulations.

As long as the issue remained a worker-safety problem, it did not attract wide attention. But then boycotters in Washington, D.C., purchased some Delano table grapes from a Safeway store and took them to a chemical laboratory to have them tested for pesticide residues. The grapes showed concentrations of a pesticide called Aldrin far above the limits set by the Food and Drug Administration. (Production and sale of Aldrin has since been suspended by the FDA because the product shows signs of producing cancer.)

The issue exploded overnight. Safeway denied its grapes were poisoned, the grower who supplied the grapes denied he had used Aldrin. Senator Murphy came to the aid of the grower and supermarket; using the U.S. Senate Subcommittee on Migratory Labor as a forum, he challenged the UFWOC to prove it was not committing a cruel hoax. Further tests of grapes from other stores by a second and a third testing firm showed the same high traces of Aldrin. Both sides had blundered into a no-man's land. There is so little knowledge about pesticides, and their effects, that confusion is the rule in most such controversies. In this specific case the test for Aldrin and the test for sulfur — which is used on the grapes to prevent mildew — are so close that an expert chemist can easily be fooled unless he is looking specifically for the infinitesimal difference between the test results on these two compounds. The grapes may well not have had Aldrin residues on them, but the argument projected the pesticide issue into the boycott.

241

The consumer-boycott aspects of the grape hassle almost obscured the more important aspects of the pesticide controversy, from a union point of view. Chavez testified: "The real issue is the danger that pesticides present to farm workers. We have come to realize in the union that the issue of pesticide poisoning is more important today than even wages." Chavez told the Senate Subcommittee that a state public health survey among 774 Tulare County farm workers revealed only 121 of them were free of symptoms that indicate pesticide poisoning may be taking place.

Workers are seldom sprayed directly; instead, most pick up the pesticide residues from the plant foliage as they work. Most of the poisoning takes place when the weather is hot and the workers are sweating; the residues are absorbed through the skin or inhaled as the dust flies from the leaves. The results are flu-like symptoms: dizziness, split vision, nausea, respiratory problems like those associated with colds. These symptoms are insidious. As the worker exposure is prolonged, the symptomatic results are cumulative. Continued exposure can result in serious illness and death. If exposure ceases, the symptoms slowly disappear. Skin rashes are common; eye irritation goes with most farm jobs.

As Chavez learned more about pesticide problems, he ordered Cohen and Huerta to write strong worker protections into the contracts.

During the winter of 1969–70 little progress was being made in the effort to get the Coachella growers back to the negotiating table. Chavez turned to the National Conference of Catholic Bishops, asking for their support of the boycott. Rather than endorse the boycott, the bishops decided to establish an ad hoc committee to attempt to bring the growers and union representatives together for talks. Bishop Joseph Donnelly was named chairman of the committee, Bishops Timothy Manning and Hugh Donohoe of California were also members, Monsignor George Higgins, of the National Catholic Conference in Washington, D.C., was made the farm labor committee chief of staff. He was assisted by Monsignor Roger Mahoney, of the Fresno diocese.

Donnelly and Higgins invited all grape growers and the union to a meeting in Fresno. Some growers did attend, but the affair did not come off well, so later in the spring of 1970 a second meeting was called. The dozen growers who had already expressed an interest in talks were invited, and so were the leaders of the Delano growers, including the Giumarras. During this second meeting the bishops talked first with growers, then with the union, and then suggested both sides join in informal exploratory talks. This was done. In the week following, Higgins and Donnelly traveled the state, talking privately to farmers, preparing the way for negotiations.

Higgins recalled: "Steinberg said he was ready to go into talks, the boycott was hurting him badly but that he would not move unless the bishops' committee sat in on the meetings. All the growers took this position; they felt they had been burned badly the year before, and that was why those talks had broken down. They didn't want to go through what they called 'that circus' again; they said the union had 20 or 30 people in the room, workers and what not. They said the union didn't negotiate, it made demands. Steinberg and the others said if we would sit in on the meetings it would insure some kind of order."

The bishops agreed, and Steinberg began negotiations with the UFWOC once more. By April a contract was worked out, and the Coachella Valley's largest table-grape farming operation was signed. A small grape ranch next to Steinberg was owned by K. K. Larson. Larson had been a farm manager and he had purchased 20 acres then, year by year, had added to his operations until he farmed 148 acres of bearing vines. He cooperated with Steinberg in the use of labor — when the Steinberg crews were finished with a job, some would move over to the Larson farm — and when Steinberg signed a contract Larson decided he would ask his workers — through a secret ballot election — if they wanted the UFWOC to represent them.

Larson, a big Scandinavian who is deeply suntanned, works with his crews, personally supervising every phase of the operation. He works for a quality product and he says of the workers and himself, "We all live off the vines, so what we do is important." Commenting on the economics of 1969 he said, "The boycott had been so devastating that we could not make mortgage payments and the banks will go along with that for a year but not two. We had to do something, but I wasn't about to make the workers go into the union."

Larson asked his local Presbyterian minister, the Rev. Lloyd Saatjian, to supervise the elections, and Monsignor Roger Mahoney was brought in as an observer. The vote on Larson's ranch was 78 favoring the UFWOC and only 2 opposing. Larson said later, "I did have an honest, secret-ballot election on my ranch, prior to the signing of the contract. I was the only one who did that; that was a legitimate election won by Chavez." He added, "Had the workers voted 'no' and the boycott been continued, we'd have been out of business and I think the workers knew that. I think that influenced their vote."

After Steinberg and Larson signed, the other Coachella growers came to the negotiating table; one by one they signed contracts. Almost without exception, the bishops' committee was in the midst of the negotiations, arranging to bring both sides together. While the bishops worked with the union and the grape growers, Dolores Huerta went underground briefly, then surfaced in Fresno county, where Cal-Mission orchard workers were striking. This 1,800-acre peach, plum, and vineyard operation was part of a 43,000-acre farming empire put together by Hollis Roberts, a big, cigar-chewing farmer who had been blown out of the Dust Bowl and who had come into California "dirt poor." Roberts was a self-made man, an arch conservative, who idolized H. L. Hunt and considered Cesar Chavez a communist threat. Yet, when the strike — and the specter of a boycott — threatened his ripe fruit crop, Roberts agreed to meet with Huerta. They began negotiations, and, just before final agreement was reached, Roberts did another surprising thing. He is a Protestant fundamentalist, yet he asked for the

Bishops' Farm Labor Committee to come into the last stages of the talks.

Higgins said, "When we arrived for the final sessions it was obvious Cesar and his people had been meeting with Roberts. We were brought in as observers. There was Cesar with his bodyguards, with their feet up on the rich furniture, and everyone was relaxed and having a drink. After everything was settled, Hollis went around to meet everyone and we were curious. He had been calling Cesar a communist, and all that, yet he had signed. Why? He explained it to us, 'Well, Reverend, I had Cesar all wrong. I discovered in dealing with him he's a God-fearing Christian. Besides, I couldn't get anybody to pick my peaches.' "

As Higgins watched Dolores Huerta negotiating contract after contract, getting them into final form before Chavez stepped in to take over the last sessions, he commented, "She's tough. Relentless. Tireless. Generally Dolores would bring in an entourage of 10 to 15 workers, and this distressed the growers. In theory the negotiations were open and these workers were ranch representatives. They nit-picked every damn word in those contracts. Dolores would aggravate the growers by calling a recess right in the room and then turn to the workers and talk to them in Spanish, filling them in, getting their counter-proposals.

"I never knew if it was an act or not, but she wouldn't answer some questions without turning first to the workers to hear their answers. On such things as the hiring hall and pesticide regulations, they would not budge. One company brought in a pesticide expert and he would try to tell Dolores what she was saying was not scientific, but she would just bluff him, drive him crazy, tell him, 'That's not what our experts tell us,' and then go right on with her demands. The growers tried to be adamant, the control of the work force and the application of pesticides were managerial prerogatives to them, but in the end they gave in . . . they had no other choice, the boycott was too much for them."

The domino theory worked. From the Steinberg and Larson contracts in April through mid-July almost all of the grape growers, except the 26 in Delano, had signed contracts with the UFWOC. Then in the second week of July the Delano growers sent word, through labor relations consultant Phillip Feick, they wanted to start talks. Chavez called Bill Kircher in Washington and asked that he help out in the talks. The grower committee, headed by consultant Feick, Bishop Donnelly, and Monsignor Higgins, and the union, repre- sented by Chavez, Kircher, Huerta, Itliong, and Cohen, started talks on July 17 in a Bakersfield motel. Kircher led off with the union's proposals, the growers countered, and negotiations were underway. During the two-day talks there were recesses and delays, but progress was made.

Kircher said, "We had it down to where we thought we had a basis for settlement. But there were two encumbrances Chavez had placed on me. The first had to do with a Chicano student walkout at the Delano High School. Some of the kids had been expelled and, because one of the school board members was a farmer negotiating with us, Cesar wanted him to order the kids back in school. I couldn't see a chance for anything so far from the purview of the negotiations.

"The other condition was that the farmers had to come to the union's new hiring hall — it was located in the new administration building at the Forty Acres — to sign the contracts. When I told them this, well they just about shit. They said 'No. No way.' But I got it, I finally got them to agree. But you know, before we could reach any overall kind of agreement, Dolores started raising issues, and the talks almost blew up. So we recessed."

Kircher was convinced Chavez had used him as a stalking horse, to feel the growers out so that when Chavez, Huerta, and Cohen finally sat down to hard negotiating they would know what to expect. Kircher had not been told this was his role, he said, adding, "I'm not bitter, but the point is they didn't tell me. If that is a negative judgment, then, so be it. That man Cesar is a great game player . . ."

Cohen disagreed that Cesar was using Kircher as a stalking horse. Cohen explained, "Cesar was trying to get the best contract possible. I think it was Feick who caused the meeting to blow up; he was very negative."

Whatever the cause, the talks were broken off, with no date set to reconvene. Chavez took off for the Filmore–Santa Paula area, in Southern California, to be with striking citrus workers who had called and asked for help. He met with the strike leaders, listened to their tactics and plans, counseled them. In the meantime Manuel Chavez, who had been down in the Calexico-Mexicali area with the lettuce and melon workers, leading strikes, had moved north with the season. He was organizing those families that travel with the strawberries and vegetable crops into the Santa Maria–Salinas areas. Gil Padilla was already up in these coastal valleys, rekindling the house meetings, getting local workers organized.

A week after the talks with the Delano growers had blown up, John Giumarra, Jr., called Jerry Cohen late one Saturday night and said he had to talk with the union representatives right then, that if the talks could not be put back together, the whole issue would take a "drastic turn."

Cohen said, "I never did learn what the drastic turn would be, but I got ahold of Cesar — he was somewhere down south near Santa Paula — and we got everyone together early Sunday morning."

The final agreement was worked out in the pre-dawn, in a Delano motel, by Chavez, Cohen, and Huerta on one side and by the Giumarras — father and son — on the other. The rest of the growers were called into a special meeting in the St. Mary's school building and the details of the agreement were spelled out for their approval. Kircher had been notified and was flying out from Washington, D.C. He arrived as the final meeting was taking place. After the growers and the union set the time and place for the official contract-signing ceremonies, Cesar and Kircher took off for the Filmore–Santa Paula–Santa Maria area to continue Cesar's series of meetings with farm workers.

Kircher recalled, "These farm workers had been making

plans for organizing in the lettuce. They were getting ready for something big. There was a rally in Santa Maria, a massive meeting in the high school gymnasium. Everyone was there, must have been 1,000 people inside. Each group of people came forward and said they supported a strike. We finished up there about 10:40 and went back to the motel.

"Manuel Chavez had been running the organizational work — he was staying at one of those Motel 6s and we went there to sleep. When we got there, about 11 P.M., we turned the TV on to see the news and goddamn there came the announcement that the Western Conference of Teamsters had signed agreements with all of the lettuce growers in the Salinas Valley. . . . I thought it was a joke, or the goddamn announcer had things balled up . . . but Cesar had this funny look on his face. . . . [We] called a guy on the Salinas paper that we knew and we asked him if it was true. He said it was, he'd gotten the press release and checked it with the Teamsters. He said the Teamsters claimed to have signed 30 lettuce growers, and the contracts covered 5,000 workers.

"So we didn't go to bed after all; we took off for Salinas. We'd stop along the way, at a pay phone, call our people, get press releases started, schedule a press conference. We got to Salinas, got about two hours' sleep, and then held the press conference to declare a strike in the lettuce. We set up a few battle stations and then took off back to Delano for the signing of the table-grape contracts."

The historic pact, ending the five-year-long Delano grape strike, was signed by all 26 of the Delano grape growers on July 29, 1970. When the strike was started, in the fall of 1965, the workers had asked for $1.40 an hour and 25 cents a field-packed box. The contract set the wage at $1.80 an hour, with 20 cents for the field-packed box. The growers also agreed to pay 10 cents an hour into the Robert Kennedy Health and Welfare Fund and 2 cents an hour into a social service fund. The workers would be dispatched from the Delano hiring hall, and they would be protected by special pesticide safety language.

The Delano contracts brought 50 percent of the table-grape harvest under the control of the UFWOC, the Coachella and Arvin contracts added 35 percent more. The remaining 15 percent that was unorganized lay in tiny 10- and 20- and 40-acre farming parcels belonging to the notoriously independent small family farmers of Fresno and Madera counties. But these growers would have to be forgotten for a while, as Chavez moved his headquarters to Salinas and prepared for the lettuce strikes and the battle to drive the Teamsters out of the fields again.

CHAPTER ELEVEN :
THE TEAMSTERS AGAIN

The Teamsters were not newcomers to the Salinas Valley agribusiness scene. Local 890 had contracts covering workers in the canneries, the fresh-vegetable packing sheds, and frozen-food processing plants; these contracts also protected the field truck drivers and the carton stitchers, who ride on the flat-bed trucks making up the cardboard boxes used by harvest crews who field pack the lettuce. And Local 890 still had the Bud Antle, Inc., field laborers under contract, as a result of the 1961 lettuce strikes by the AWOC and United Packinghouse Workers. At the time the Teamsters signed Antle they offered similar field labor contracts to 110 other Salinas Valley growers. The farmers rejected the idea of unionization, condemned Antle, and expunged his name from the influential Growers-Shippers Vegetable Association membership list.

The AWOC-UPHW effort was easily beaten back, and the Salinas growers went about their business. The Teamsters showed no wider interest in field labor, and there matters rested for nearly a decade. But when the Coachella grape

Teamster in Coachella stomping Chavez effigy.
El Malcriado Photo

growers gave up the fight and began negotiating with the UFWOC, the vegetable and fruit growers in the Salinas Valley began to worry; then as the Arvin and Delano grape growers began negotiating contracts, the Salinas growers began to get strong indications they were next on the UFWOC list.

During July of 1970 the Growers-Shippers Vegetable Association — representing 29 of the largest vegetable-farming operations in the valley — was in negotiations with the Teamsters, attempting to renew the contracts covering workers in the packinghouses, canneries, and freezers and on the trucks. Although these were Local 890 contracts, Bill Grami, director of organizing for the Western Conference of Teamsters, came down from Burlingame to sit in on the talks. Negotiations broke down and the workers went out on strike, tying up the harvest for a week. At some point after talks were resumed and before a settlement was reached, Grami informally let the growers know the Western Conference — not Local 890 — was interested in organizing field workers.

The Teamsters' sudden public emergence in the fields of the Salinas Valley and the resulting Teamster-grower field labor contracts came at a bad time for Chavez. The UFWOC had to establish hiring halls to dispatch thousands of grape workers, and it had to create the administrative machinery to govern the workaday union and train the ranch committees to enforce the contracts the union had just signed. No one really knew how many workers would pass through the hiring halls as the union met the farmers' demands for work crews because of the instability and high mobility of the work force. Among the 26 growers signed in late July in Delano was the Giumarra Vineyards. Just this one company annually goes through 8,000 workers to meet the seasonal labor fluctuations that do not exceed 2,000 workers at any one time. In varying degrees this kind of turnover had to be expected on each of the ranches. The union's task was awesome.

The Teamsters' move into the lettuce fields grabbed the headlines and obscured the organizing efforts the UFWOC had going among the vegetable, strawberry, and cantaloupe workers. Chavez's swift reaction, his quick move to Salinas, leaving the very complex Delano problems to others, was difficult to understand. Why hadn't he reversed the priorities, why hadn't he focused his own attention on building a strong operational union in Delano and let Manuel Chavez and Gilbert Padilla, who were already in the Salinas area, direct the fight against the Teamsters?

Chavez answered with a history lesson: "We had workers in the avocados, the lettuce, and the row crops and soft fruit. We'd signed them all quietly. In 1967 there were strikes in the strawberries in Santa Maria and we had to go in there and tell them they had to cool it, they had to wait because we couldn't help them just yet. In 1968 the lettuce workers in the Imperial Valley wanted to strike and we told them to wait.

"See, in 1970 the grapes were won, but . . ." Cesar paused, then explained, "Well, you have to go back about three months, to the early spring. When the strawberry and lettuce workers saw that we were not getting bitten off, when they saw that while we weren't winning, we weren't being destroyed either, they began to make demands on us, and we had to tell them we could not handle two strikes at once, that they would have to wait until we finished the grapes. They agreed, but they extracted an agreement from me, too; I agreed that as soon as we started to win we would turn to their problems.

"Within a week after we'd signed the grape contracts in April, a delegation of about 30 lettuce workers came to Delano, so I asked them to give me another month so I could get some more contracts signed. On Cinco de Mayo [the May 5th Mexican holiday], we were down in the park in Delano having a rally and a delegation of about 80 lettuce workers came and we made a plan, and drafted a letter and a telegram and about two weeks later I sent the letter to the Western Growers Association, saying we represented the workers and wanted a meeting, but nothing happened. . . . [We] found out later that when the letter came, the growers decided to call the Teamsters . . ."

The lettuce workers were migrants, most of them either were single, or had left their families in the Calexico-Mexicali area as they followed the seasons. These men travel in cohesive crews from Phoenix and Yuma through the Imperial Valley and north to Salinas and back. There are similar crews following similar routes in the cantaloupe and watermelon harvests. The crews that harvest the strawberries, the soft tree fruit, and the onions, garlic, and tomatoes are entirely different; they are made up of casual workers, primarily families willing to work on a piece rate of pay; a nickel a pound, 30 cents a bucket, a dollar a flat. Some of the families are migrants from Texas and Mexico, but most live in one of the California farming valleys and travel out to work. The piece rates are set so only the fastest workers can make a modest day's pay; as a result, the parents bring their children with them and the whole family works. The smallest children pick into their parents' buckets or baskets, they fetch and carry water bottles and lunch sacks. These families frequently work on a single Social Security card; this allows them to avoid deductions and gives the farmer a single padded payroll entry on his records to show he is meeting the minimum wage.

Because of the complexity of these various work forces, the UFWOC approached the job of building its organizational base from two directions. Manuel Chavez was assigned to move with the migrants, to organize the lettuce workers and cantaloupe workers, starting with the season in Arizona and along the California-Mexican border and moving north. Chavez established a farm worker service center in Calexico and a medical clinic in Mexicali, and he conducted hit-and-run strikes wherever he could, building a cadre of experienced *huelgistas* who could, when the time came, run a general strike.

Gil Padilla was assigned to the coastal valleys to work with those families who had settled out, but still made their living as seasonal workers. Padilla worked through all of 1968 and 1969, ranging from Oxnard north to Gilroy and Hollister. "We were organizing committees out of the contacts Cesar had established during the house-meeting days; each one of the committees had to have at least 25 dues-paying members. The committees were supposed to go out and sign up new members, you know, organize on their own.

"We had committees in all those towns, King City, Watsonville, Salinas. In Santa Maria we had a goddamn good organization. There were 200 or 300 people in that committee; we had a credit union and a service center there. We had rallies and Cesar would come over. When the word came about how the Salinas growers were signing with the Teamsters the people were really mad. Because of the problems with the new contracts in Delano Cesar tried to ask them to hold off with a Salinas strike, but they said, 'No, we've waited too long now.' The farmers were trying to make them sign cards with the Teamsters and they were saying, 'Hell, no. We're with the farm workers union!' "

There was no doubt the farmers and the Teamsters were working in concert. Cal T. Watkins, personnel manager for Inter Harvest — a 20,000-acre vegetable-growing subsidiary of the United Fruit conglomerate — was a member of the Growers-Shippers Vegetable Association's negotiating team. He said that once the contracts covering the packing sheds, freezers, and trucks had been successfully renegotiated, on July 22nd, the GSVA sent a special committee to the Western Conference officials to see if something could be worked out to bring the field workers in under the jurisdiction of the Teamsters' union. The committee reported back the next day that the Teamsters were not only willing to represent field workers, they were ready to have the growers sign recognition agreements *immediately*. Watkins said all 29 firms formally recognized the Teamsters, even though the union "did not claim to represent any agricultural employees at this time [July 25th]." Teamster-grower field labor contracts were signed and announced publicly on July 28th, the day before Chavez and the Delano grape growers signed collective bargaining contracts.

Chavez could not ignore the challenge. He moved his headquarters to Salinas, and by August 1st he was personally leading marches through Watsonville, holding rallies in Salinas and Hollister, and directing the strikes against the Teamsters and the lettuce growers. The UFWOC leadership all over the United States was ordered to drop everything and come to Salinas.

Within the week Grami was announcing the Teamsters had signed 60 growers, and were out after more. An 18-man Teamster task force was going through the fields signing up workers. UFWOC organizer Manuel Olivas charged the Teamsters, aided by growers and their foremen, were coercing the workers, forcing them to sign cards. Olivas said, "Some of the field workers are afraid of losing their jobs, three men have been fired already . . ."

Padilla was right. Many of the workers were refusing to sign with the Teamsters. Cal Watkins said that after a week or ten days Teamster organizers had signed only 108 of Inter Harvest's 1,000 field workers. Many of these lettuce workers got mad and walked off the job.

Padilla said, "They just started walking off, and they came to our office in Salinas and Cesar had to immediately set up some staff there. All the workers from all the companies started coming out . . . and we had to get them organized for a strike. There were thousands of them coming, and we had to find out where they were coming from, what ranches they had struck . . .

"Cesar was bossing the strike, and we set up a special office in the old MAPA [Mexican American Political Association] headquarters. Our first job was to locate the ranches. The people didn't know the addresses where they worked but they would just give us a description, like 'You go down that road by the railroad, and go over a ditch and turn that way . . .' that sort of thing. We went crazy trying to pin the locations down, because it was important to tie the man to the place he struck. We got a big map, and we color-coded the strikes and then assigned each picket captain two or three ranches and told them to get those workers who had struck those ranches to form the picket lines . . ."

The AFL-CIO executive council was meeting in Chicago as

the Teamsters moved into the Salinas lettuce fields. Chavez flew to Chicago, expecting to stand beside George Meany as the federation president read a strong statement denouncing the Teamster raid and pledging the federation support for the UFWOC. But it wasn't to be. The executive council vacillated; a weak statement was issued hailing the victory in the Delano grapes and declaring the full weight of the federation was behind the UFWOC effort to organize all farm workers in the United States, but no mention was made of the Teamsters.

Bill Kircher was furious: "When I first reported the Teamster sign-up to Meany, he said we'd have to do something about it. I told him we could run the Teamsters out and he told me to write up a strong statement. . . . [The] morning I was to read the statement to the council I got a phone call saying could I come down [to Meany's room] because Joe Keenan [president of the electrical workers, an AFL-CIO vice president, and a member of the executive council] had gotten a call from someone in the Teamster hierarchy."

For reasons that still are not clear, Keenan had received a call from Tom Flynn, a Teamster International vice president and director of the Eastern Conference. Keenan explained to me, "Flynn said they'd heard about the statement and asked that we defer making it until he'd had a chance to talk with me, to work something out. He said there'd been a mix-up somewhere. Later I got a call from Frank Fitzsimmons asking us to hold off. I went to Mr. Meany and Mr. Meany agreed to defer and he asked me to go into it and see if I could work out some kind of understanding, so Al Woll and I got into it." Woll is the AFL-CIO's chief counsel; he was also general counsel to the Teamsters before they were expelled from the federation.

Kircher speculated that Einar Mohn had called Flynn and asked him to head off the AFL-CIO statement. Mohn was the Teamster International's first vice president and he was director of the Western Conference. Mohn, a soft-spoken, rotund fellow, has a "good guy" reputation and in the farm worker jurisdictional wars, at least, is considered the chief architect of the various peace pacts that have been attempted. Grami, on the other hand, is lean and tough, an articulate, bright, and aggressive man who is obviously ambitious. Kircher — who has no love for Teamsters in general and Bill Grami in particular — speculated it was Grami making a power play against Mohn that had triggered the "mix-up." Certainly it was Grami who set the grower-Teamster contract wheels in motion. Kircher believes Mohn, to head off the Grami power play, appealed directly to Teamster International's officers for help.

Whatever the internal politics, Grami was ordered to set up a meeting between the Western Conference and the United Farm Workers and to do it in a hurry. Grami called Delano that night — Cesar's daughter Eloise was being married at the time — and talked to UFWOC attorney Jerry Cohen. Grami asked for a meeting some place halfway between Burlingame, on the San Francisco peninsula, and Delano. The Black Oak Motel in Paso Robles was chosen. It was about a three-hour drive for each side. Cohen said it was late by the time he and Cesar arrived and the meeting lasted for several hours. General areas of agreement were worked out on the jurisdictional questions, based upon the original agreement at Perelli-Minetti Vineyards in 1967. But there were problems with how to get the Teamsters to disengage from the farm contracts. At about 2 A.M. on Sunday morning, August 9th, Cesar put in a call to Monsignor Roger Mahoney, in Fresno.

Mahoney said, "He told me they had been meeting, that they had general areas of agreement worked out, but they thought it would look better, from a public relations standpoint, if the bishops' committee were to bring the two sides together for talks." Mahoney called George Higgins and he agreed to fly out from Washington, D.C., immediately. Mahoney set up meetings for the next night in Salinas.

Although all of this was clandestine, there were so many conflicting interests within the arrangements it was impossible to keep the meetings secret. Someone leaked the story to a reporter in Washington, D.C.; the resulting news dispatch *suggested* some talks might be underway. I called Mohn in Burlingame the next day and he confirmed talks were being held but would only add, "We are trying to reach an agreement that will protect our interests."

Chavez denied any agreement had been reached, and hinted a general strike was "hours away." On August 9th, after calling Monsignor Mahoney, Chavez tried to bolster his bargaining position by ordering 300 strikers to picket the Fresh Pict Farm, owned by the Purex conglomerate.

On August 10th the bishops' committee announced it was bringing the two sides together for meetings that night. The Monday night meeting lasted until dawn Tuesday; it was agreed the Teamsters would pull back out of the fields and the UFWOC would not organize workers in food processing, produce sheds, or freezers. By mutual consent the parties agreed to disagree over who should have the workers on machines in the fields. A secret side agreement was made wherein the Teamsters would assist in getting farmers to rescind Teamster contracts and enter talks with the UFWOC. No specific language was included on the 1961 Bud Antle–Teamster contract, but the Teamsters say Chavez agreed to leave this established contract alone.

Chavez ordered most picket lines and all of the boycott activity halted, to take the pressure off and give the Teamsters a chance to convince the growers they should switch to the UFWOC. While Chavez hoped for an orderly transition, all was not well within the Teamsters. Monsignor Mahoney said it was obvious Grami was not happy with the idea of the peace pact. Others reported hearing Grami say he would not sign papers rescinding the lettuce contracts; Grami would leave that to Einar Mohn because he did not want his name on them. And that is the way it was worked out, according to Cal Watkins. On August 14th, Inter Harvest asked Grami for a contract rescission; Watkins said the UFWOC was still picketing Inter Harvest and he wanted to settle the dispute. Grami at first agreed to rescind the contract, but then, after receiving a phone call, the Teamster hesitated. He said the continued UFWOC picketing was disturbing and the Teamsters might be having second thoughts. Grami backed away from signing rescission orders. A week later Einar Mohn terminated the Inter Harvest contract, freeing the company to negotiate with the UFWOC.

The new UFWOC–Inter Harvest contract covered 1,500 to 2,000 workers at the peak of harvest and it set a base pay of $2 an hour. This ranges up to $2.75 an hour for tractor drivers and up to $3 an hour for field foremen. The company contributed 10 cents an hour for health and welfare benefits, and provided vacations, holidays, and other fringe benefits. Within the next few weeks Fresh Pict, Pic 'N' Pac (a big strawberry operation), and several other large growers switched to the UFWOC under similar terms, but 170 vegetable and soft-fruit growers who had followed the GSVA lead into the Teamster lair were standing firm.

The UFWOC continued its limited selective picketing. Both Grami and Mohn charged the Chavez forces had violated the jurisdictional pact 29 times and pointed to the UFWOC picketing of Bud Antle as proof of their allegations. Chavez denied there was any agreement exempting the UFWOC from organizing Antle workers, and he countered with allegations the Teamsters were not pushing the growers out of bed, as had been promised.

On August 20th grower Herb Fleming said all 170 growers were going to honor the Teamster contracts; they considered them binding agreements. The UFWOC countered by calling a general strike and ordering all lettuce boycotted. This was the signal the workers had been waiting for; 7,000 men, women, and children walked off their jobs in the lettuce and strawberry fields. From Santa Maria north 200 miles to Salinas the coastal valleys were scenes of chaos as roving bands of pickets tried to prevent farmers from importing strikebreaking crews; lawmen and Teamster "guards" appeared in the fields, and along the back roads, carrying guns. The UFWOC office in Watsonville was blown up; UFWOC counsel Jerry Cohen was jumped by a 300-pound, 6 foot–2 inch "guard" who held him in a bear grip while another guard beat him unconscious. Cohen was hospitalized for four days with a brain concussion and cuts and bruises.

Strike costs were spiraling and the call for help went out to the AFL-CIO unions in Los Angeles and San Francisco; Chavez accepted a $150,000 interest-free loan from an order of Catholic priests near Santa Barbara. The growers went into court in an attempt to get the strike declared illegal; they argued it was a jursidictional dispute between two unions and California law protected employers from such action. The lower courts agreed, and enjoined the UFWOC from picketing or boycotting. The union ignored the order. Bud Antle, Inc., acting alone, went into court with a similar argument and Judge Gordon Campbell ordered the UFWOC boycott against the Antle products stopped. Chavez ordered the strike line activities increased, in defiance of all court orders, and he specifically stepped up the boycott against Antle. Judge Campbell ordered Chavez into court December 4th to show cause why he and his union should not be held in contempt.

Too late, the Antle lawyers saw what was coming. With Chavez in jail, his followers would certainly make a great issue out of the fact that it was the Antle company that had put him there, and this would not help the sale of $30 million worth of fresh vegetables that the company marketed under its own, highly visible labels. The Antle lawyers told reporters they did not want Chavez jailed, and they suggested Judge Campbell would hand out punishment enough if he just fined the union. But neither the judge nor Chavez was to be denied.

On December 4th the UFWOC turned out 3,000 farm workers; they ringed the Monterey County courthouse, in Salinas, they lined the front entryway and the hallways. Kneeling or standing, they remained absolutely silent as Chavez and Cohen went inside. The hearing lasted three and a half hours, and, when Chavez refused to call off the Antle boycott, as ordered, the judge ordered him jailed. As he was being led away Chavez shouted, "Boycott the hell out of them."

The UFWOC workers set up a "vigil" around the jail, union

priests said a Mass and were arrested by police for failing to get city permits for public meetings. The UFWOC held rallies, and the widows of Robert Kennedy and Martin Luther King, Jr., came to visit Chavez in his cell. Chavez issued a statement assuring his followers he was being treated well and explaining he was prepared to "pay the price for civil disobedience . . . jail is a small price to pay to help fight injustice . . ."

The New York *Times* editorialized:

> The imprisonment of Cesar Chavez . . . is an exercise in legalism of the kind that serves only to discredit the law. Mr. Chavez, as firm in his dedication to nonviolence as Mahatma Gandhi, is a symbol of emancipation for the most exploited of the nation's workers, the agricultural laborers . . .

The editorial called for passage of federal labor laws to protect the rights of farm workers in their effort to gain collective bargaining agreements with their employers, and noted that had such laws existed the lettuce workers in Salinas would have been able to record their union preferences, and "Mr. Chavez would have the law as an ally, not an obstacle, in his drive for economic justice."

By December 24th even Judge Campbell had had enough; the thought of what Chavez's supporters might do if their leader was still in jail on Christmas Day helped the judge make up his mind to release Chavez, pending the outcome of the appeals filed by the union's attorney. Cohen and his staff had done their homework well. They managed to consolidate all of the cases except Bud Antle, and then they advanced their position through the appellate procedures to the California Supreme Court.

The process took two years, but in the end the UFWOC position was upheld; California law, while it protects employers from two unions fighting for jurisdiction over workers, does not tolerate the creation of a "company union" by an employer. The court, in a 6 to 1 decision, ruled the growers had invited the Teamsters into the fight in an effort to block Chavez and the UFWOC; therefore the injunctions against the UFWOC picketing and boycotting were invalid. The six Supreme Court Justices reported they found "no suggestion in the record that the growers . . . attempted to ascertain whether their respective workers desired to be represented by the Teamsters or indeed that the question of their field workers' preference was even raised as a relevant consideration." The court took judicial note of the Teamster-Antle contracts in 1961 and testimony that this was an apparent move to avoid the AWOC and United Packinghouse Workers' efforts to organize lettuce field workers. Then the six justices made this telling observation:

> Although there is some dispute as to the precise number or percentages of field workers favoring either the Teamsters or the UFWOC, it appears clear that by mid-August at least a substantial number, and probably the majority of the applicable field workers desired to be represented by the UFWOC rather than the Teamsters.

In Washington, D.C., Meany and Fitzsimmons found the fight over the lettuce workers a messy, embarrassing affair, and they continued to push for some kind of jurisdictional settlement that would hold together. By mid-March of 1971 both Grami and Chavez were persuaded to sign a revised agreement that created machinery to settle any disagreements through arbitration directed personally by Meany and Fitzsimmons.

The Teamsters pulled back, at least part way, announcing the contracts with the growers were being held in abeyance. Meany sent Joe Keenan to California to personally get the UFWOC-grower talks started. Negotiations were held first in Monterey then moved to Bakersfield and Los Angeles. Both sides reported "some progress" was being made, but the talks dragged on, through the summer of 1971 and into the fall and were finally stalemated. No more meetings were called. The grower-Teamster contracts remained dormant, the UFWOC-Teamster jurisdictional pact operative.

The fight in Salinas and then the attempts to reach some kind of settlement had drawn the public's attention away from Delano and the UFWOC's effort to establish administrative machinery needed to service the contracts. In Chavez's absence Larry Itliong had taken over the Delano operations and the establishment of satellite field offices that contained both hiring halls and service centers. After the Salinas strike action had slowed down, Padilla was assigned to the Tulare-Fresno-Madera county area where 8,000 small family farms grow tree fruit and grapes. Most of the ownerships are in small parcels. These independent operators consider Chavez an evil genius bent on taking their land and their livelihood.

These small farmers grew the remaining 15 percent of the table-grape crop left unorganized by the UFWOC. Each of these farms has several crops, a few acres of peaches, a few plums, and some vineyardland. The owners do much of the work themselves, but they need extra help to prune, to thin the fruit before it ripens, and finally to pick the crop. Some hire and direct the work themselves; others work through a packinghouse. These packinghouses finance the farmer's annual operational costs, they hire and supervise the extra labor and the harvesting of the crop, and, at the end of the season, they tote up the books, make the deductions, note how much of the operating account has been used, and then issue the farmer a check.

While the small growers are not vulnerable to boycotts individually because several hundred of them may market their fruit through a single packinghouse that has its own labels, the packinghouse itself is vulnerable. Padilla selected the eight largest packinghouses in the area and struck their field operations. All of the fruit packed and shipped by these firms was added to the boycott lists. The "big eight" gave up without too much fight and signed a contract with the UFWOC. This made many of the small growers furious; they withdrew from these houses and sold their fruit through those operations that were still independent.

The smaller packinghouses and most of the growers resisted Padilla's advances; when the UFWOC pickets would appear, the farmers and their wives gathered in counter-picket lines. The growers formed associations expressly for the purpose of fighting Chavez and the UFWOC; the associations imported strikebreaking labor — including large numbers of illegal aliens. Tractor tires were slashed and vandals sawed down trees and vines; the growers blamed the union and established armed night patrols. The union denied its members had anything to do with the vandalism and continued the strike.

The widespread attack was not working well, so the UFWOC narrowed its focus, singling out the 1,700-member Allied Grape Growers Association, an old cooperative that owned a part interest in the United Vintners. This company operated a large winery. The primary owner of UV was Heublein, the liquor conglomerate. Heublein also owned a large vineyard that it had acquired when it bought controlling interest in UV. Chavez ordered the boycotters to concentrate on all Heublein products, in the hope that the company would in turn pressure Allied Grape Growers into signing UFWOC contracts. The big company protested, contending it was willing to sign a UFWOC contract covering its own vineyards, but it could do nothing else. Behind the scenes Heublein did pressure the Allied Growers, but to no avail.

The Heublein boycott was not popular with Chavez's supporters. First the Catholic Bishops Farm Labor Committee, then the AFL-CIO, protested the boycott was unfair; Heublein had contracts with several AFL-CIO unions and the company repeatedly expressed the desire to recognize the UFWOC and negotiate a contract covering its vineyard workers. George Meany, angry because the UFWOC had unilaterally called the boycott without consulting the federation, ordered all AFL-CIO unions to ignore the Heublein boycott. Not long after, the company and the union signed a contract and the Heublein boycott efforts were discontinued.

By the spring of 1971 the union was running strikes in San Diego, Imperial, Tulare, Fresno, Madera, Monterey, and Santa Barbara counties. Although the move against Allied Grape Growers had not worked, many of the strike efforts

— combined with the threat of boycotting — brought growers to the bargaining table. By summer the union had more than 100 contracts to administer. Chavez had turned the talks with the Salinas growers over to Cohen and Kircher and was devoting his full attention to the union's administrative structures. There were real problems. Most of the hiring hall administrators had never administered anything more complex than a picket line. The ranch committees — the backbone of the Chavez system — were not working out well; they were uncertain or vindictive or apathetic. Some simply relied on the foremen to tell them what they should do. Chavez called Fred Ross to take over the training of the ranch committeemen.

Ross recalled, "The workers on the ranches had elected ranch committees, but the committees were meeting only once a month; they were yelling and screaming at each other. They weren't organized, they didn't know what it was they were to do, they were afraid to go up against their employers, or in some cases they were pushing the employers too hard. No one had come to lead them, to train them, so that became our job.

"This was the first time we'd gotten so close to so many of these workers. They'd been imported as strikebreakers, and now, overnight, they were blanketed by a union." Ross pointed out that many of the Delano ranches now under contract had been struck for five years, some of the original workers had become strong union members, some had given up the field work to devote full time to the UFWOC, but most of the workers had scattered, to find work outside the strike area. The 400 to 500 percent turnover on each ranch each year complicated the union's task of equitably establishing work patterns and seniority systems.

Ross added, "What had happened was that the original strikers, the boycott workers, and the college kids had handed these workers a union. So in order to make these workers union conscious, they had to go through a lot of the same thing that the original strikers had gone through. We were fighting Safeway [for selling lettuce] at the time, so we made these workers go out onto the picket lines; we found 10 or 15 workers who were potential organizers and we taught them how to hold house meetings, how to go through ranches, crew by crew, teaching people the history of their own union, and how to administer their own contracts.

"There were a lot of problems with the seniority system, whether the seniority should relate to the time in the union, or the time working on a particular ranch," Ross said. Those original strikers who had picketed for a while, supported the union, then gone off to work elsewhere but had continued to pay union dues, wanted the right to go back to work. Those who had been loyal to the union for a while, but then drifted away, thought they had some rights. Those at work on the ranches formed the ranch committees and set the policies. When some workers came back and found they had to pay back dues, they were angry. Others found the seniority system worked against them. Migrant families used to working together were split up, the father dispatched to one farm, the mother to another. The smaller children could no longer work. Frequently the workers protested.

Ross said, "Our toughest job was to convince the ranch committees they had to deal with these issues themselves, not come to us or to Cesar."

It was during this time that the movie producer helped the union purchase the 300-acre tuberculosis sanitarium in the Tehachapi Mountains, east of Bakersfield, and convert it to a national union headquarters. Chavez explained, "It was my idea to leave for La Paz because I wanted to remove my presence from Delano, so they could develop their own leadership, because if I am there, they wouldn't make the decisions themselves. They'd come to me."

The Forty Acres became the Delano hiring hall and service center. The union medical clinic remained on the site. Itliong, whose base of power within the union rested primarily on his long-lasting relationships with the older Filipino crew leaders, maintained his office in Delano, refusing to move with the rest of the "national staff" to the mountains. He was unhappy with the move and with the way the union was being administered. He felt many of the Anglo volunteers, like Drake, Chatfield, and Ganz, did not understand farm workers and that they exerted undue influence on Chavez.

Itliong said, "We, in the top echelon of the organization, make too many of the rules and we change the rules so very quickly that the workers themselves don't understand what the hell is going on. Since I am close to the workers, I begin to understand this feeling; they become very unhappy about this sort of thing." He went on to explain that he felt the move to La Paz took Chavez too far from the people, that the bureaucratic structures imposed to administer union affairs were further screening Chavez from direct contact with the farm workers. Eventually these feelings led Itliong to resign from the UFWOC.

Chavez suffered the agony of this growing bureaucracy; he conceptually saw a union run in the most democratic terms, but in practice he had a difficult time trying to maintain his own distance; his tendencies were to step in and make decisions, but he knew instinctively the new union must suffer its own mistakes if it was to grow. Even though he had removed himself from Delano, he maintained a close supervision over it, and all of the other field offices. Through frequent staff meetings and meetings of the executive board, he developed his own personal involvement with the tiniest of union details.

This tactic angered and frustrated Kircher. He had offered Chavez 35 AFL-CIO administrators to act as a training cadre for the farm workers and Chavez had rejected the offer. He felt the farm workers must make their own mistakes. Kircher watched as the farm workers stumbled through their administrative tasks, he watched as Chavez personally conducted interminably long meetings. Kircher said, "He ran the credit union meetings. Now I know credit unions are important, but God almighty a couple of administrative officers could run it, but no, Cesar had to be there. . . . [Here's] the top guy, spending hours of his valuable time, in a damn credit union meeting, going over every detail."

Chavez feels that it is his attention to detail that keeps him in touch with the union's various activities and with the people who carry out the day-to-day routine. Once, very early in the morning, I asked him what the stack of paper on his desk was; he patted it, replying, "I receive all the correspondence. I didn't used to do this, but I do it now. Every piece that comes into the movement that is not clearly assigned, you know? Then I assign the letters with a message to the people to take care of it. . . . The ones that are mine, I dictate answers, then I make memos. A letter will trigger a memo, like I'll dictate an answer and also send a memo to let so-and-so know what we are doing.

"What I do is come in about three o'clock in the morning, and I can work without interruption until about eight; that's when I do all my paper work."

I was amazed. Couldn't he delegate much of this work to others?

"Oh, I delegate a lot of it. The only thing I do here is, if someone writes a letter, I make damn sure he gets the right answer, and I also want to know, to keep myself informed. I have to read the mail, all the reports. I can't have someone else do that. I wouldn't get the impact. It is not so much delegating authority as it is being informed."

When I talked to Padilla about Chavez's attention to administrative detail, he laughed, nodding his head, and started telling about the telephones. It seems almost everyone within the union has run afoul of the phone budgets and Chavez had ordered the offending phones shut off. Padilla said, "In Selma we needed more phone money to do the job right, but as a board member I knew we didn't have it. When he turns the phones off, he is teaching you a lesson, making you think. He knows we need more, but he can't give it."

I asked Padilla if Chavez was something of a dictator at times.

"Yeah, sort of. But we have a democracy, we have a board that talks things over, and when we make a decision, he enforces that decision. What he does is call you in to La Paz, and he says for you to give him a list of what is happening, everything, and he checks it, all of it. He's up day and night, and then he talks to you about it, you can argue, but once it is set, that's it."

Chavez is a teacher. He has patience and a sense of time that can be — and often is — exhausting, and he understands that the farm workers must be allowed the time and the experience to learn how to put a union together and operate it. In the process he can be witty (his humor shows frequently in little, pointed jokes that coax and prod), or he can be surprisingly abrupt.

One major problem that had to be ironed out in the beginning was the operation of the hiring hall. Chavez explained, "Each field office is an administrative unit; once we reach agreement with the workers [through their ranch committees] on procedures of the dispatch and dues collection, then the field offices do the actual dispatching and collection of dues, but only according to those regulations the ranch committees agreed on. We have found it is important for the ranch committees to have a representative in the hiring hall to watch the dispatch, so that everyone, including the workers, knows it is going by the rules. Otherwise some of the workers may start raising hell with our guys.

"We have had to fight the companies to get them to talk to the ranch committees; the companies want to straighten out their problems directly with me, or someone else here at La Paz; but we are saying that it is the local ranch committee that is in charge, the company must deal with the ranch committee. And the workers must make the committees they've elected responsible for the grievance procedures, for running the meetings, and carrying out the mandates of the workers."

In the early summer of 1971 I made an inspection trip through the farming areas to see how the contracts were working. In the Calexico UFWOC office I found Roberto Garcia — a former Salinas lettuce striker turned organizer — in charge of the hiring hall. His staff was dispatching 500 workers into the melon harvest and 7,000 pickers into the lettuce fields owned by Inter Harvest, Fresh Pict, and

D'Arrigo Farms. At the same time he was running strikes against three melon and lettuce farms, and he was helping Manuel Chavez in the continuing effort to organize the green-card aliens living in Mexicali and commuting into the U.S. for work.

The pace was hectic, the emphasis was on striking and organizing the Mexican commuters. The union and the service center had adjacent offices, on a side street, in an old hotel building, not far from where labor contractor Jesus Ayala parked his buses each morning. The street corner labor shapeups were an integral part of the union's environment.

The UFWOC "hiring hall" was a battered little desk in a small office; the workers gathered outside, on the sidewalks. The dispatchers were various organizers assigned to desk duty on what appeared to be a haphazard rotation system. Garcia told me the dispatch was on a first come–first served basis and he made no mention of the union's rather complex seniority system. Each morning before dawn the workers milled around the offices; some were dispatched, most were waiting for picket-line duty assignments. The cars to be used for the picket caravans were gassed up at the station across the street and then queued up. The workers, carrying strike placards and *huelga* banners, climbed into the cars; after a last-minute scramble for seats, then they went off in search of strikebreaking crews. They knew generally where the melon pickers were working on the three ranches under strike, but in the vast, flat emptiness of the Imperial Valley, search was required to find the precise locations.

After spending a morning with the pickets — they may have bothered the strikebreaking crews a little, but no one walked out of the fields — Garcia took me to watch union melon crews at work in the cantaloupe fields. These men work in crews of 14. During the early part of the picking season the contract called for $2-an-hour pay scale, but when the weather turned hot and the pace of picking reached a furious peak, the crews would be working at a piece rate — 54 cents a 90-pound "pack-out box" — and they would earn $30 to $40 a day. The men work bent double, loading the huge picking sacks, running with their loads up ramps, and dumping them into a truck that moves with the crew.

One member of each crew was a UFWOC steward; he enforced the contract provisions and kept discipline in the crew. When a grievance arose, when there was some dispute over pay or working conditions, or the crew boss or foreman was pushing too hard or was abusive, the steward would try to settle the issue with the company supervisor. Failing that he could, and often did, order the crew to stop work until formal grievance procedures could be utilized.

At Inter Harvest, Cal Watkins said one of the biggest problems the company faced was a growing sense of militancy among the crews. "They'll sit down at the least little thing," Watkins said, adding, "They are feeling their power too much, and you have to go and talk them back to work, you have to point out the contract calls for grievance procedures, not sit-downs."

At Inter Harvest and Fresh Pict and other big multiple-crop operations, the UFWOC had created a ranch committee for each crop or series of crops. The result was three or four ranch committees on each of these big operations. Watkins found this "too damn democratic to be efficient." But he said the union contract was not causing insurmountable problems, adding, "We don't find the hiring hall a stumbling block, although they are obviously short of administrative experience."

Herb Lee, manager of the Fresh Pict farming operations said, "The contract is all right; if we had a good hiring hall and a hard-headed business agent it would be all right, but they are using organizers to administer their contracts."

At first the union had insisted on a dues-checkoff system — the employer deducted the union monthly dues from workers' paychecks — but because of the high worker turnover and mobility any one worker might pass through several company payrolls in a month. Each company would deduct the same month's dues. The system could not work unless all farms were organized under contract and a fully computerized dues payment system was worked out, so the union asked that the companies scrap the idea. The union then collected the $3.50-a-month dues itself, on a quarterly basis, affixing a "dues stamp" to the back of the worker's membership card. If the worker was not paid up, he could not be dispatched; his card was taken from him and placed in the inactive file.

Fresh Pict and Inter Harvest had 12-month vegetable-production operations, and their crews moved with the seasons from the Yuma-Imperial areas north through Oxnard up into the Salinas Valley. The companies computerized their employee lists and hired and laid off workers by a seniority system based on time with the company, rather than time with the union.

Overall, the union's seniority system was confusing, because it seemed to vary from farm to farm, from hiring hall to hiring hall. Some UFWOC people told me seniority was based on time in the union; others said it was a combination of time in the union and on a particular ranch. The problem was complicated by the fact that farm workers must move from employer to employer, from union job to non-union job.

The attitudes of growers toward the union varied considerably. Where Watkins and Lee, as corporate managers, were more accustomed to the idea of unions, the family farmers — the owner operators — were more personally involved. John Kovacevich owns 700 acres of grapes and 300 acres of tree fruit in the southeast corner of the San Joaquin Valley, near Arvin. He employs 20 full-time workers and during the harvest season his payroll goes up to 500 workers. Kovacevich and his father developed this farm, and Kovacevich has a strong feeling for it and for the way of life he lives. He is considered a fair, reasonable man by the UFWOC. When asked why he signed with the union, he replied candidly that he had no economic choices left, the boycott had taken his markets from him. He said when the question of unionization was put to his workers he told them if they did not sign with the union he would be out of business.

After explaining that, Kovacevich added, "I will have to be

272

fair and say that quite a few of those people became very loyal to Cesar and the United Farm Workers."

It was Kovacevich's feeling that a joint hiring hall, operated by the farmer and the union, could be workable. He said that UFWOC hiring hall operations were very uneven. "It depended upon who was running it. They had some real fine fellows running it, and they had some fellows you just couldn't work with at all. We started with Dave Burciaga, a fine man. Roberto Garcia was darn hard to get along with. We were always wrong, there were constant grievances. At times we'd get together with Cesar and get it all straightened out . . . but we just couldn't live with it at times. One day you put in an order and the next they'd send out double what you asked for, then insist on you paying all those dispatched. I had to show them the dispatch order and *make* them live up to it."

Kovacevich's complaints were similar to other owner operators in other areas. The shifting of power away from the grower and placing it in the hands of the workers, through the ranch committees and the hiring halls, was traumatic. Employers like Ernest Gallo — the E. and J. Gallo Winery — are strong, autocratic men who would rather deal with other strong, autocratic men. They are problem solvers; when a question arises they seek answers and make decisions; rule by committee, rule by inexperience, rule by inefficiency, drives them up the wall.

Undoubtedly there were union administrators who did see opportunities to "get even" for past wrongs; there were some who let their racial hatred stand in the way of good judgment and some who saw chances to acquire and exercise power at a personal level. The hiring halls in 1971 and 1972 were dealing with 40,000 to 50,000 workers in 26 different locations. The system developed problems and was modified. For instance the change from dues checkoff to the quarterly dues payment caused another problem; the migrants returning to Mexico or Texas each winter did not pay dues while they were out of California. When they came back in the spring they were faced with at least a $10.50 charge per worker to catch up on the back dues, and often they had to come up with another $10.50 for the current quarterly installment. The worker unrest over this issue became so strong the dues structure was changed again, in 1973; now members pay a flat 2 percent of their income as they earn it.

The first grape grower to sign with the UFWOC, Lionel Steinberg, felt the union system was working "reasonably well" and that the hiring hall was able to meet 80 percent of his peak labor needs. He said the hiring hall was also stabilizing the work force. "Where we used to go through 2,000 men and women just to keep 500 working, the hiring hall has smoothed things out so we don't need these high numbers anymore."

Steinberg computed the cost of the union contract was 30 cents for a 22-pound box of grapes that sold for from $7 to $8, and cost about $5 to grow. Within that 30 cents there was a 10-cent-an-hour contribution to the Robert F. Kennedy Health and Welfare Fund. Leroy Chatfield, administrator of the fund, reported there were 55,000 worker cards in the files in the summer of 1971; the fund then was disbursing $60,000 a month in medical benefits that ranged from $5 for a visit to the doctor's office up to $300 for maternity benefits and $400 for surgery. Workers had to put 250 hours a quarter in to qualify for major benefits, but only 50 hours a quarter to qualify for the minor benefit program. The plan was designed for workers who were without employment for weeks at a time, and the union was opening medical clinics of its own and designing a prepaid health care plan.

Clearly through 1971 and 1972 the United Farm Workers had begun to consolidate its gains, had begun to build itself into a powerful and increasingly more permanent force as it signed more contracts and spread the influence of the hiring hall further afield. No matter what the problems expressed by the farmers against the union — and there is no doubt many of these complaints were justified — it was the influence of the hiring hall and the seniority system that was bringing about change. No one expressed this better than John Giumarra, Jr.

John is a young, clean-cut attorney who looks more like a stockbroker or account executive than a farmer. He moves easily in the country club set, likes golf and good food, and operates his workaday world from a soft leather chair in a wood-paneled office in the opulent new Giumarra Vineyards office building east of Bakersfield. Toying with a silver letter opener and swinging gently back and forth in his big office chair, Giumarra said, "The hiring hall has changed the whole way of operating, the whole relationship. Now any time an employee wants to work he has to go down to the hiring hall and be dispatched. Since the people tend to work in crews, teams in effect, when we would want a particular crew to go to work, we would have to send a written dispatch down to the hiring hall, and then the whole crew would have to go in, get dispatch cards filled out, and be sent back to the ranch. The hiring hall became a bottleneck in every farm operation."

When things did not move fast enough for Giumarra, he personally took a crew into the hiring hall. He described what he felt was a chaotic, inefficient scene that had bogged down completely: "It was like a herd of cattle in there. I literally went behind the counter and went to the window and started dispatching my own workers, getting them union forms, collecting dues, making change, to facilitate what was going on."

I asked UFWOC attorney Jerry Cohen about Giumarra's complaints. Cohen, sitting on a broken kitchen chair in a paint-splattered old room in the La Paz administrative building, his feet propped up on a beat-up old desk, said: "We're willing to work out some changes, if the farmers are talking about specific problems, but I don't think they are talking about specifics, so much as I think they want to get rid of the whole goddamn system. We're talking about power, now, power of the hiring hall and of the union."

A couple of hours later I was walking with Cesar, up a hilly road. We paused under the shade of an oak, and he explained, "For 80 years farm workers thought the grower was invincible, but now the myth is broken. It was shattered when we found we could win. Now the workers are no longer afraid; they want to take on the growers."

Corky Larson, wife of Coachella grape grower K. K. Larson, talked about the union and about agribusiness. "The lack of ground rules has prevented orderly unionization. In 1968 the growers felt they had the upper hand in the dispute, and they wanted no legislation which would facilitate unionization. By 1970 the UFWOC had found real power in the use of the secondary boycott. With its availability as a tool, the UFWOC felt legislation would dilute, rather than enhance its power."

Without realizing it perhaps, Mrs. Larson had spoken for most of California agribusiness. The Salinas–Santa Maria growers might try jumping into bed with the Teamsters as a way to avoid Chavez, but that, at best, was a drastic solution and it did nothing to take away the secondary boycotts and strikes — the tools the UFWOC used to develop power enough to move farmers to such desperate acts. An increasing number of agribusiness leaders knew they needed some countering force that only new legislation could provide; their primary job was to take away Chavez's power tools.

U.S. Senator George Murphy was talked into introducing such a bill, but even with the $1 million public relations campaign by Whitaker and Baxter, the Murphy bill never got off the ground. Something more subtle, more dramatic was needed, something like an apparently complete reversal of agriculture's traditional anti-labor stand. Quietly, with the cooperation of both the Nixon and Reagan administrations, farm groups began to put together ad hoc committees to draft amendments to the National Labor Relations Act that would shield agriculture from the likes of Chavez. The move was led by California agribusinessmen and the American Farm Bureau Federation. This was to be a multi-pronged legislative attack; as the Nixon Administration introduced the agribusiness package in Congress, similar bills would be introduced in the farm state legislatures.

The California ad hoc committee included seven agribusiness groups and was chaired by Robert Brown, executive director of the California Taxpayers Association, an urban-based conservative organization with ties that spread across the industrial spectrum. The committee's direct link to the Reagan Administration was Allan Grant, a thick-set dairy farmer out of the Tulare County Farm Bureau, who had slavishly worked his way to the presidency of the California Farm Bureau Federation and the chairmanship of the state board of agriculture. Grant, as a member of Brown's committee, arranged for the committee's proposals to be critically reviewed by the state board of agriculture before they were presented to the legislature. All of this was done quietly, without public notice.

News of California agribusiness's switch in its absolute opposition to including agriculture in the National Labor Relations Act — and coincidentally the existence of the ad hoc committee — was revealed almost by accident. Early in 1971, El Centro farmer Mike Schultz, while talking to Los Angeles *Times* labor reporter Harry Bernstein, said several farm groups were seeking the protections of the NLRA. While Schultz could not elaborate, that small bit of information was dramatic enough: After 35 years the farmers were reversing their position.

The *Times* story caught everyone by surprise. Brown was just returning from the National Council of Agricultural Employers convention in Atlanta when I reached him by phone. He was evasive, and underneath he seemed furious that the news was out, but he tried hard not to let it show.

When I asked why the California ad hoc committee had been kept out of sight, Brown replied, "We're not trying to keep anything from the press, but now wasn't the time to be talking."

While at the NCAE convention Brown had talked to representatives from 37 farm states. The NCAE was coordinating the state efforts and, from its Washington, D.C., office, lobbying for the national legislative goal. During the convention, top U.S. Department of Labor officials had come down to discuss the Nixon Administration's legislative package. It would be "similar to the NLRA" but would have special provisions designed to meet agriculture's special problems. Heavy emphasis was placed on the "similar to the NLRA" because agribusiness needed to build a smoke screen for its real designs.

The effort was being given a big ride; Assistant Secretary of Labor W. J. Usery and Undersecretary of Labor Laurence Silberman were out giving speeches on the new Nixon farm labor package: It would exempt small farmers who employed 500 mandays of labor or less any quarter; it would establish union representation election machinery that would make it difficult, if not impossible, for seasonal workers to vote; it would require workers to give ten-day notice before striking and provide the farmer with a 30-day cooling-off period before going into binding arbitration, thus sidestepping the words "no strike at harvest" while providing that protection; and finally the proposal would create a special agricultural labor relations board, controlled, of course, by the U.S. Department of Agriculture. About the only thing similar to the NLRA in the Nixon proposal was the outlawing of the secondary boycott.

The federal package was a mild version of the proposals being advanced by the agribusiness coalition in the various farm states. Many of the state bills would extend the cooling-off period to 60 days; some beefed up the anti-boycott language to make it illegal to even utter the word "boycott" or to carry picket signs advocating such a boycott. Some of the state bills included provisions governing what issues could and could not be brought into collective bargaining sessions. The NCAE helped set up nationwide speaking tours for men like Grant. The message was clear: If Chavez and the UFWOC were not headed off, the farmers of Iowa or Kansas or Idaho might be next.

The agribusiness efforts were opposed by the AFL-CIO and its state federations, not only to help the farm workers, but to head off any cumulative anti-labor effect the passage of such laws might have. This put the federation in a strange position: It was supporting the farm workers by opposing these proposed laws while at the same time it had to oppose

278

Chavez's position on the inclusion of farm workers under the NLRA.

The Farm Bureau and other agribusiness interests based their campaign on the issue of secret-ballot elections; they contended the farmer was trying to secure this right for his workers while Chavez, because of his NLRA position, was opposing secret-ballot elections. It was not elections that Chavez opposed, but the Taft-Hartley Amendment which stripped away the right to conduct secondary boycotts and opened the way for states to pass anti-union, "open-shop," right-to-work laws that seriously weaken union strength.

The California agribusiness coalition poured another $1 million into its effort to push through a state agricultural labor relations act. The same crew bosses and foremen who had put together the company unions in opposition to Chavez appeared on behalf of the agribusiness interests, bringing with them 400 anti-Chavez farm workers. The UFWOC countered with a whirlwind lobbying effort within the state capital, and the bills were defeated. Agribusinessmen expected this and immediately announced they would take the issue directly to the voters, through an initiative process.

In Oregon a similar Farm Bureau bill had passed through the legislature and was on Governor Tom McCall's desk. If McCall did not veto the bill within one week it would become law. Chavez ordered Jerry Cohen into Oregon to convince the governor he should veto the measure. Cohen activated the Portland boycott to his cause, and started a direct pressure telephone campaign. Thousands of supporters from all over the United States called the governor's office. Cohen ordered an evening prayer vigil on the steps of the capitol in Salem, and he launched an attack on the Oregon Farm Bureau. The Farm Bureau rose to the bait and Cohen was off and running in the press. The whirlwind campaign impressed Governor McCall, and he vetoed the bill.

Arizona was another matter. This was a right-to-work state, under section 14-B of the Taft-Hartley Amendment, and notoriously conservative. The legislature whipped out the Farm Bureau bill, hardly paying any attention to the

AFL-CIO threats of a nationwide boycott of all Arizona products. Chavez sensed a national issue could be made in Arizona, and he sent Jim Drake in to evaluate the situation.

Drake said, "We had a lot of debate whether or not to try to do away with the bill, or to pick on all of the legislators who voted for the bill, or narrow the attack by taking just one political 'hostage' and making him an example. So we decided to go after the governor, to recall him because he had been so bad. He had refused to see Cesar; he signed the bill without reading it. He was a very good symbol, he'd called John Birch Society Day for two years in a row, so it looked like a good place to fight."

When Governor Jack Williams signed the bill, on May 30th, Cesar Chavez started a fast that was to last 24 days. Drake explained: "The fast was undertaken because Cesar wanted to change the system; he wanted to get people over their fears of organizing, so they would be willing to fight for the union, and he figured the best way to do that was to expend himself. We never lost sight of the fact that we did not want a new governor, but that we wanted to organize the people and in the process send a clear message to all politicians that they had to be responsive to the people, to the workers."

The union built its "Arizona Campaign" around the fast; Cesar was moved into a small, air-conditioned room in the Santa Rita Center, on Phoenix's south side. The logistics of the fast were left up to Leroy Chatfield and Cesar; Marshall Ganz took charge of mobilizing the people to come into the Mass; Dolores and Richard Chavez were out in the fields, organizing the people, getting them turned onto the idea of a union; Drake was assigned the political work, the registration of voters, the gathering of the 175,000 signatures they felt were needed to come up with the 108,000 qualified signatures required for a recall election.

The fast attracted thousands of farm workers, just as it had in Delano; the staff and union priests conducted nightly rallies and celebrated the Mass. The fasting and the harshness of the new law did project the issues onto the national scene.

In June the Democratic Party built a lettuce boycott–United Farm Workers plank into its convention proceedings; in August Secretary of Agriculture Earl Butz, stumping in Florida, attacked the lettuce boycott. As the issues swirled around in the media, Drake put together a coalition of Navajos, blacks, Chicanos, disgruntled mine workers, and steel workers and set about recalling Governor Williams.

Drake said, "We went knocking on doors. We'd ask if they favored the recall of the governor. If they did, we asked if they were registered to vote; if not, we would send somebody around to register them and then have them sign the petitions. We registered nearly 100,000 voters and we secured 176,000 signatures."

But the recall election was never scheduled; first the validity of large blocks of signatures was questioned by state election officials and the UFWOC filed suit to prove that the signatures were valid. The legal hassling stalled the recall movement, but the message was clear: 176,000 voters in Arizona were not happy with the Williams administration. And farm workers in Arizona were, for the first time, aware that they had some political clout.

The California farmers were also going to the people, by the initiative process; they, too, needed large blocks of signatures to put their farm labor proposal on the November 7, 1972, ballot. Within the context of the proposal, the issues were almost identical.

Allan Grant explained: "Growers are supporting the agricultural labor relations act — Proposition 22 — for two major reasons: They strongly believe farm workers should be entitled to vote . . . by secret ballot . . . on whether or not they want to be union members . . . and secondly [farmers] feel just as strongly that the secondary boycotts should be illegal . . ."

UFWOC supporters like Father James Vizzard, of the National Catholic Rural Life Conference, came into California to oppose Proposition 22. Vizzard argued the proposition would limit the secret-ballot elections to permanently employed farm workers by a series of exclusions that would make it all but impossible for seasonal workers to vote. Vizzard charged the proposition would restrict the rights of free speech and free assembly by limiting or prohibiting boycott actions. The farmers would have to be given ten-day strike notice and then they could use a 60-day cooling-off period to avoid strikes at harvest.

Leroy Chatfield was put in charge of the UFWOC Anti-Proposition 22 campaign. Chris Hartmire donated office space in the migrant ministry's suite in Los Angeles. Chatfield put together a statewide organization built around the boycott structure; there were 40 separate committees, each responsible for organizing a specific area, each reporting in daily. Chavez had ordered this issue must take precedence over any other and had put the full resources of the union behind Chatfield. Chatfield began registering voters. By the time Chavez called a general board meeting to discuss the progress of the campaign, Chatfield had 40,000 to 50,000 new voters registered.

Chavez wasn't impressed. Voter registration was not the kind of issue that would catch fire, not against the well-financed, well-staffed grower campaign. From the time the growers hired professionals to circulate their petitions — paying them so much for each signature obtained — the agribusiness campaign was built around the secret-ballot issue and around consumer protection against the boycott. Nothing the union had come up with in its first two months of campaigning had begun to make headlines or attract attention.

Chatfield recalled the board meeting, "After the board members agreed with Cesar that I hadn't come up with enough effort, he told me to go out and find an issue that would make headlines. That afternoon, driving back to Los Angeles, I was in a funk. I had done the best I could on the voter registration and he didn't think it was good. I had to come up with something, and my mind was a blank."

Chatfield and his staff, faced with an extensive "Yes on 22" billboard campaign, copied the "human billboard" tactics used earlier by Marcos Muñoz in the Boston boycott. Hundreds of volunteers, each equipped with a "No on 22" sign, would mass in single file near freeway off and on ramps, around supermarkets, and along busy streets. Once 350 of these human billboards completely encircled the Los Angeles Coliseum just before a Ram football game.

But this still was not creating a big public issue. Then the break came. As the news accounts began to tell the farm workers' side of the story, people began to call the UFWOC office to apologize for signing the petitions. Chatfield said, "They told us they had thought they were helping the farm workers, or that they thought they were signing a protest over the high cost of food, or something like that. It began to dawn on us that we might have stumbled into something."

Leroy's wife, Bonnie, went to the public records and extracted a long list of the petition signers. Then, using the phone books, she began to call around and ask questions. She heard more tales of fraud. Chatfield contacted California Secretary of State Jerry Brown. The office of the secretary of state polices election laws, but Brown was skeptical. This was a cat-and-dog fight and either side might be using him. (Brown's father, the former governor Edmund G. Brown, had suffered the same doubts years before.) The Chatfields persisted. They went out to the petitioners they could find and took affidavits and brought these to Brown; finally he was convinced. Brown filed suit to get the issue taken off the ballot.

While Brown's suit was thrown out of court, it raised enough questions to bring the matter to the attention of several district attorneys in the state. In Los Angeles the grand jury investigated the charges and returned an indictment. The resulting news stories were "the issue" Chatfield had been seeking. Big headlines suggested fraud, and the UFWOC made the most out of the controversy. This put the agribusiness campaign on the defensive. The pressures built up as charge and counter-charge were hurled back and forth. Chavez alleged the names of dead voters were on the petitions; Chatfield claimed entire pages of petitions had been signed in the same handwriting.

Even though they had turned the situation back on the farmers, Chavez was extremely anxious about the campaign. He felt the law, if passed, would spell the end of the union. Chavez personally stumped the state at a fierce clip, turning himself over to each of the boycott–anti 22 committees to do with him what they felt was best; he talked and marched and was interviewed until he was near exhaustion. Chavez spent the last few days of the campaign in Los Angeles.

Chatfield said, "He was really uptight. He was pacing the floor, and asking if were doing everything we could. I'd never seen him so worried. We didn't know what to do with him, how to make the best use of him. We put him on the human billboard for a while, that sort of thing."

Chavez kept asking Chatfield if he was doing all that could be done. Chatfield finally snapped back, "Yes, goodammit, everything's being done that can be done." The UFW efforts were more than enough.

On November 7, 1972, the California voters soundly rejected Proposition 22. The United Farm Workers had proven, both in Arizona and California, that they could mount a political campaign and, given an issue, carry that campaign to success. The message was not lost on agribusiness.

CHAPTER TWELVE :
AGRIBUSINESS CONSPIRACY

The UFWA–Schenley Ranch contract first negotiated in 1966 and renegotiated in 1969 had a June 21, 1972, expiration date. During the term of the second contract, Schenley Industries sold the 5,000 acres of vineyards to Buttes Gas and Oil, a small, aggressive conglomerate that had already "taken a position" in agribusiness and was expanding. The UFWA contract with Schenley had a successor clause that carried it through the sale; Buttes renamed the ranch White River Farms and made a few management changes, but the transition was orderly and did not disturb the work force.

Early in the summer of 1972 UFWA negotiators sat down with ranch managers to renew the contract. Progress was slow. Out in the vines work progressed and the crop matured. When the grapes were ripe ranch managers ordered the harvest started, and on August 10th the UFWA hiring hall started dispatching harvest crews into the White River vineyards.

Dolores Huerta explained, "We didn't have a contract yet, but we didn't want a strike. We didn't need any more problems at the time; Proposition 22 was just getting hot, and then, remember, Schenley was our first contract. We'd been in there six years, and the ranch committee was working well. The people had a lot of feeling for that contract."

The Schenley Ranch had become the working model for the UFWA's democratic form of unionism. Through their ranch committee, the workers policed the contract safety clauses, especially those regulating the use of pesticides; they exercised grievance procedures, and they supervised the union hiring hall's worker-dispatch system. When the contract talks were opened in June the ranch committee had a direct input into the negotiations. The talks went smoothly for a while, then hit a snag, in mid-August.

Chavez, Huerta, and the ranch committee went to the workers. Chavez said, "We told them what was happening. We had a hunch management wanted a strike. The workers agreed to let the ranch committee offer 20 cents [an hour] less than our standard contract, just to avoid a strike. But once we gave them [company negotiators] wages, they came back and wanted language, so we said, 'To hell with you. We aren't going to argue language.' I think they wanted a fight."

The company denied this, and blamed the union for the breakdown in negotiations. The talks were discontinued

August 28th and the ranch committee called the workers out of the vines; the UFWA struck White River Farms. Farm managers immediately began to recruit and haul strikebreakers into the vineyards. For the first time in six years the $3 million wine-grape crop was being harvested by nonunion crews. These crews were short handed, inexperienced, and intimidated by the *huelgistas:* Farm associations throughout the San Joaquin Valley began recruiting more experienced workers for White River Farms. Each morning several busloads of workers were dispatched from Fresno, Reedley, and Parlier.

The small farmers in these associations were not content with just recruiting and hauling strikebreakers into White River Farms; they wanted to confront Chavez directly, personally. One Sunday morning 600 farmers, their wives, and children gathered at White River Farms just after dawn; they sharpened the hooked blades on their grape knives, took up the dishpan picking containers, and trooped into the vineyards to help personally with the harvest. It was like an old-fashioned communal harvest among frontier settlers come to help a neighbor in need.

But if farmers are thought of in human terms, this neighbor was not a farmer; Buttes Gas and Oil was and is a multi-leveled corporation designed by urban executives to make profits from petroleum and land ventures. A Buttes report states all farm costs are written off over the "useful lives of the properties." For Buttes, farming is a tax shelter: ". . . no income taxes have been paid by the company or its subsidiaries for the years 1967 to 1971 . . ."

For the traditional farmer the useful life of his property dates back to his father and grandfather and extends forward — he hopes — to the lives of his children and his grandchildren. Unfortunately, the small farmer is in direct, unfair competition with the corporate giants who, because of their outsized farm-to-market operations directly influence or control the market prices. These corporations consume the small farms they drive out of business; they displace the small farmers. Yet, in times of labor crisis, these giants manipulate the surviving small farmers, pushing them into the forefront of the fight. They are the shock troops.

Chavez observed, "The corporations have the small farmers fighting the union because as they fight us, they divert their attention from the real issues for the small farmer. These small growers are being exploited by the same forces that exploit the workers. To make it more ridiculous, the corporations and the organizations like Farm Bureau use the small growers as spokesmen to peddle all of the nonsense they have developed about the small independent farmer standing against the union threat to the nation's food supply.

"The small farmers think that if they get rid of our union their problems are over, but they are wrong. They will never make it that way. The small farmers will never make it unless they stand up to the conglomerates." Chavez believes small farmers can, by organizing into collective bargaining associations, compete with the conglomerates in the marketplace and, at the same time, deal more effectively with organized farm labor's demands. By pooling their labor needs into a master contract, a group of small farmers would cut costs and make their operations more efficient.

Chavez explained, "One disadvantage the little guy in agriculture has is that he has to pay a premium to get workers to come to small jobs. In our hiring halls, when a job order comes in for 50 workers, the workers look to see where the job is, and they always take the large farm first because the job lasts longer. If the small growers would get it together, they could offer more work over longer periods and they wouldn't have to pay premium wages."

Ironically the small growers did organize, not to negotiate with Chavez, but to fight him. When the Buttes strike started at White River Farms the Central California Farmers Committee and the Nisei Farmers League recruited and bused hundreds of farm workers into the strike area. The big buses bringing the strikebreakers to the farm were met by a great mass of UFWA pickets, former White River Farms workers who were angry and sullen. They stood defiantly in the driveways, trying to block the buses; they called the U.S.

287

Immigration Service, reporting illegal aliens were being transported into the strike.

On the morning of September 25th the U.S. Border Patrol set up a roadblock on a county road, near the farm entrance. As the buses rolled toward the ranch, they were stopped and searched. Border Patrolmen found 68 illegal Mexican aliens. They were taken off the buses and the drivers were allowed to proceed. As the buses slowed and turned into the ranch, 200 screaming, yelling *huelgistas* mobbed up in front of them; the drivers stopped, then tried to bull through the crowd, slowly. Rocks and clods pelted the sides of the bus and smashed windows. The sheriff's deputies on duty radioed for help, but by the time the reinforcements arrived Dolores Huerta and Richard Chavez had managed to regain control of the strikers.

With Huerta and Chavez in the lead, the *huelgistas* marched down a farm road, part way onto the ranch; they knelt in the white, powdery dust and began a prayer vigil. Deputies moved in, informed them they were on private property, and, when they refused to leave, the lawmen arrested 141 of the strikers, including Huerta and Chavez. During the next week 128 more UFWA Schenley workers were arrested for mass picketing, against court-imposed restrictions on UFWA activities, or for trespass. Buttes managed to continue the harvest, but, by the time the last gondola was loaded with grapes and driven to the winery, the company estimated it had lost $1 million due to the strike. The UFWA lost its first contract.

But the action at White River Farms was more than just another local strike; it was the place where agribusiness began to put together what was to become one of the largest anti-labor conspiracies ever assembled, a conspiracy that was to involve the Teamsters and the Nixon Administration. First the Council of California Growers, then the California Farm Bureau Federation involved themselves in the dispute; Secretary of Agriculture Earl Butz, stumping in California for the reelection of Congressman Bob Mathias, used the White River Farms strike to express not only his opposition to Cesar

Chavez, but to set out the Nixon farm labor doctrine: "Such actions should be outlawed. It is not fair for a farmer to work all year to produce a crop and then be wiped out by a two-week strike."

The *Chavistas* were the enemy; the UFWA controlled 55,000 jobs in the grapes, vegetables, and tree-fruit crops, and its influence was spreading. Because of this, California agribusiness leaders felt it was imperative to move on as many fronts as possible. The President was cooperative. Nixon had appointed a young lawyer, Peter Nash, chief counsel for the National Labor Relations Board, and in March of 1972 Nash moved against the UFWA, in an unusual way; he declared that because the AFL-CIO had chartered the United Farm Workers, raising the organization from its status as an organizing committee to that of a full-fledged union, the UFWA was covered by the NLRA. Nash filed suit in federal court to block the UFWA's boycott against wineries. This legal end run was interesting because it displayed the hypocrisy of the Nixon Administration; as long as it served agribusiness interests Nixon opposed protecting farm labor under the NLRA, but when such a move could be used to bolster the farmers' fight against unions the switch was attempted. But the law was clear. Farm workers were specifically exempted from the act. The suit was dropped, but the Nixon efforts did not cease; the administration came up with its own versions of the Farm Bureau anti-labor bills that would outlaw boycotts and harvest strikes.

The Democrats, preparing for their nominating convention, drafted a platform plank supporting Chavez and the UFWA's boycott of lettuce. The Teamsters took exception. So did Secretary of Agriculture Butz; in a Florida speech, he said most of the lettuce was harvested by Teamster union crews and this fact was clearly marked on each box by a red-white-and-blue Teamster label that also carried a "Re-elect the President" political plug.

No doubt some Teamsters supported Nixon; Teamster President Frank Fitzsimmons, puffed up by Nixon's attention, personally contributed $4,000 to a Democrats-for-Nixon fund. However it was unusual — at that time — to hear agribusiness spokesman Earl Butz supporting any organized labor effort in farming. Later it became obvious that the most politically corrupt, most discredited presidential administration in the history of this nation was in an alliance with the scandal-ridden Teamsters' union to help agribusiness rid itself of a farm workers effort to form a democratic union.

Since the Salinas lettuce growers' talks with the UFWA had been discontinued in 1971 the Teamsters had never been very far back in the wings. Technically they still held the contracts covering lettuce workers on 170 farms, but these contracts had not been enforced. Bill Grami was anxious to get back into the field labor fight. As he pointed out, 100,000 of the 400,000 Teamsters in the Western Conference worked in agribusiness-related jobs, in the canneries, the produce sheds, cold-storage plants, and freezers. Grami said he wanted to organize field labor to protect the Teamsters' flank; strikes in the fields would disrupt the flow of work to the Teamsters.

During the Proposition 22 campaign the Teamsters kept a low profile; while the issue was so patently anti-labor even they had to oppose it, Western Conference boss Einar Mohn was careful to point out that their opposition in no way meant they were supporting Chavez. An uneasy truce prevailed, until after the election. The voter rejection of Proposition 22 triggered the next step in the escalating conspiracy against the Chavez forces. Because of the unprecedented UFWA victory — this was the first time farm workers had ever put together enough political power to beat their bosses — agribusiness was pressured to take even more desperate steps to head off the *Chavistas*. Quietly, they turned once more to the Nixon Administration for help.

On the surface, the American Farm Bureau Federation announced Teamster President Fitzsimmons would be the principal speaker at its Los Angeles Convention on December 12, 1972. The invitation had been suggested to the Farm Bureau by Undersecretary of Labor Laurence Silberman.

Chavez believes Charles Colson, then a special counsel to the President, put the deal together, using Silberman as a go-between. Colson, who when he quit government went into a law firm that was given a $100,000-a-year retainer by the Teamsters, denied the allegation: "We had absolutely nothing to do with the strike."

Chavez countered: "Colson was Nixon's hatchet man on unions. We say Colson did bring them together, he was one of the administration officials who set up the meetings with the Farm Bureau in Los Angeles; we say at that meeting in Los Angeles they put their thing together to destroy this union. We know that right after Fitzsimmons attended that Farm Bureau convention in Los Angeles they began moving into the fields and signing up workers, and they tried to negotiate with growers even before our contracts expired . . ."

Fitzsimmons billed his talk to the farmers as the "opening of communications" between his union and the AFBF. At times during the speech the Teamsters' president sounded like a tough labor leader scolding the collected agribusinessmen for their anti-labor biases. But in the end he became more obvious: He attacked Chavez, the UFWA, and its supporters; he called the boycott a fraud; he proposed an alliance between organized labor and agribusiness; then he urged the Farm Bureau to support legislation that would subject agriculture to regulation under the National Labor Relations Act.

The farmers seemed to get the message. The convention delegates voted to reverse the long-standing AFBF opposition to the NLRA. While this appeared to be a major turnaround, it wasn't made without some reservations and some strings that were strongly attached to pet phrases like "no strikes at harvest." Even so, it was change.

Two days later Fitzsimmons and the Western Conference leadership created their own Agriculture Workers Organizing Committee. A tough organizer named Ralph Cotner was made Imperial Valley area supervisor and told to recruit a seven-man field staff to work the Coachella vineyeards. At the time, the UFWA contracts still had nearly four months to run before they expired, on April 15, 1973. The Teamsters made their move quietly. While Cotner began to put his organizational effort together, Bill Grami made a diversionary move far to the north and west, in the Salinas Valley.

On January 17th, Grami and a spokesman for the 170 lettuce growers announced they had renegotiated the *unexpired* 1970 lettuce contracts. The Teamsters said they were sending organizers into the fields to sign up the 30,000 field workers who they claimed were represented by these contracts. Once again, the Teamsters and the growers had the cart before the horse. These were the same workers the California Supreme Court said preferred the United Farm Workers in 1970, and there was no indication the workers had changed their minds; yet the Teamsters were going back into the fields to sign them up *after* the contracts had been signed.

The news in Salinas covered Cotner's work in the Imperial Valley. On January 24th, Cotner and three other Teamsters met for two hours with 25 growers in a motel banquet room, in Indio, to discuss what the Teamsters could do for the farmers. Under the Teamsters, there would be no union hiring hall, growers would be free to use the crew boss–labor contractor system once more, be free to return to the traditional labor practices of agribusiness. Cotner warned the growers that Teamster contracts would force them to pay higher wages and provide health and welfare fringe benefits, and he said the Teamsters would provide worker signatures to show they represented the majority of the field laborers.

At the time, Ray Huerta was in charge of the UFWA Coachella Valley hiring hall. He had 31 contracts to administer, covering approximately 6,500 dispatches a season. During January, February, and March the pre-season work requires only a few hundred workers in the valley. Huerta said, "We heard Cotner and his people were passing the petitions, but we felt it was the packinghouse workers they wanted and we couldn't get involved. But then we saw it spilling over into the fields and we began checking. Cesar met with the growers, and asked them what the problems were. They said the hiring hall, but they were sneaky, saying things could be worked out, and that they were going to stay with the UFWA . . ."

On March 16th a Teamster organizer told the Riverside *Press Enterprise* that the Teamsters were replacing the Chavez-led union and that they had already signed 84 percent of the work force. Later the Teamsters began to claim 4,103 workers had signed their petitions. The UFWA said the petitions were a fraud, that many of the signatures were forged. *Press Enterprise* reporter Dick Lyneis said, "The number did seem high, so I called the farm labor service and I asked how many workers were there, at that time, in the Coachella Valley. They estimated 1,200 to 1,500, yet Cotner had told me he had three times that number of signatures."

These unverified petitions became the Teamsters' offer of proof not only to the growers, but to the public as well. The big union muscled right in, pushed the UFWA aside, and signed contracts with the vineyardists. The war was on. Months later, after all of the details of this move came out, Los Angeles *Times* labor reporter Harry Bernstein called the Teamsters' moves into both the lettuce fields and the grape vineyards "a sordid story that makes a mockery of trade union traditions." The *Nation* magazine criticized the Teamsters for their ungainly leap back into farm management's bed.

Fitzsimmons, angered by Bernstein's opinions — written for the *Progressive* magazine — and the *Nation*'s editorial comment, defended the move: "It is a question of which union farm workers feel they need to achieve economic and job dignity through collective bargaining. What is important are the needs and wishes of the workers involved."

Through it all, AFL-CIO President George Meany remained silent. It was as though he and Fitzsimmons had never agreed the UFWA had jurisdiction over the fields. But Meany was having trouble understanding Chavez and his followers; he publicly supported the UFWA, but privately Meany found the farm worker fights noisy, bothersome affairs. He had been angered by Chavez's switch in position on the NLRA and by the UFWA's unilateral boycott action against Heublein. The UFWA didn't act like a union, its secondary boycott tactics against entire supermarket chains put pressure on other AFL-CIO unions.

The pressures that had moved Fitzsimmons to back away from the 1970–71 fight were clearly absent in 1973. Meany's long silence not only encouraged the Teamsters, it raised some serious questions for the UFWA. Why the tight lip and low profile? Did Meany intend to abandon Chavez and the farm workers?

The official answer, as relayed by AFL-CIO publicist Al Zack early in February, was a terse: "No comment."

Bill Kircher would only explain, "When they were an organizing committee we had a direct responsibility, but that relationship ceased when they got their charter. They are now a fully autonomous union."

The words sounded strange — and strained — coming from a man who for years commuted between his Washington, D.C., office and the Delano grape vineyards in an effort to help the farm workers organize and fend off the periodic Teamster raids. Asked if the federation was still contributing the $10,000 a month to the UFWA, Kircher said, "No. We can only subsidize organizing committees."

When asked why the AFL-CIO was issuing no statements protesting the Teamster move back into the fields, Kircher said, "You'll have to ask the president that question."

Meany would not comment. At the time neither he nor the AFL-CIO executive council knew anything about the Teamsters' plans to move in behind the UFWA vineyard contracts; the federation leaders felt an accommodation was still possible in the lettuce dispute, but they were in no big hurry to put the pieces back together again because, as one AFL-CIO official expressed it: "Cesar Chavez is not the world's greatest trade union leader. He never asks us for advice, he goes on his own. . . . Meany and Fitzsimmons had the farm worker pact put together and Crazy Cesar blew it apart with a candlelight march on Bud Antle. . . . [he] clearly could have left Antle alone . . ."

Even Chavez and the UFWA had little inkling of what the Teamsters were up to in the Coachella Valley during the first two months of 1973. Chavez explained, "Our contracts were expiring and we had to get ready for the negotiations. I went around and talked to every grower in Coachella, in Lamont, every grower in Delano. I told them I thought it would be a good idea if we avoided one farmer paying 10 cents more than another. I said we wanted an industry-wide contract.

"As we went around, we began to pick up information that the hiring hall was going to become an issue. Way back in the middle of 1972 people were warning us, we had an idea this was going to happen. Growers would tell us they were having problems with the hiring hall, but they would always tell me that they knew the workers wanted our union."

During January and February, Chavez was also meeting with the ranch committees, supervising them as they elected delegates to a negotiating committee. This committee worked through a UFWA industry-wide contract proposal and elected a 10-member negotiating team. Chavez said a total of 300 workers were involved in the process. By the time the contract talks were started in late March the union felt it had a solid industry-wide position that expressed the desires of the grape workers.

Chavez said, "The first meeting we had they wanted us to give the whole thing to them, and they would give us their entire counter proposal. Dolores didn't trust them, but Jerry and I said 'What have we got to lose?'

"But that's as far as we got. They never would look at the whole proposal, all we got from them is talk about the hiring hall. I said, 'Okay, let's leave the hiring hall over here and see how far we can get on other things, but they would go two or three steps and then return to the hiring hall . . . but I don't think that was it, you know? The real thing is they had to justify what they were doing. They had a plan, they were going to get rid of the union and this was the time to do it. We talked about a joint hiring hall. Well, we would rather have our own hiring hall, not a joint hiring hall, but it was a calculated risk that we took. We asked for a joint hiring hall, but they didn't buy it."

As the negotiations failed to move off center, grape growers from Coachella, Arvin, and Delano began to publicly question which union really represented the farm workers. On April 9th David Smith, an Indio attorney representing Coachella growers, said that until the jurisdictional issue was resolved he was not going to continue the negotiations; Al Caplan, labor relations man for some Arvin-Delano growers, followed Smith's lead. The rest of the growers then withdrew to reassess their positions. Cohen and Chavez stormed out.

John Giumarra, Jr., in an interview nearly a year after his 11,000-acre company had signed with the Teamsters, said, "There was no need for a hiring hall. The union claimed it needed it to do away with the labor contractor, but that is just a baloney argument."

When asked about the joint hiring hall proposals, Giumarra became irritated, arrogant: "What the hell is a joint hiring hall? It was never defined in Coachella. . . . [The] point is why is a hiring hall needed? For what purpose . . ."

John Kovacevich was easier to talk to, more candid in his answers; he made it clear the hiring hall and the shift of power from the employer to the union were the issues concerning him. The dissolution of the old paternalistic system bothered him, and his feelings came out in comments like "Before we had the union the kids could come out on weekends and cut a few strings for dad, cut canes and rake them, help their father and *increase his income 30 to 40 percent.* Under the union contract they could not come into the fields."

I emphasized the income percentages to make a point; the farm worker husband historically has depended upon the work of his wife and his children to make enough for the family to survive. The farmers see the system in this traditional context and when they talk to their workers they sometimes do hear fathers complain the UFWA hiring hall has disrupted family work patterns. The Teamsters' offer to return to the old crew boss–labor contractor system was attractive to the growers, and to those migrants who worked in family groups.

As the Teamsters moved into Coachella, Chavez called for help from the clergy. Chris Hartmire began bringing in volunteers and supplies. Monsignor George Higgins headed up a group of 25 churchmen and labor leaders who went into the vines on April 10th to take an informal poll among the workers. Higgins said the group split up and contacted workers in 31 different locations; the poll revealed 795 workers preferred the UFWA, 80 preferred the Teamsters, and 78 workers wanted no union at all. Higgins said, "It is clear to us that the great majority of the farm workers in the Coachella Valley want to be represented by Cesar Chavez and the UFWA and they resent the intrusion of the Teamsters' union."

The grape growers' obvious run into the arms of the Teamsters finally provoked George Meany; he sent Kircher flying out to California to stand once more with Chavez, and Kircher brought with him 25 trained AFL-CIO organizers. On April 13th, two days before the contracts expired, Chavez called a strike rally and more than 1,000 workers jammed into the Coachella high school auditorium; they overwhelmingly voted to go out on strike against any grape grower signing a Teamster contract.

Chavez committed $1 million of the UFWA's funds to the fight. By April 18 Meany was pledging "all the assistance we can provide" from the AFL-CIO. Meany found the Teamster actions "disgraceful." He said, "They are clearly union busting in a concerted campaign to wipe out the United Farm Workers. This is the most despicable strikebreaking, union-busting activity I have ever seen in my lifetime in the trade union movement."

Meany backed up his pledge of support a few days later by announcing the federation membership was levying a special assessment to raise $1.6 million for the UFWA strike fund. The Coachella strike became the first well-financed, well-planned farm worker rebellion in history. The strikers were paid from

$35 to $75 a week for picket line duty, and they had a strong legal staff behind them with the ability to bail pickets out of jail.

Chavez explained the heart of his strike strategy: "We give the staff the general policies, then give them the freedom to make the decisions on the spot. And remember, all the things that we are doing may change from day to day. We have to be flexible. We have to be able to react. It is much easier now because we have the farm worker leadership, and we meet with the ranch committees and we pool our ideas on how we should conduct the strike."

Chavez and Cohen were casting about for issues and tactics that would project the strike out into the national arena. Meany's anger and support helped, but they needed something more explosive, more emotional. From the beginning, the courts and law enforcement officials had been used by growers to restrict the strike activities through the use of an extraordinary civil injunctive procedure. The judges would limit the number of pickets the union could place and restrict the use of sound amplifiers and then order the sheriff to enforce this civil injunction.

In most civil actions a judge would not make such an order. Normally when he restrains or enjoins litigants from further action in a controversy a judge enforces the order himself, by citing the parties back into court if one or the other violates his order. However, there is an obscure code section that allows the judge to assign enforcement of civil orders to the sheriff, if extraordinary circumstances prevail.

Cohen argued the judges had erred both by issuing the injunctions that limited or prevented strikers from assembling on a public roadway and speaking freely — through voice amplifiers — and by sending lawmen out to enforce these abridgments of the workers' constitutional rights. Cohen advised Chavez the union had a strong legal position to back up any mass exercise in civil disobedience the UFWA might conduct against the court orders.

He explained, "In California you have two ways to test a

constitutional issue like this; you can appeal to a higher court, which takes a long time, or you have the right to violate the court order and raise your defense. See, in California the right to violate the court order in a case like this is not implied, it is explicit. The California Supreme Court has held that, especially where First Amendment rights are concerned, the people have the right to violate such orders because to wait for court processes would finesse them around their constitutional rights."

Chavez and the strikers liked the idea. It was decided that wherever pickets were enjoined from gathering or using sound equipment, they would purposely violate the court order. Cohen said, "First we tried it in Coachella. During the first week of the strike the injunctions were just as bad as anywhere else, the judge had us down to one picket every 300 yards, or something like that, the same crap. So we violated the law and the judge reversed himself, after we argued the case. He gave us notice we had unlimited picketing on the other side of the road, we had two pickets at each entrance, and he gave us the use of the bullhorns and access to the camps. That made for a pretty damned effective strike. But that was Riverside County. In Kern and Tulare counties the judges just got more restrictive . . . and the cops began to pound on us."

The Coachella and Arvin strikes were violent. The strikers, like those at White River Farms, the year before, were workers who had been covered by UFWA contracts and had seen those contracts stolen by the Teamsters. They were bitter. As farm labor from the Mexican border was hauled into the strike area the turmoil and tension mounted. The Teamsters imported "guards" to protect the strikebreakers working in the vines. These guards — huge, muscular young men who dressed and acted like extras from a Hell's Angels movie — set up "counter picket lines" to oppose the *huelgistas*. A special squad of these guards — 30 bigger, beefier, meaner-looking creatures with long hair and scruffy beards — traveled the back roads by truck, armed with clubs, chains, and tire irons.

These were the guys Chavez called "goons." Whenever they spotted a UFWA picket line they would jump out of their truck and try to scare the pickets; they would grunt and snort and paw the ground; they dragged effigies of Chavez around to stomp on. The strikers were intimidated, but they did not give up. Seafarers Union president Paul Hall sent a planeload of his bully-boy sailors out to Coachella and he offered to have them break a few Teamster heads and legs. Hall, a tough-talking guy who uses four-letter words in combinations seldom heard, had led his sailors against the Teamsters in other fights and "whipped the shit out of them. You gotta break those bastards' legs, that's the only thing they understand."

Chavez rejected the offer. He explained, "They would have run the Teamsters out of town, they've done it before, in Puerto Rico and Chicago. The sailors have taken the Teamsters on in violent confrontations and they have beat them. Maybe we would have won the strike that way, but we would have lost a lot too. We don't want to do it that way, we would find it very hard to have been a part of something like that. See, every time the Teamsters beat up one of our guys they lose. Sure we are concerned about the guy who was beaten, but we are not frightened. The whole idea of nonviolence is you are not afraid, if you become afraid you start doing things you are not supposed to do . . . violence is a trap. We convert farm workers to nonviolence and they can see what happens, they can see our strength . . ."

John Bank, a Catholic priest who acted as the UFWA press liaison during the Coachella strikes, gave an example of how the union tactics worked. He said one morning early he drove out to a picket line and watched a young UFWA striker standing on top of a car, using a bullhorn to make her words reach into the vines, where the strikebreakers were at work. She yelled: "Remember when we were all in the union and we used to shout, 'Viva Chavez!' Is there anyone in there who still shouts 'Viva Chavez'?"

A woman crew boss stood up and shouted back, "Abajo [down with] Chavez!"

Bank said, "Instantly workers all over the fields stood up yelling 'Viva Chavez! Viva Chavez!' The Teamster guards rushed from their positions facing our pickets and ordered the workers to go back to work. But they kept shouting 'Viva Chavez!' and every worker left the grape field to join the picket line. . . . The young Chicana put down her megaphone, climbed down from the car roof, and said softly, "Si se puedes. [We can do it.]."

The Teamsters countered UFWA picketing with terror tactics. The "goons" began pounding on anyone they could catch. One afternoon Bank and a reporter were sitting in a restaurant frequented by the Teamsters. A dozen of the Teamsters' heaviest came waltzing into the place, and, when the 300-pound leader spotted Bank, they started to play a grotesque game of ridicule. Bank was their target. Finally the 300-pounder sat down across from Bank, laughed at him, then swung a fist hard into the priest's face.

Bank said, "It shattered my nose completely."

There were several minor clashes between the Teamsters and the UFWA pickets; then on June 8 members of the two unions met head-on in a pitched battle in the middle of Highway 195, east of Mecca. It took 40 Riverside County deputies and California Highway Patrolmen to break up the fight. No arrests were made. The pushing and shoving, the swinging of fists, and throwing of rocks flared up here and there as the UFWA pickets massed to challenge the strikebreakers. Because the Riverside County sheriff did not have to enforce the court orders, his deputies could maintain a neutral position; they were even handed, arresting both UFWA and Teamster members whom they caught violating the criminal laws.

On June 19, just before dawn, about 500 UFWA pickets began gathering in front of the Ruth Young Farm Labor Center, a camp near Indio operated by the county. The farm workers inside the camp were mixed in their loyalties; some were UFWA sympathizers, others worked behind the UFWA strike lines. A bomb exploded under the hood of a car belonging to Santiago Serana, a UFWA member. No one was in the car at the time but the explosion sent ripples of fear and anger through the pickets.

Teamster counter pickets, led by Bill Grami, arrived to confront the UFWA. Someone threw a rock. It hit Grami a glancing blow on the forehead, staggering him.

Someone yelled, "Grami's shot."

Dazed from the blow, blood running from his head, Grami was taken to a car and rushed to a doctor's office. United Press International flashed a report: Grami had been shot. When facts were checked, the report was corrected. Sheriff's deputies said Grami had been hit by a rock and was not hurt seriously.

On June 21 two Teamsters organizers were arrested by Riverside deputies on assault charges and for kidnap and attempted murder. Captain Cois Byrd of the sheriff's office said the Teamsters had abducted a worker; mistaking him for a member of the UFWA, they had stabbed him six times with an icepick and then beat him. The victim survived. On June 23 the UFWA set 400 pickets around an asparagus field southeast of Thermal; 180 counter pickets were brought in by the Teamsters.

Captain Byrd said one of the Teamsters threw a firecracker. "It seemed to be the signal; they charged into the United Farm Workers when that cracker exploded."

The Teamsters, armed with chains, clubs, and tire irons, worked their way through the strikers; 25 or 30 people, most of them UFWA strikers, were injured before lawmen could quell the riot and arrest six Teamsters and five UFWA pickets. Teamster area supervisor Ralph Cotner told reporters his "guards" had intercepted the UFWA pickets as they moved into the field to beat up the asparagus workers. Captain Byrd disagreed. He said it was obvious the Teamsters planned the attack and the firecracker was the signal for the charge.

One Teamster became disgusted with such tactics. He told reporter Dick Lyneis that Cotner was the man who was responsible for ordering the violence. Cotner denied the charge. Grami told Lyneis that he had issued orders against the use of violence, adding, "I can't understand the confusion in carrying out my orders. Maybe I just don't want to believe that instructions for violence were given contrary to my orders."

By mid-June the violence had spread north, to the Arvin area in the San Joaquin Valley. Pablo Espinosa, area supervisor for the UFWA, said, "The goons came here and they beat the hell out of our strikers. One day one of our pickets was talking on the speaker and the goons came along in a car, got out, and one of them just walked up and jerked the cord out, grabbed the microphone, pulled and tried to break it. For the goons any guy with the complexion of brown was a target. Our people were really frightened. Those guys were ugly. They were huskies. They looked like a gang."

On June 28th a large group of Teamster guards charged into pickets around the John Kovacevich ranch, near Arvin. Espinosa, who was on another ranch at the time of the incident, rushed to the scene, "When I came up the people were all crying and there is blood on the street. I don't see how a guy who weighs 300 pounds can beat the hell out of a little guy . . . a man 60 years old. He [Juan Hernandez] didn't even try to put up a defense. They fractured his cheek bone and he was in the hospital. The sheriff made an investigation, but Juan couldn't remember which one hit him in the face because it was like an explosion and he went black."

Twenty-five Teamsters were arrested by Kern County sheriff's deputies, and the resulting publicity — coming on top of the stories of other terror tactics — forced the Teamsters to disband their terror squad. But this did not stop the picket line violence. From Bakersfield through Visalia to Fresno the county jails began to fill as deputies from the three counties confronted the *huelgistas*. Too often the confrontations turned into battles as club-swinging lawmen made mass arrests. The domino theory was at work: as the farm contracts expired the growers signed with the Teamsters, as the Teamsters came into the vines the UFWA set out picket lines, the judges issued restrictive injunctions, and the lawmen started mass arrests. The jails became furnaces in which the steel backbone of the UFWA was forged. Out of the turmoil a new attitude began to emerge; by going to jail the people found a new toughness, a new will to defy the established order.

Ernesto Loredo described leading 289 *huelgistas* to jail in Tulare County, and in the process his own attitude, his own depth of feeling, emphasized what was happening within the movement. Loredo and his picket captains kept their protest going, even after they had been locked up. He explained, "We learned that if you stop up the water and then flush the toilet the pipes empty and you can talk from one floor to another. The women were in cells directly above us, on the next floor up, so we coordinated what we were doing. We were rattling and hollering '*Viva Chavez! Viva la Huelga!*' you know, and singing songs, and the jailer tells us to stop. They asked me to stop the others, they say that if we don't stop they will put us in the hole.

"I tell them, 'You can kill us, if you want to. You are not going to scare us anymore. We know what we are here for, so that is it. You do what you have to do. And we will do what we have to do. Okay? If we are doing something wrong and you want to do something about it, don't tell me about it. Just do it.' "

From April through August, lawmen arrested 3,500 men, women, and children. Among the strikers were dozens of Catholic priests, nuns, Protestant clergymen, and volunteers to *La Causa* who went willingly to jail, with the farm workers. Commenting on the thousands of workers who were jailed, Chavez said, "We built a perpetual strike. It's amazing. In the beginning they were afraid of anyone who even mentioned the word strike, but this summer they *voted* to go to jail. We told them it was hard in jail, that they would have a record the rest of their lives . . . they went to jail and afterwards they got out and they started talking about it. It was amazing to hear mothers and grandmothers talking about how they had been in jail, to see them hold up their clenched fists and say they were no longer afraid. That is the kind of commitment you cannot destroy."

While the strikers, the Teamsters, and the table-grape growers met head-on in the Coachella and Arvin harvests, the Teamsters' Joint Council 38 began a flanking movement farther north in the San Joaquin Valley, in Merced and Fresno counties. The target was the farm land operated by E. and J. Gallo Wineries. Gallo has its headquarters in Modesto and it produces one third of all the wine consumed in the United States. The company buys and crushes 25 percent of the wine grapes grown in California, in addition to farming its own 3,500 acres of vineyards. Gallo also has 1,500 acres of apples and 1,500 acres of general farm land.

The Gallo farming operations — employing 150 permanent workers and up to 600 seasonal workers during the harvests — had been under UFWA contract since 1967. Prior to the expiration of the UFWA contract, in mid-April, UFWA negotiators opened talks with the company. But little was accomplished during the two months of negotiations, and talks were broken off. The company then notified the UFWA that the Teamsters were claiming to represent a majority of the Gallo workers and that Teamster-Gallo contract talks were being scheduled. The UFWA went out on strike, on June 27th. Chavez personally walked the picket lines and led a protest rally in which 300 UFWA supporters crowded into the small auditorium to vent their anger. Their protest availed them nothing.

A Gallo-Teamster contract was negotiated, and Jim Smith of Joint Council 38 — the same man who had worked with Al Green in the old AWOC–Teamster joint move into the Tulare County citrus crop — reported the Gallo workers ratified the new contract 158 to 1. A year later I talked to Ernest Gallo, chairman of the company's board of directors, asking him to shed some light on the controversy.

Gallo said, "We knew Cesar Chavez to be a man with honorable motives, and we held him in high regard, personally. We have always favored farm labor unionization, and we were delighted when Chavez started his movement. . . . [But,] we also know that he has encountered many difficulties administratively in developing his young union."

Ernest Gallo and his brother, Julio, have earned reputations for their aggressive, competitive management of what has grown into the nation's largest, most powerful winery. Ernest Gallo is a man of taste, a man of authority; he is used to making decisions and giving orders. After a 40-minute interview, it was obvious he was a man who would prefer to deal with men who also make decisions, who have the authority to issue orders and get things done. Dealing with a committee of farm workers was not his idea of efficiency.

Yet a committee of farm workers is what Gallo, and all of the other farmers, had to contend with once they signed with the UFWA. They found that Chavez discouraged direct calls to his office by either the farmers or the farm workers. The farmers had to deal with their own workers. Gallo did not understand Chavez's theories on union democracy; this farmer-businessman-vintner felt the hiring hall staff had not been trained well, that too often those in power had been capricious, arbitrary, vindictive, inefficient. He said, "There was never enough supervision, and leaving it up to the ranch committee was entirely impractical."

The contract expired. The switch was made to the Teamsters and the UFWA started a major boycott effort against all Gallo wines, but most especially those "pop wines" — the fruit-flavored, low-alcohol, cheap wines — so popular with young people. Gallo responded: "Because we have honored and respected the wishes of our farm workers to change unions, we have been caught in the middle of a jurisdictional dispute between two unions. This in turn has subjected us to vilification and character assassination."

But there was an absolute difference of opinion over just who was and who was not a Gallo worker. At the time of the strike the UFWA had objected to the Gallo company's eviction of 71 families from company-owned housing. These were UFWA members who had worked on the Gallo ranch and who had gone out on strike when no contract agreement was reached. Although Gallo did not remember the number was 71 — he thought it was about half that number — he acknowledged the striking workers had been put off Gallo land. Gallo explained that all striking workers had been notified by telegram that if they didn't return to work immediately they would be discharged from the payroll and replaced by crews that would work. The strikers stayed out; the new crews were hired.

I asked Gallo if the striking workers had been allowed to vote on the Teamster contract ratification. He said "no." Only those workers on the job at the time, only the strikebreakers, had signed Teamster authorization cards and ratified the contract. There is great irony in this; if the National Labor Relations Act had covered farm labor the Teamsters could not have raided Gallo. The NLRA protects the striking workers in their efforts to economically force employers back to the bargaining table. If the Gallo workers had, in fact, wished to switch to the Teamsters union, under the NLRA procedures they could have petitioned the National Labor Relations Board for a decertification election. The irony comes in the fact that both Ernest Gallo and the Teamsters publicly favor including farm workers under the NLRA. It is Cesar Chavez who continues to oppose such a legislative move.

The Gallo boycott caused George Meany problems because the company had contracts with other unions; the old federation president wanted to settle the jurisdictional fight and get on to other things. All during the Coachella and Arvin strikes both Kircher and Joe Keenan were keeping Meany informed on what was happening. Keenan was also trying to work with Einar Mohn on getting the jurisdictional talks started again. After some preliminary meetings, they succeeded. It was obvious both sides wanted to disengage: Fitzsimmons was personally taking a lot of heat from the Catholic church; his image as a trade union leader was tarnished by the terror tactics in the vineyards. Chavez wanted a settlement so he could get back to the business of organizing farm workers; the Coachella strikes had not produced the definitive statement of UFWA strength that he had hoped for, and his union had been unable to drive the

Teamsters from the fields through economic pressure on the growers.

On August 1, in Chicago, Meany announced that a basis for agreement had been reached. He said that when he and Fitzsimmons met in Washington, D.C., the following Friday, he would have in his hand a letter signed by Chavez authorizing Meany to personally arbitrate any disagreement that might arise out of a UFWA–Teamster jurisdictional agreement. Meany was putting his own reputation on the line and he told reporters, "This kills whatever arguments the Teamsters have about Chavez's irresponsibility."

Fitzsimmons seemed to agree with Meany that a basis for an agreement had been reached; he ordered all Teamster organizing halted while Mohn and Chavez personally worked out the final jurisdictional language in a series of meetings in the Western Conference headquarters in Burlingame. Jerry Cohen was with Chavez at the first negotiations. He said, "It was kind of weird, the Teamsters had pledged — Fitzsimmons had promised Meany — that they would not sign any more sweetheart contracts, that they would hold with the status quo. On the basis of that pledge, Meany had asked Cesar if we wouldn't meet with the Western Conference, because there was a chance to settle it.

"So we went up on August 9 and we met with Mohn, Andrade, Grami, and Al Brundage, their attorney; and Al Woll and Joe Keenan from the AFL-CIO were there. After the first meeting, Mohn talks to Woll, who comes up to our room and tells us Mohn has said a mistake has been made, the Teamsters have mistakenly signed 29 contracts with Delano growers.

"Cesar and I burst out laughing. Woll could not understand why we'd started laughing. He looked at us and said, 'What the hell is funny? We've been double crossed.' We asked him what the hell he expected from the Teamsters. We'd been through this so many times before, we weren't surprised. We just took off, Cesar blasted the hell out of them, and we left. How the hell can you negotiate with guys like that?"

It had been Jim Smith of Joint Council 38 who had been down in Delano working on the growers. Grami said that he had personally instructed Smith not to sign the contracts, but there had been a mix-up in signals. Both Mohn and Grami issued statements saying Smith had made a mistake. Fitzsimmons repudiated the contracts verbally, and then formally by letter. He wrote the growers, "The Teamsters have no interest in organizing your employees in the vineyards in and around Delano."

Kircher laughed the loudest. He cited similar Teamster raids in other industries, adding: "This is their tactic, this is why you can't deal with them, this is why you have to go for their fucking jugular. You don't talk to Teamsters, you fight them."

Chavez had little time to dwell on the latest Teamster duplicity. He ignored Fitzsimmons's countermanding move, and turned his attention to the strikes. The situation in the vineyards around Arvin and Lamont, in the southeastern corner of the San Joaquin Valley, was getting critical. The August sun had temperatures up over 100 degrees, the Kern County deputies were enforcing the injunctions with vengeance; after several skirmishes in which UFWA pickets were bloodied, the union began to level charges of brutality against the lawmen. Deputies using mace and clubs hauled hundreds to jail; farmers hired private guards and began carrying guns themselves. Some strikebreakers were armed.

On August 14 Nagi Daifullah, a UFWA striker from Yemen, died of a skull fracture after he scuffled with a Kern County deputy sheriff outside a bar on the main street of Arvin. Pablo Espinosa said, "According to our people, it was in front of a beer joint, just down the street from our union headquarters. Some claim Nagi threw a bottle at the sheriff. He had been drinking. He is a little guy, maybe 130 pounds, and this deputy went after him, chased him, and hit him over the head with a flashlight."

The official police report was similar to Espinosa's version of the story, with the exception of how the deputy struck Daifullah. Law investigators contend the flashlight blows struck the farm worker on the shoulders and then he fell, during the scuffle, and hit his head on the pavement. The report indicated his skull must have been fractured during the fall. The death was ruled accidental. Whatever the cause, the UFWA went into mourning.

Espinosa said, "We told the people we want a silent picket line. No shouting. No *huelgas*. No words. We want to wear the black flag. This is a tradition. We wanted a silent vigil."

Each picket line that was set out the following morning received these instructions. Among the silent pickets was Juan de la Cruz, a 60-year-old farm worker who had joined the union not long after he and his wife started working on the DiGiorgio Arvin ranch in 1963. Señora de la Cruz explained, "When we first came, we were only six in the union here. We made the meetings in one house, and we organized all of the people in the fields that we could. We first met Cesar Chavez in a meeting. We had heard a lot about him, and when he came that time, he made a big meeting here in Lamont."

Señor and Señora de la Cruz were strong members of Chavez's NFWA even before they met him. Because neither tried to hide their loyalties as they worked on the DiGiorgio farms, Señora de la Cruz said they were fired. Both husband and wife went to work on other farms; they traveled to San Francisco with other strikers to picket the DiGiorgio offices and to bolster the boycott of DiGiorgio grapes. Señora de la Cruz proudly explained that they both had voted against the Teamsters in the DiGiorgio elections in 1966.

After Nagi Daifullah's death, she and her husband had joined the silent picket lines. On the second day, August 16, at about 2:30 P.M., the UFWA pickets were standing by their cars, on the Weedpatch highway, near where it crosses Valpredo Road; they were waiting for quitting time so that the Giumarra workers might pass by and see that someone had died, that someone was being mourned. The picket cars all faced north. A pickup truck approached them, also traveling north. A young man on the passenger side leaned out, pointing a .22 calibre gun at the pickets.

Funeral march for UFW picket slain in summer of 1973.
Photo by Michael Mally, Los Angeles Times

Señora Juan de la Cruz sprinkles earth on coffin of her murdered husband—a UFW picket. Joan Baez and Chavez stand behind priest. *Photo by Bob Fitch, Black Star*

Kern County (California) police and UFW pickets, summer 1973.
Photo by Bob Fitch, Black Star

Señora de la Cruz said, "I see the gun, because I see the boy. He had the gun in the hand. I hear first shots, four of them. Then when he passed by he turned and made another shot. He was going this side and he turned and he shoot back." She demonstrated the assailant's turning motion. The final shot struck her husband in the heart. He died an hour later, in the Bakersfield hospital.

Five thousand farm workers turned out first for Nagi Daifullah's funeral on August 17th; then three days later they attended the requiem Mass for Juan de la Cruz, and then formed a funeral cortege, carrying the body through Arvin, down Bear Mountain Boulevard to the Arvin Cemetery. In the procession were 10 Catholic priests, including three bishops. Chavez, in his eulogy, said, "We live among people who hate and fear us, people who will spend millions of dollars to make sure Juan's sacrifice will be in vain . . . but because of the spirit and dedication of people like Juan de la Cruz we cannot lose."

Chavez called an end to the one-sided war; he ordered the *huelgistas* off the picket lines and into the boycott efforts; rather than risk more lives he called off the strike. Those families who volunteered for boycott assignments were dispatched to New York or Chicago or Seattle; those who could not travel to one of the 40 or 50 boycott cities scattered across the nation were asked to help raise funds and food for those who had gone out, and the workers who stayed in the valley were expected to picket local stores and march in demonstrations.

The death of Juan de la Cruz, the Teamster terror tactics, and the arrest of 3,500 farm workers and UFWA supporters all were used by the United Farm Workers to load the bad-guy image of the Teamsters and thereby increase public pressure on Fitzsimmons, Mohn, and Grami. But Fitzsimmons, who would like to be known as a good trade unionist, was caught between the tarnishing of his public image and the pressures from the agribusiness-Nixon coalition who wanted the Teamsters to hang in there and continue to disrupt and distract the Chavez efforts. When Fitzsimmons repudiated the Teamster contracts with the Delano 29, Chavez was once more persuaded by the AFL-CIO to sit down with the Teamsters and try to work out a jurisdictional agreement.

Jerry Cohen recalled, "When Cesar and I flew back to Washington, D.C., we didn't know how the lettuce would be resolved. We weren't giving up on the lettuce because we had people in there who wanted our union. But we were prepared to make a trade: our jurisdiction in the vineyards and fields would be recognized, and the Teamsters would give up the lettuce contracts as they expired in 1975. Most of the heat was on the Teamsters, they wanted to protect those lettuce contracts, they didn't want to give up Gallo, because they had other relationships in there. At first they didn't want to give up anything but Delano. Then it was Delano and Arvin. Then things began to move."

The talks progressed rapidly, a final statement of agreement was patched together and announced by the AFL-CIO: The Teamsters recognized the UFWA's jurisdiction over all vineyard and field workers, the UFWA would have immediate jurisdiction in the table grapes, the Teamsters would withdraw from the lettuce fields by stages, as their contracts expired. The UFWA would drop the lettuce boycott and formally recognize the Teamsters' jurisdiction in the canneries and related agribusiness enterprises. Fitzsimmons and Meany were named the final arbiters of any jurisdictional disputes that might arise.

Like all the previous agreements, this one began to unravel before both sides had left the building and hailed cabs. Fitzsimmons announced the agreement had to be checked over by Teamster lawyers and he said the Teamsters wanted the AFL-CIO to agree to indemnify the Teamsters if growers sued for breach of contract. No one is quite sure why Fitzsimmons was having second thoughts. Meany believes Lee Shaw, an influential Chicago lawyer who has represented agribusiness interests, and Dusty Miller, a top Teamster official, convinced Fitzsimmons that backing out of the grape contracts would cause more problems that it would solve. Other sources say the Nixon Administration — acting

314

through Colson — convinced Fitzsimmons that he should back off from the agreement; it is said Nixon did not want Fitzsimmons, his strongest labor ally, reaching any agreements with George Meany, one of Nixon's most ardent foes.

Whatever the cause, Fitzsimmons reversed fields once again: "We intend to keep our obligations morally as well as legally as far as the farm workers are concerned." Ten days later Fitzsimmons met in San Diego with California agribusiness leaders, and, a week later, he made the reversal complete. He repudiated his own repudiation of the Delano 29. He said once again the Teamsters had a moral and legal obligation to honor all their agribusiness contracts.

The Teamster tactics had thrown the UFWA boycott into utter confusion. Consumers who would normally have supported the Chavez cause had read so many conflicting statements and stories over the previous three years they had no idea if they could or could not eat grapes and lettuce and drink wine. The UFWA had contracts with some wineries, but several of these were expiring. The boycott lists of products to shun changed frequently, its secondary boycott tactics against individual stores or chains also changed rapidly; sometimes boycotters were picketing grapes harvested by the two Coachella growers who remained with the UFWA — one of these, K. K. Larson, has since switched to the Teamsters, contending his workers wanted the change.

The Teamster-Nixon-agribusiness conspiracy had worked, at least temporarily. The Teamsters had most of the contracts, the boycott efforts had been defused, the legal and physical energies of the Chavez forces had been diverted from the primary union task of organizing workers and servicing contracts, and the UFWA financial reserves — including the $1.6 million grant from the AFL-CIO — had been depleted. The long strike and boycott efforts had used up people, too; many of the original volunteers had dropped by the wayside, Jim Drake had taken a six-month rest, and Leroy Chatfield quit in utter exhaustion. Bill Kircher was no longer available to help out. He had moved from the federation's top organizing job over to an executive position

315

in the culinary workers' union. The move was made, at least in part, because Kircher's close association with the farm workers had put him into an awkward position with Meany and the executive council.

Kircher had acted as a buffer between Chavez and Meany for eight years. It was Kircher who tried to educate the federation executive council on the problems of farm labor; he tried to explain Chavez's often mercurial moves to these old labor leaders who remembered the romance of their own organizing days, but not the mistakes, the confusion, the setbacks, and errors of judgment.

Cohen said, "Kircher was really a great friend, and I am sad he's not working with us anymore. I feel Bill is upset with Cesar and with the AFL-CIO too. He got caught in the middle. He tried to do too much; he should have exposed Meany to us more directly. He took a hell of a burden on himself. But Bill's history with the Teamsters goes back a long way; people in the other unions knew how much Bill hated the Teamsters and they weren't sure if this was Bill's fight, or not. Now that he's not standing between us and the federation, I think the AFL-CIO people are getting a pretty fast education about the Teamsters and the farm workers . . . but there is still a lot of misunderstanding about us."

This lack of understanding became obvious after Coachella. Most people who know farm labor patterns and history also know that no labor leader in the world, given the proximity of the open Mexican border, could shut off the flow of workers into the strike area. Every labor contractor operating out of the Calexico-Mexicali shapeups is anti-Chavez. The thousands of workers coming through to work each morning are powerless; to work they must go with a contractor and to ask a contractor where the work is only invites trouble.

Both Cohen and Chavez took pride in the partial disruption of the Coachella harvests, contending the strikes cost the growers millions of dollars in lost market revenues. By historical perspective, this was at least a partial success. Yet George Meany felt the $1.6 million had been wasted. He told reporters: "After all it was Chavez's own people who went to work behind the picket lines in Coachella, and that didn't indicate much support from the workers for Chavez . . . that situation in Coachella was almost a disaster."

Months later, during a luncheon with a selected few from the labor press, a more relaxed Meany was asked what he thought of Chavez as a trade union leader. Meany replied: "I don't know. I know that we spent a lot of time with Cesar. We've helped him every way we can. . . . I admire him. He's consistent, and I think he's dedicated. I think he's an idealist. I think he's a bit of a dreamer.

"But the thing that I'm disappointed about Cesar is that he never got to the point that he could develop a real viable union in the sense of what we think of as a viable union. Now maybe that is being unfair, because of the type of people that he had to deal with, and the type of employers that he was dealing with.

"You know he's fighting not only the ranch owners, he's fighting the Teamsters, the Bank of America, and the State of California, beginning with the governor, right on down. He's got a hell of a problem out there. . . ."

Meany has made it clear the AFL-CIO will continue to support the Chavez-led union; he has sent out a "white paper" denouncing the Teamster raids, and he has urged federation member unions to support the boycott of grapes and lettuce. Chavez in turn has agreed the UFWA will give up the secondary boycott tactics against retail outlets where other AFL-CIO unions have membership. This compromise brought to an end the UFWA boycott of Safeway stores.

In mid-August, after he had called off the bloody grape strikes, Chavez returned to La Paz to personally supervise the tightening up of the union's administrative machinery. He and the executive board decided the United Farm Workers needed to hold a constitutional convention to allow the workers to construct a constitution and to reaffirm their belief in a union of their own creation. There were internal problems, like the dues structure, that had to be changed; and the convention would allow the UFWA to tell the world

317

that, although the contracts were lost, the workers still had a viable union that represented people who had gone out on strike for a better way of life.

Chavez assigned his administrative assistant, José Gomez, the task of putting a convention together. Because of its central location, Fresno was picked as the site. Chavez personally inspected the city's large new convention center and liked what he saw; the main hall was a large arena flanked by galleries that could hold thousands of visitors. As he walked across the arena floor he noticed a big black cube suspended from the ceiling. He asked what it was, and, when he learned it was an electronic score board, he quipped: "It should read Teamsters 220, United Farm Workers 14."

Even though the UFWA no longer held many contracts, the ranch committee was still the basic structure in the union's concept of democracy. Each ranch that was, or had been, under contract, was assigned a number of convention delegates according to the total number of workers employed on that ranch during the previous year. It was then the job of the ranch committees to conduct delegate elections and submit the results to the convention credentials committee; a total of 414 men and women were elected and seated as delegates as the convention opened, September 21, 1973.

The convention was impressive; the big hall was decorated in great *huelga* flags and symbols; the black Aztec eagle was everywhere. A huge mural, done in Diego Rivera style, depicted the history of the union's struggle against the growers, the police, and the Teamsters. The 414 delegates sat at long rows of tables, while in the galleries hundreds more gathered to watch the proceedings. Chavez, flanked by the union's executive officers and staff, stood on the high podium, conducting the convention business.

Chavez told the workers: "The life of our union is at stake. We have given the fight everything we have. The forces who oppose us in the rural areas where we strike — the sheriffs, the district attorneys, the courts, the Teamsters with their violence, the violence of the growers, the killings and beatings — force us once again to go to the cities and take

318

UFW Convention, Fresno, 1973. *Photo by Ronald B. Taylor*

Farm worker delegates, UFW Convention.
Photo by Ronald B. Taylor

our message to the American public. . . . [The] only weapon we have left is the boycott."

The delegates began the long task of reading and debating each of the 82 sections in the 111-page UFWA constitution. Hour by hour, the delegates stood up to speak from the floor microphones; when they were impatient, or out of turn, Chavez gaveled them to order, reminding them that Roberts' Rules of Order prevailed.

At one point early in the proceedings a delegate rose and angrily asked, "Who is this Roberts? And why are we following *his* rules and regulations?"

It was a serious question. Chavez gave it a long, serious answer, explaining the need for rules and procedures in such a debate. The delegates worked on, long into the night, recessed, and started early the next morning, and the next. One session lasted an incredible 22 hours. Each day's work session was interspersed with speeches from famous supporters, like Senator Edward Kennedy and UAW president Leonard Woodcock. Paul Hall was there, representing George Meany. The convention went into overtime, but finally the work was done, and the delegates were satisfied. They had put their knowledge, their experience, and their feelings into the document that would govern their union.

After the convention, Chavez returned to La Paz to continue his effort to shape up the union's administrative structures. Although the UFWA no longer had 26 hiring halls, it kept service centers in each of these areas to maintain contact with the workers. In addition, the union had three medical clinics, was adding a fourth, and was establishing a pre-paid medical plan. Each area director was now ordered to focus the union's attention on worker services, and the area directors were to encourage house meetings and participation in local boycott efforts. While dues income had obviously fallen off dramatically, UFWA fund-raising efforts were bringing in enough to cover the $225,000-a-month expenditures without dipping into the union's reserves.

There was a serious personnel problem at La Paz. Jack Quiggly, the union's business manager, was quitting because of differences with Cesar. Quiggly had come into the union two years earlier, at a time when the business affairs had been drifting badly. He set up the union's accounting systems, established a quarterly budgeting system, and acted as the chief disbursement officer. During the Coachella and Arvin grape strikes Quiggly and José Gomez were left in La Paz to keep the administrative machinery functioning, in Chavez's absence. Upon his return, Chavez questioned some of their decisions. Gomez threatened to quit if two staff people he had fired did not stay fired. Chavez backed down.

But in Quiggly's case, the differences were too basic, too sharply defined, for the business manager to remain on with the union. He explained, "We had been making a great many decisions back here that traditionally had always involved Cesar, so when he came back . . . he became afraid the business office had taken over a great deal of the union administration and he felt he had to reassert himself. We ran headlong into one another. . . . [He] feels he must have control over all aspects of the union."

Quiggly believes Chavez's need for tight personal control is one of the factors limiting UFWA growth. "Up to this point a strong, personal leadership was important, but if we are going to go on and build we are just going to have to draw on the collective judgments of diverse experience. We have enough money (at the time there was $700,000 in reserves) to spend a little money to make more. If you spend some money on adult staff who have some experience and you have administrators to run the offices and the field offices, you pay them modest salaries, it would pay off in better relations with the growers, better administration of the contracts.

"Instead of paying volunteers $5 a week and then paying their bills, why not pay them a salary? It's not a big deal. Remove the hassle. Then the Teamsters can't come in and take over because the United Farm Workers is known for the radical kids that it puts into the jobs that pay $5 a week.

"Cesar has those of us here who can handle administration, who can do it relatively easy, and do it with his concerns in mind. So we ought to handle that stuff. He is far too important and far too capable in the larger issues to be tied up with paper clips and light bulbs."

Asked about Quiggly's comments, Chavez said, "He was a little upset with me because things were not going well and I called his attention to this and I told him things had to be done better. I am saying that everything has to be done better. I've become more critical."

The union has always had a problem in handling some Anglo volunteers who were obviously working through their own mixed feelings about social reform, feelings that didn't always relate to the needs of farm workers or the union. I asked if this was the case with Quiggly.

Chavez replied, "No. No, it wasn't that. He had too much to do. He couldn't do everything, but he didn't tell me, you know. It wasn't his fault. He is very sensitive. I had to tell him certain things. He was understaffed. And when we left to go on the strike, he didn't communicate with me. He didn't keep in touch with me, so he had to do certain things that were wrong, and I had to call him on it."

When Chavez took over the administrative helm, he did so with characteristic passion. He insisted that every issue must come to his attention, and to insure that it did, he ordered department heads to write every action down in memo form, with copies to his office. He started getting up at 3 A.M. and working through the great mountains of memos, mail, and other paperwork. At 7:15 one morning, when I arrived for an interview, there was a stack of yellow slips in a file folder on his desk. I asked what they were.

"These are the receipts that come in from New York [boycott office], they are contributions, $10,000 worth, but they didn't balance. See, I am helping out the accounting department. They have been having a little difficulty getting things organized. We have written them letters, we have called them, and they don't change. They are not doing it right, so it comes to me, and I put pressure on them."

These words were spoken three months after Quiggly had quit. The accounting department and budgeting processes had been turned over to farm workers and volunteer staff people, and they were learning how the system worked. About the same time Cohen was getting upset with the bureaucratic paper shuffling. He resented the number of memos and forms he had to fill out.

Cohen said, "The intent behind the memos was good, but you can overdo that sort of thing, so Mandy [Cohen's wife] and I decided on a little hoax. We made up a memo of our own and circulated it. The memo stated: 'In our zeal to streamline the administration of the union we have neglected to inform you that from now on you will be referred to by number, rather than name . . . from now on you will be known by the number of your telephone extension. Non-working wives will be known by their husband's number, followed by a lower case 'a'. *Si Se Puede* 4.' [By signing the memo "4" — Cesar's extension — Cohen had made it appear to come from Cesar's office.]

"Well, some people around here are so intimidated by Cesar and by memos they believed it. Not all of them, but enough. They were going around cussing, saying this was going too goddamn far. Some gal down in accounting had two telephones and she didn't know what to do; she asked her supervisor and actually got an answer." Cohen started laughing, "Well there was some real turmoil for two or three hours, until we let them know it was a joke.

"Cesar got the point. He was a little mad, but he knew it was funny. He found out some of the people were laughing like hell, but the fact that some people believed it shocked him, and it showed him that some people around here are intimidated by his presence."

As Chavez worked on the UFWA administrative problems, the Teamsters began expanding their field operations. Fitzsimmons approved the creation of Farm Worker Local 1973, named for the year they grabbed off the UFWA contracts, and committed $100,000 a month to finance the effort. Local 1973 was headquartered in Salinas, but had field offices in all of the farming valleys. The local was structured to make it appear competitive with the UFWA in services to the workers.

Grami bragged, "We have 308 contracts with growers who hire 50,000 workers in the peak of the season."

As usual, the numbers were confusing. If the Teamsters had 50,000 dues-paying members among the farm workers, that would translate into $400,000 a month income, but when Local 1973 filed its first annual report with the U.S. Department of Labor it listed a total dues income of only $638,838 for the entire lettuce and grape harvest seasons. The number 50,000 referred to jobs, not workers; each worker covered by Teamster contract might work on several of those jobs, as he or she moved from crop to crop, place to place. Given all the vagaries of farm labor employment, the Teamsters probably had no more than 15,000 workers employed under contract at any one time.

Some of these workers were members of the Teamsters, some were not; many were members of both the Teamsters and the UFWA. The Teamster contracts gave the workers wages and fringe benefits that appeared comparable to the UFWA contracts, but only full-time farm workers received anywhere near the full range of benefits the Teamsters bragged they offered. Seasonal workers did not qualify for various health, welfare, and pension benefits until they had worked specific lengths of time; and these qualifications frequently excluded the migrant from benefits.

But the major difference in the UFWA and Teamster contracts was the Teamster concession to the growers allowing them to return to the crew boss–farm labor contractor system that gave the boss absolute control over the worker. Another difference between the Teamster and UFWA organizational structure and attitude came in the area of worker involvement in union affairs. The Teamsters run a top-down organization; Teamster organizers come in and sign growers to a contract, then organize the workers and pass out benefits to those workers who prove to the union they are qualified and worthy.

Nowhere did this Teamster attitude toward farm workers come out so clearly as when Einar Mohn was interviewed by Jane Yett Kiely, a theological student in Berkeley who was working on a farm labor report for Safeway Stores. Safeway was then under UFWA boycott, and was trying to gather as much information as it could about the struggle. Kiely asked Mohn what role he thought farm workers should play in the Teamster union that represented them. Mohn replied:

> We have to have them in the union for a while. It will be a couple of years before they can start having membership meetings, before we can use the farm workers' ideas in the union. I'm not sure how effective a union can be when it is composed of Mexican-Americans and Mexican nationals with temporary visas. Maybe as agriculture becomes more sophisticated, more mechanized, with fewer transients, fewer green carders, and as jobs become more attractive to whites, then we can build a union that can have structures and that can negotiate from strength and have membership participation.

Mohn's words were the governing credo in Teamsters Farm Worker Local 1973. Through 1973 and 1974 there were no membership meetings. The workers didn't elect officers or delegates to any convention or caucus, nor were they likely to for years to come. From the outset, the local was placed in "trusteeship" by the Western Conference, subject only to the autocratic rule of Einar Mohn, and through him, Bill Grami. After Mohn's retirement, Teamster president Frank Fitzsimmons appointed M. E. "Andy" Anderson boss of the Western Conference. There were rumors at the time that the farm labor jurisdictional fights between the Teamsters and the UFWA had been used by Grami and/or others, to pressure Mohn into retirement. Although Mohn denied this, events that transpired soon after his resignation indicated the farm workers were, in fact, pawns in some larger power game within both the Western Conference and the International Brotherhood.

Late in the fall of 1974, Farm Worker Local 1973 went through a dramatic upheaval that may have been understood within the Teamsters' private councils, but certainly left the farm workers puzzled. Cono Macias and 29 other organizers, most of them Mexican Americans, were fired by Anderson in an "economy move." Anderson then appointed Ralph Cotner — the man Grami indirectly blamed for the violence in Coachella — as the new operating head of the farm workers organizational efforts. The move appeared to push Grami out of farm labor — he technically heads the Western Conference warehousemen's division — and Macias felt the Cotner takeover meant the Teamsters were backing away from Grami's avowed effort to organize all farm workers in California, then the United States.

Whatever the Machiavellian designs within both the Western Conference and the International Brotherhood, it was obvious the farm workers were not involved, nor did they know what was happening. They had had no voice in the creation of Local 1973, they had no voice in its operations, and, in the fall of 1974, no one had asked them if a major shake-up was needed to improve the union's ability to service the farm labor contracts. Macias and his followers became the victims of the "*gabacho* way" they so assiduously followed — used for their "Mexicanness" in a work force that is primarily of Mexican descent, they were cast aside when no longer needed.

There are no indications the growers were involved in any of the Teamster plots and counterplots; agribusiness had little concern for the internal union workings. The farmers still preferred no union at all, but, given the need to head off Chavez's concepts of union democracy and the UFWA's growing power, the Teamsters were an acceptable alternative. Agribusiness leaders were hoping for legislation to protect the industry from Chavez, or any other labor movement as aggressive as the UFWA, but their desperately constructed coalition of anti-Chavez forces had crumbled under the weight of Watergate, and the 1974 off-year elections further eroded the agribusiness political power base in both California and the nation.

Politically the tide seemed to be turning in the UFWA's favor. The Chavez forces were still weak because the loss of the grape contracts had been a serious, damaging blow; for a year the union staggered under the impact of this blow. Covering up like an old punch-drunk fighter, it struggled to regain control. The UFWA made all of the familiar moves, through the spring and summer of 1974, but there was no real punching ability there, no zing. Nothing seemed to work right. Chavez tried without success to make an issue out of the half million illegal aliens at work on the farms throughout the Southwest. Thousands of these illegals were used as strikebreakers. The lettuce and grape boycotts went nowhere. Manuel Chavez was everywhere, doing his thing: strikes in the melons, in the tomatoes. But none of the strikes did more than flare briefly and die out. The Gallo wine boycott sputtered along.

Then a spark of life began to burn; students' rejecting the pop wines made by Gallo began to cut into sales and the company began to react. Both youth and housewives make up the backbone of the customer support of boycotts, and they were rejecting Gallo, in some areas, in some stores. California state tax figures showed that the Gallo market position — relative to all other vintners — slipped 7 percent during 1972–73. The news was encouraging to the farm workers' union and it came at a time when a new plan, a new sense of direction was beginning to take shape.

Proposition 22 had shown the UFWA had some political muscle; for the first time in the long history of farm labor, the workers had whipped the bosses in a political fight. But the victory was a negative one, and now Chavez wanted to make a positive effort, to create a California law that favored farm workers. With the help of Cohen and Jack Henning, head of the California AFL-CIO, Chavez proposed a law that would create a three-man labor relations board to conduct secret-ballot union-recognition elections.

All of the previous state or federal legislative attempts had language that outlawed the secondary boycott and provided legal machinery to prevent strikes at harvest. Most of these bills had excluded seasonal farm workers from the balloting. Chavez had opposed each of these efforts, and remained outside the law, fighting his guerrilla war. The success of his tactics can be measured by how far agribusiness has moved in its legislative positions in the past decade. Between 1965 and 1975, farmers have completely reversed themselves; they have come to accept the idea the NLRA can protect them against Chavez and the UFWA. As Chavez maneuvered them to within sight of his own legislative goals, he opened up a political front. Cohen was put in charge, and this brash young lawyer stormed the California legislature. Just as he had applied pressures against Oregon's Governor Tom McCall, he began to apply direct pressure on California's Democrats in the state Assembly. The Chavez secret-ballot election bill — *sans* any language on boycotts or strikes — was introduced by a UFWA friend, Assemblyman Richard Alatore, a Los Angeles Democrat.

Cohen contacted all of the boycott staff in California's cities and had them focus a telephone and letter-writing campaign on the assemblymen. Jerry Brown, the former California secretary of state who had helped bring out the allegations of fraud in the Proposition 22 campaign, was the Democratic candidate for governor and considered head of his party in California. One of Brown's top aides was Leroy Chatfield, the former UFWA staff man. Cohen asked Chatfield to get Brown to both endorse the farm labor legislation and lobby for its passage. Brown seemed to hesitate; he didn't return Cohen's calls.

Cohen conferred with Chavez — who was in Boston on a boycott tour at the time — and they decided to apply some direct pressure on Brown. Cohen ordered the San Francisco boycott staff to put 20 pickets in Brown's offices on the mezzanine of the swank Fox Plaza in downtown San Francisco. Both news wire services, the New York *Times*, and one of the city's major radio stations have offices in the same building. The UFWA pickets could hardly be missed. They were told to stay in Brown's offices until they got a commitment from him.

Cohen said, "It was kind of like blackmail, but damn it, we needed help. We had to put the heat on Jerry Brown to make him twist some Democratic arms, so we did it."

329

The key to getting the needed legislation past the combined opposition of agribusiness and the Teamsters was heading off amendments that would either water the bill down or load it with controversial issues that had no chance of passage. With the farm workers personally moving through the legislative offices, lobbying for secret-ballot elections, Cohen and Alatore pushed the bill through the friendly labor committee, past the ways and means committee, and out onto the floor of the Assembly where it was passed by a 43 to 31 vote.

The Teamsters and agribusiness had more strength in the state Senate. They managed to defeat the measure 19 to 16 in the upper house, but Cohen and the farm workers were quite happy about the showing they had made. Cohen said, "We'll get 'em next year. We're putting together a legislative package, and we'll get it through. The climate isn't right in the Congress yet for federal legislation, but here in California we think we can do it."

Jerry Brown's election in November of 1974 gave Cohen's words added emphasis; with Brown in the governor's office openly working for a farm labor union recognition bill in a legislature controlled by the Democrats, the UFWA's proposals would have a real chance of passing. And Cohen's moves to put a UFWA legislative package together indicate that Chavez has apparently decided to move in that direction, finally to come out of the jungle into a labor relations environment regulated by law, but only if laws could be passed that would assure an environment that represented all farm workers in the United States.

There can be no suitable ending for a book like this, gathered and written while the struggle goes on, but some concluding thoughts and observations are possible. Chavez has implanted in the minds of the American farm workers the seeds of an idea, the seeds of a labor rebellion. He and the several thousand tough-minded, dedicated workers who follow him have proven that men and women of the fields can stand together and fight for something they call social justice.

Chavez has become a legend. He is a rebel who fits no mold. In the popular press he is one of the best known labor leaders in the United States, in the urban *barrios* he is a respected grandfather figure who has been disappointingly nonviolent. Unlike other ethnic radicals who emerged in the 1960s, Chavez has endured. *La Causa* has endured. Chavez has given enormous time and energy in developing this cause, and his effort has become a part of the Chavez myth. But such personal expenditures also appear to be having some kind of diminishing return.

There are those within the movement who want to see him relax his control, at least a little, who want him to spend less time with the details of the union — purchasing paper clips and light bulbs — and more time on the broader leadership issues, more time with the people in his symbolic role as the man who led them out of bondage. If *La Causa* is to make the transition from cause to stable union structure, its leadership must begin to accept the idea of a membership and union bureaucracy beyond the absolute control of any single individual. Chavez has been trying to delegate more and more authority, but in this effort he is clearly a man at odds with himself.

If the cause of the farm worker is to survive, it must have the protection of the law. Chavez has recognized this and has begun the move in that direction. It is time for organized labor to get behind this move in a meaningful way, time for all labor leaders to support farm workers with the sweat of their bodies; tough-sounding rhetoric and a few bags of silver are not enough.

When George Meany says, "This is our fight and we are involved and are going to stay involved until the sour grapes of oppression taste sweet again. The growers know that if the UFWA is destroyed the spirit of the farm workers will be broken and the workers will be more manageable," the words sound responsive.

When Meany says, "Cheap labor is the reason growers forged an unholy alliance with the Teamsters to break the UFWA, and cheap labor is the reason growers now seek a

331

return of the [Mexican] *Bracero* program . . . ," it sounds as if he is beginning to understand farm labor. Meany has pledged the federation's full support for an international primary boycott of grapes and lettuce. He should also pledge the federation's finances and great political power structures to the task of creating legislative measures that would allow farm workers to pool their collective power to force agribusiness to the bargaining table.

The AFL-CIO should make such legislation its primary goal. It is time the liberals in the state and federal legislatures stop talking about migrants as the forgotten people and start passing laws that will truly help these seasonal workers. It is not enough to appropriate millions of dollars for migrant education classes or migrant health clinics; while such programs may be useful to workers, in the immediate sense, the same way a Band-Aid may be useful to cover an infected wound, they do not cure the basic problem: *pay scales that produce poverty*. Such programs are direct employer subsidies that help perpetuate the agribusiness slave rental system.

Because few employers willingly give up economic power and advantage, farm workers can never be free to earn a decent living until laws are passed allowing them to create a union of their choosing, a union that can exercise a counterbalancing, collective strength. Without laws guaranteeing secret-ballot choice of unions, and without laws protecting the workers' right to strike and boycott, the growers will continue to dominate the power struggle. Without laws restricting the flow of aliens north from Mexico — laws that impose criminal penalties on the employers of illegal aliens — the farm workers will remain powerless, the UFWA will remain a band of guerrilla fighters reacting to the great conspiracies hurled against them.

SUGGESTED READING

Dunne, John Gregory, *Delano: Revised and Updated* (New York: Farrar, Straus & Giroux, 1971).

Galarza, Ernesto, *Merchants of Labor: The Mexican Bracero Story* (Santa Barbara: McNally & Loftin, 1964).

Grebler, Leo, Joan W. Moore, and Ralph C. Guzman, *The Mexican-American People: The Nation's Second Largest Minority* (New York: The Free Press, 1970).

McWilliams, Carey, *Factories in the Field: The Story of Migratory Farm Labor in California* (Santa Barbara: Peregrine Publishers, 1971).

McWilliams, Carey, *North from Mexico: The Spanish-Speaking People of the United States* (New York: Greenwood Press, 1968).

Matthiessen, Peter, *Sal Si Puedes: Cesar Chavez and the New American Revolution* (New York: Random House, 1969).

Taft, Philip, *Organized Labor in American History* (New York: Harper & Row, 1964).

Taylor, Ronald B., *Sweatshops in the Sun: Child Labor on the Farm* (Boston: Beacon Press, 1973).

In addition to the above reading list the serious student of farm labor is directed to the labor committees of both the U.S. Senate and House; each has in the past had subcommittees on migratory labor and agriculture labor that have conducted extensive hearings. Of special value: U.S. Congress, Senate, Committee on Labor and

Public Welfare, *Migrant and Seasonal Farmworker Powerlessness, Hearings* before the Subcommittee on Migratory Labor of the Committee on Labor and Public Welfare, 16 volumes (Washington, D.C.: Government Printing Office, 1970).

INDEX

Bureaucratic problems: 214–215, 267, 322–324
Burial insurance: 111, 130
Buttes Gas and Oil: 284–285, 286, 288
Butz, Earl: 281, 288–289, 290
Byrd, Cois: 302

California: agriculture in, 38–41; Department of Public Health, 241; Farm Bureau Federation, 288; farming towns, 108–109; Highway Patrol, 6, 59; Proposition 22, 281–284, 285, 290, 328; Senate hearings, 196
California Migrant Ministry (CMM): 102–103, 104, 111–112, 116–119
Californians for Right to Work: 236
California Rural Legal Assistance (CRLA): 206
Camacho, Epifanio: 132
Campbell, Gordon: 260–261
Cannery and Agricultural Workers Industrial Union (CAWIU): 48–58
Caplan, Al: 296
Catholic Bishops of California: 167–168
Catholic Church: 81, 167–168, 242–243, 260. See also Bishops' Farm Labor Committee
La Causa: Catholic Church and, 168, 226; cultural base, 131, 168–169, 182–183; growth of, 106–129, 180, 209, 331; origins, 78–105; social revolution, 182–183
CAWIU. See Cannery and Agricultural Workers Industrial Union
Central California Farmers Committee: 287
Chambers, Pat: 48, 49, 51, 52, 54–57, 58
Chatfield, Bonnie: 283
Chatfield, Leroy: 205, 206, 216, 223, 224, 274, 280, 282–284, 315, 329
Chavez, Anna (daughter): 85
Chavez, Cesar Estrada: 17–18, 23, 92, 221, 222, 228, 311; arrested, 65–66, 260–261, 288; attention to detail, 140–141, 215, 267–269, 322–323, 331; cost consciousness, 186, 268; CSO at Sal Si Puedes, 82–86, 105; Delano grape strike, 125–129, 136–137, 145–146, 154, 181–182; DiGiorgio election, 183–184, 190–202; family, 77, 82, 85, 108, 213–214; fasts, 23, 220–229, 238, 239, 280; march to Sacramento, 168–180; on merger with AWOC, 197; national recognition, 13, 144, 174, 179, 183, 209–214, 223, 331; and NFWA, 105, 107, 110–119, 121, 123, 125–129; at 1966 Senate hearing, 158–159, 164–165; and nonviolence, 137–140, 149, 181, 220, 225, 229, 300; organizing strategy, 35–36, 90–93, 113–115, 141, 169; on picketing, 136–137; and Teamsters effort, 189–190, 252, 254–255, 258,

260–263, 293–298, 304, 308–309; worker transportation, 1–8
Chavez, Dolores (wife of Richard): 280
Chavez, Eloise (daughter): 257
Chavez, Fernando (son): 77, 82, 108
Chavez, Helen Fabela (wife): 77, 82, 85, 108, 112, 213, 216, 221, 226, 238; arrested, 143; with NFWA, 116
Chavez, Juana (mother): 59, 64, 226
Chavez, Lennie (brother): 64
Chavez, Librado (father): 59, 62, 226
Chavez, Linda (daughter): 82
Chavez, Manuel (cousin): 34, 61, 112, 137, 207, 215, 219, 247, 248, 252, 253, 270, 328; designs flag, 115–116
Chavez, Richard (brother): 21, 61, 64, 76, 82, 108, 216, 280
Chavez, Rita (sister): 64, 82, 108
Chavez, Sylvia (daughter): 77, 82
Chavez, Vicki (sister): 64
Chevaria, Art: 199, 200
Child labor: 2–4, 11, 30
Chinese, as farm workers: 41–42
Christian Brothers Winery: 184, 205, 206, 207
Church support: 14, 81, 118–119, 153, 168, 190, 304. See also Bishops' Farm Labor Committee; California Migrant Ministry; Catholic Church
Civil rights movement: 106, 121, 140
Clark, Ramsey: 218
Clinics: 211, 216, 219, 253, 266, 274, 321
CMM. See California Migrant Ministry
Coachella grape strike: 15, 16
Coca-Cola, UFWA contract: 13, 33–34
Cody, Abp. John: 190
Cohen, Jerry: 92, 207, 223, 224, 225, 246–247; and NFWOC lettuce effort, 257, 259–261, 265, 275, 279, 295–296, 298–299, 308, 314, 316, 324, 328, 329, 330; and P–M boycott, 206; and pesticide issue, 240–242
Cohen, Mandy: 324
Colon, Maria: 234
Colson, Charles: 291, 315
Communists, early role: 48–49
Community Service Organization (CSO): 80, 82; at Sal Si Puedes, 82–84, 89, 105, 209
Company unions: 160, 184, 236, 261
Conference on People Who Follow the Crops: 103
Congress of Racial Equality (CORE): 140, 145, 150, 210
Connors, Donald: 202
Consumer Rights Committee: 235
Contracts, labor (see also "Sweetheart contracts"): drafting, 184–185, 217, 242; Teamsters', 30
CORE. See Congress of Racial Equality

Grami, Bill: (*Cont.*)
257–259, 262, 290, 292, 302, 308–309, 313, 325, 326

Grant, Allan: 159, 234, 238, 277, 278, 281

Grants: early aversion to, 117; OEO, 130, 150–151

Grapes of Wrath (Steinbeck): 41

Great Depression: 46–50, 59

Green, Al: 106, 197; and AWOC, 101, 119, 128, 146, 171–172; and Teamster efforts, 125, 152–153, 305

Green, William: 71

Grievance procedures: 20, 21, 33, 185, 271, 285

Growers (*see also* Agribusiness): aversion to ranch committees, 21, 28, 306; groups, 97, 236–237, 251, 276–277, 287; and local media, 209; opposition to reform, 159–160; reaction to boycott, 231–237, 276–284; reaction to Delano strike, 149–150, 155–156, 183–184; reaction to NFWA successes, 177–178, 183, 196, 271–276; role in DiGiorgio elections, 195–197; small, 263, 272–273, 286–287

Growers-Shippers Vegetable Association (GSVA): 251, 254, 259

Guevara, Ernesto ("Che"): 131

Guines, Ben: 101, 120–121, 124

Gutierrez, José Angel: 220

Hagen, Harlan: 150, 158–159

Hall, Paul: 219, 300, 321

Hartmire, Wayne C. ("Chris"): 103–104, 112, 117, 118, 120, 128, 141, 147, 177, 186, 187, 193, 194, 213, 282, 297

Harvest of Shame (CBS-TV): 41, 106

Hasiwar, Hank: 69, 73, 86

Havens, Dave: 117, 118, 121, 122

Hemmett, W.D.: 54, 55

Henderson, Donald: 73

Henning, Jack: 328

Hernandez, Delores: 55

Hernandez, Juan: 303

Hernandez, Julio: 113, 115, 185, 217

Heublein: 13, 264

Hi-C, citrus workers: 33–34

Higgins, Bp. George: 242–243, 245, 246, 257, 297

Hiring halls: 16, 18–20, 29, 30–31, 133, 185, 207, 211, 245, 246, 248, 251, 265, 269–270, 273, 274, 275, 285, 292, 294–296, 321

Hoe, short-handled: 2, 63, 114

Hoffa, James: 188–189, 190, 198

Hoffman, Alex: 206

Hoffman, Cecil, Jr.: 193

Houghton, Ronald W.: 194–195

House meetings: 110, 113, 114, 115, 121, 215, 247, 310

Housing. *See* Labor camps

Howard, Delos: 51, 53

"Huelga!", use prohibited: 142–144

Huerta, Dolores Fernandez: 87, 91, 105, 176, 179, 213, 226, 238; contract work, 184–185, 217, 242; DiGiorgio election, 191, 192–193, 194; early efforts, 87, 90, 103; with NFWA, 110–111, 113, 115–116, 120, 121, 123, 184–186; at Senate hearing, 148; and UFWOC, 197, 203, 207, 217, 229–230, 244–245, 246, 247, 285, 288, 295

Huerta, Ray: 292–293

IAF. *See* Industrial Areas Foundation

Imutan, Andy: 98, 101, 197, 217

Industrial Areas Foundation (IAF): 78–79, 82

Insurance programs: burial, 111, 130; medical, 216, 274

International Brotherhood of Teamsters: alliance with growers, 5, 200, 254, 288–293, 325, 327, 330; citrus effort, 125, 152–153, 171; contracts, 30, 203; Delano boycott, 149–150, 152; Delano raids, 188–191; DiGiorgio elections, 190–202; Farm Worker Local 1973, 324–327; and lettuce growers, 15, 100, 248–249, 290, 293–294, 299–304; and Nixon administration, 288–291, 313–315, 327; talks with UFWOC, 207–208, 256–258, 308, 314; terror tactics, 299–304, 313

International Longshoremen and Warehousemen's Union: 149–150, 189–190

International Workers of the World (IWW): 42–45

Irrigation, subsidized: 39–40, 75, 109

Irving, Leonard: 71

Itliong, Larry: 8; and AWOC, 98, 101, 103, 120–121, 124, 173; and Delano strike, 125, 128, 145–146, 154, 158, 173; and Sacramento march, 171; and UFWOC, 197, 216–217, 246, 263, 266–267

IWW. *See* International Workers of the World

Japanese, as farm workers: 41–42, 45

J.D. Martin Ranch: 122–124, 130

Jersey City, boycott in: 232

J.G. Boswell Company: 39, 89

John Birch Society: 210

Jones, Nick: 199, 230–232, 235

Karter, Thomas: 151

Keenan, Joe: 256, 262, 307, 308

Kennedy, Edward M.: 321

Kennedy, Ethel: 261

Kennedy, Robert F.: 106, 175, 198, 228; assassinated, 24, 239; and Chavez fast, 225–226; 1966 hearings, 11–12, 160–161, 165–167